I0818981

THE DINING ROOM

THE DINING ROOM

Exploring the Design of
Twelve Iconic Rooms
in Search of the
Perfect Dining Experience

John Ota

appetite
by RANDOM HOUSE

Library and Archives Canada Cataloguing in Publication is available upon request.

ISBN: 978-0-525-61342-8
eBook ISBN: 978-0-525-61343-5

All drawings by John Ota
Cover art: Claude Monet's dining room by John Ota
Cover based on a design by Leah Springate
Text design by Leah Springate
Printed in Canada

The authorized representative in the EU for product safety and compliance is Penguin Random House Ireland, Morrison Chambers, 32 Nassau Street, Dublin D02 YH68, Ireland, https://eu-contact.penguin.ie

Published in Canada by Appetite by Random House®,
a division of Penguin Random House Canada Limited.
320 Front Street West, Suite 1400
Toronto, Ontario, M5V 3B6, Canada
penguinrandomhouse.ca

10 9 8 7 6 5 4 3 2 1

appetite
by RANDOM HOUSE

Penguin
Random House
Canada

For Chris, my brother and co-pilot

dining room: a room used for eating meals

—*Merriam-Webster Dictionary*

"Dining with one's friends and beloved family is certainly one of life's primal and most innocent delights, one that is both soul-satisfying and eternal."

—JULIA CHILD

CONTENTS

INTRODUCTION

RIGHT FROM THE BEGINNING, I was obsessed with dinner.

Some babies learn to talk early. Others learn to sit up early. I learned to hold a spoon and feed myself early. So it is no surprise that dinner holds a special place in my heart.

When I was growing up, dinner was the main event of the day. My whole schedule revolved around dinner and being at the table. It was like the sun rising in the morning and setting at night: It always happened and I looked forward to it. I realize now that I was a fortunate person to live in a house where my family valued gathering for dinner and where this guaranteed meal was secure.

As an adult, my love for dinner has not changed. In fact, it is only intensifying. Every night, food is the last thought on my mind before I fall asleep: *Hmm, what's for dinner tomorrow night?*

I first became fascinated with the social significance of dinner and the dining room when I was an architecture student. On a tour in Chicago of the Robie House, designed by Frank Lloyd Wright, I learned that Wright wanted to reinforce the closeness of the Robie family unit, which he felt was sacred, through the design of the house.

For the dining area, Wright designed a sleek table and accompanying chairs with unusually high backs. More than just stylish flair, the high backs of the chairs had another purpose: to create another set of walls—a room within a room around the dinner table. Wright wanted the family to feel a sense of protection and togetherness; the family was not to be disturbed during their meal.

I had never before considered the importance of the dinner table and chairs in architectural and philosophical terms. Up until then, I had just thought of them as generic pieces of furniture. But Wright made me realize that dinner and the dining area had powers beyond a time to eat.

Indeed, historically, the dining room has been used to encourage gathering, discussion, and cultural exchange. It has provided a platform for events that have changed the world.

In AD 117, when ancient Romans kept a room specifically designated for dining in their homes, Emperor Trajan held lavish banquets with leaders to solidify his empire that stretched from Britain to Baghdad, and Kublai Khan welcomed Marco Polo to China with magnificent dinners, his journals describing great parties in a dining area that could seat six thousand guests. King Henry VIII of England used dinner as a way to demonstrate his power and influence, putting foreign guests in awe with extravagant feasts in his massive dining hall, where he would present platters of roasted swans and peacocks, with the colorful feather display intact.

As many of us know firsthand, dinners and the dining room have also created spaces for celebration, laughter, and happy memories.

For myself, at the dining table of our New York tenement, my former roommate Becky Harrison casually took her shoe off to smash cockroaches as they crawled up the wall, all the while conversing with our guests, laughing and spooning ice cream into her mouth without skipping a beat. Then, at my first Christmas dinner in Franny's family's dining room, I was employing my best table manners (like chewing twenty-five times before swallowing), and looked up halfway through the meal to see that her entire family had vacuumed up their turkey and stuffing and were impatiently waiting for me to finish. "Hurry up, John," my future brother-in-law Brian said, annoyed. "You're delaying dessert!" All of them wore huge grins, wined up and looking a bit demented, wearing those silly hats out of the Christmas crackers.

But my favorite dining room was in the home where I grew up, a modest house built in 1910 in a working-class neighborhood of Toronto, Canada. The dining room was the focus of the house, a place for more than just eating—we all finished school projects and dutifully plowed through our homework at that table. But as I've mentioned, dinner was a main event for our family.

We did not have a lot of money, but food was plentiful and dinners in this room were always lively when, every evening at 6 p.m., my mom called out in her sergeant-major voice, "Dinner! Come to the table! Now!" Those were the magic words that my dad, two brothers, grandmother, and I—and the occasional boarder—had been waiting for all day. From all over the house, rapid footsteps would pound down the stairs, doors opening and slamming, toilets flushing, and dogs barking as we followed the aroma of soy sauce, honey, and green onion from salmon teriyaki and the pure essence of steamed white rice to the dining room.

I didn't realize it at the time, but with our chaotic reports of the day, recitals of jokes, and lectures on table manners, we were bonding. This was a place to gather every night with the family I love.

This was also where we gathered with friends and extended family for special celebrations: anniversaries, birthdays, graduations, church luncheons, parties, bridal showers, and even my aunt's surprise wedding. The room had monstrous spider plants spilling out of pots, bright yellow and red string macrame festooned across the room, purple and black Marimekko fabric hangings; the lime-green oak table was laid with psychedelic placemats, mismatched silverware, and glasses of different shapes and sizes.

Now Franny, my wife, has a significant birthday coming up. I want to get this one right. Over the years my birthday dinner parties for her haven't gone quite to plan.

One year, I threw a garden party for her birthday—and it rained a downpour. (Did you know that helium balloons stop floating once they've been rained on?) Another, we invited our friends to a fancy bed and breakfast. But there was one problem: water contamination—we could not drink the tap water.

But the most compelling reason for having this special birthday celebration is that the previous year, Franny had a stroke. A serious one. In those first twenty-four hours, I thought I might lose her. She insists she doesn't remember much, which is a good thing. But I do.

Thanks to first responders, nurses, doctors, and physiotherapists, Franny was patched up. She still has some lingering aphasia or word-finding challenges, but she has recovered about 99 percent of her formal self. We know we are lucky. Still, I have never forgotten those hours when she was in such distress.

So I think it's time for a huge celebration . . . and a new dining room.

To celebrate this significant birthday, I want to give Franny an all-out dinner party that she'll never forget. To make it extra special, I want to truly understand all the elements that go into a great dinner and dining room. Of course that means outstanding food and drink, but I also want to explore the history of dinner and the dining room, the furniture design, decor, and etiquette. And there are so many intricacies surrounding this special meal that remain a mystery to me: invitations and outfits, table arrangements and seating plans, manners and conversation, entertainment and background music, and of course, the menu.

Eating, architecture, and entertaining are my favorite things in life. There is nothing I like better than joining friends and family around a table to dig into a sumptuous, multicourse meal—roasts, sauces, vegetables, breads, salads, fruits, sweets, and drinks—in a beautifully appointed room as we revel in each other's company and stimulating conversation into the wee hours of the morning. (Yes, I'll have another cognac, please.)

But in our go-go-go society of today, dinner and the dining room are falling out of fashion. Open-concept houses eliminate the dining room, family room, and living room walls, creating one large ground floor space: the great room. While this creation of open-concept spaces seems to have become the dominant trend in house design over the years, I'm not convinced that the dining room is extinct just yet.

It might be that the unifying and celebratory values of the traditional dining room are still with us, just in a different form. I need to find out.

More than anything, I want to understand how dinner and architecture bring people together. I want to explore the ways that we can come together to create comfort, strengthen ties, and build personal relationships. I want to use dinner and the dining room as vehicles for people to open up to each other, let down their guard, and talk about life and possibilities for the world. And I won't stop at conventional dining rooms as we know them: four-walled rooms with a long wood table designated for eating. Any place we gather to eat, drink, and share time with friends is fair game—inside the house, out front of the house, out back, or even in the garden. If we can have a great meal together in an unusual setting, I want to know about it.

So I am embarking on a journey. I hope to visit the most famous dining rooms and dinner sites in world history. I also want to step into the houses of people from different cultural backgrounds and experience their dinner customs and cuisines. My goal is to learn from these spaces to help make Franny's birthday dinner—and our new dining room—a success. I believe that houses and their rooms and furnishings have a soul, that they are not inanimate objects. (When we had to sell my childhood home after my mother died, the last thing I did was walk around the empty house, thanking all the rooms and kissing each door.) And so, along with some architectural and design pointers, I hope to discover the spirit and good feelings that once emanated from these iconic dining rooms.

Finally, to deliver the centerpiece of Franny's special night (and maybe to satisfy my hunger pangs along my journey), I plan to make a dish from each historical dinner. Will it be tasty enough to make the cut for the birthday menu?

Through my lens as an architectural writer, I want to explore how design affects, maybe even encourages, camaraderie and togetherness with my wife and friends within this special room. I want to enhance the great pleasure of eating as well as enjoying time with people. As I search for a perfect dinner and dining room, I have developed a set of goals that I believe a dining room should achieve:

> *Create a center of hospitality: Discover the meaning of hospitality, how it has changed over the centuries and how we can explore a new meaning of hospitality today.*

Be a place to slow down: Create dinner surroundings that will help me relax, take time to savor food, encourage conversation, and disconnect from the hectic, always moving outside world.

Rejuvenate traditional ideas: Over the years, the dining room has taken different forms. I want to take the best aspects of this room and transform it into a twenty-first-century space for company, discussion, and camaraderie.

Solutions to our ever-changing, fast-moving world might be more complicated than dinner and dining rooms, but I have always found that sharing a meal is a good place to start. Eating is something we all have in common.

I'll start simple for Franny. One night, one dinner, one room.

But of course, I'll make sure they're the perfect ones.

1

GEORGE AND MARTHA WASHINGTON'S GARDEN AND DINING ROOM AT MORRIS-JUMEL MANSION, 1790

New York, New York

DO YOU BELIEVE that dinner has the power to bring people together? George and Martha Washington did.

What might have been one of the most important dinners in the history of the United States was also an understated one. On Saturday, July 10, 1790, the new American president and his wife invited members of his first presidential cabinet for an outing in the country and dinner at the majestic Morris-Jumel Mansion, which still stands in New York City today as a historical house museum open to visitors. (New York was the capital of the United States at the time; Washington, DC, was still a dream).

This meeting of the minds was a family affair; it included wives and even children. Today, the gesture of such a dinner with the cabinet would be incomprehensible. It would be too informal, personable, and family-oriented. But this was the new United States of America, led by the forward-thinking Washingtons.

So, when I learn that the Morris-Jumel Mansion hosts an annual George Washington Dinner in the style of this cabinet soiree, it's clear I have to find out more. After all, President and

Mrs. Washington were well-known for their generous hospitality: Washington felt that, as president, he had an obligation to feed anyone who visited his house, even if they arrived unannounced; meanwhile, Mrs. Washington was known for greeting guests at her front door with a glass of lemonade sprinkled with cinnamon. With Franny's upcoming birthday in mind, I am looking for all tips to make guests feel welcome.

My research is nearly thwarted, though. When I call the folks at the Morris-Jumel Mansion to ask whether the dinner will be taking place this summer, Vincent Carbone, director of public relations, doesn't sound hopeful.

"We've had a tough year," he explains. "We had a pipe burst in the house this winter, we're undergoing renovations, and our curator position is vacant."

This news leaves me feeling discouraged, crestfallen.

As we chat, I describe my background working with historical architecture, food, and museums, and ask if I can be of assistance. With that, Vincent makes me an unusual offer. "You seem very enthusiastic and knowledgeable. Would you give us some advice on setting up the historical menu? Can you cook? Also, we need a dinner speaker. Do you think you could give dinner remarks?"

I have long been a supporter of historical house museums, and I do whatever I can to help—especially if there is food involved.

My response is immediate: "I'll be there."

I confess that for a long time, I never really understood Washington. Perhaps he suffered from overexposure, appearing everywhere from the dollar bill to signs for cities, states, and universities. He even played a role in American architecture: Along with Thomas Jefferson's Monticello home, Washington's Mount Vernon house is considered one of the two early American houses to have had an immense influence on the future of home design. My architectural history professors, however, tended to gloss over Washington's simpler, straightforward Georgian style, preferring to concentrate on Jefferson's more cerebral and eccentric building features; many consider him to be America's greatest architect.

But it all changes for me when I learn, doing research for this important dinner, that Washington had severe tooth problems: His diary records references to toothaches, painful gums, tooth removal, and use of dentures. Here was a man leading an entire nation, fighting for a revolution, establishing a vision for a new country, at the head of a starving Continental Army in the middle of savagely cold winters—and all the time his teeth hurt. As someone with my own share of dental horror stories, I immediately feel his pain.

In fact, as I learn more about Washington, I am becoming a great admirer of his leadership skills and his personal commitment to the ideals of the new republic. As general of the Continental Army, he and the Founding Fathers fought a revolution to achieve a new society free from aristocracies and monarchies.

As the first president, Washington established crucial precedents that set a direction for the new nation and, over two hundred years later, continue to the present day. Among them, the reason behind this very dinner: It was Washington's idea to form a presidential cabinet, minds he could trust when making decisions for the new country. Today, there are enough cabinet members to fill a boardroom, but in 1790, Washington chose only four people to advise him: Secretary of State Thomas Jefferson, Secretary of the Treasury Alexander Hamilton, Secretary of War Henry Knox, and Attorney General Edmund Randolph. As it happens, Edmund Randolph was absent from this dinner. Vice President John Adams, however, *did* join the dinner.

Another precedent came from Washington's fear of a future president uncontrollably seizing power for themselves (in the way kings had). He took steps to try to prevent this from happening, limiting a presidency to a maximum of two terms. Like many of his fellow Founding Fathers, Washington believed the president should be a common man, subject to all the laws of the land. By all historians' accounts, Washington was an ethical and unselfish president.

So with all my admiration, I can't keep myself from bounding up the steps from the bleak subway station, blinded by the summer sun as I emerge onto 168th Street and Broadway. I arrive in the middle of a bustling New York City street scene set with five-story brick tenements, colorful Dominican grocery stores, and thumping rhythms of Latin music. I am in the Washington Heights neighborhood.

Walking along Broadway, I am surrounded by the George Washington legacy: Signs lead to historical Fort Washington; dry cleaners, fried chicken stores, and car repair shops proudly carry the Washington name; and just a few blocks north is the George Washington Bridge.

I turn off the main street onto Jumel Terrace and step into another world, a shaded neighborhood of flourishing trees, cool breezes, and elegant brownstone townhouses. At 65 Jumel Terrace, I pass through iron gates into a walled park with winding paths, a forest of mature trees, and a magical sunken garden dappled in sunlight. Before me, a monumental house set in a lush green oasis emerges. I have arrived at the Morris-Jumel Mansion in Upper Manhattan.

The first thing that strikes me is the impact this classical house has on me. I adore the grand facade: It is dominated by a portico porch and triangular pediment supported by four robust classical columns. The wood exterior is painted white to simulate stone, giving the mansion a stately presence. Thrilled to visit this majestic dwelling for the first time, I try to imagine

General Washington's initial impression of the house in all of its architectural glory.

After all, according to the historical plaque at the front gate, Washington was not the first resident of Morris-Jumel Mansion. The 8,500-square-foot home was designed and built by British colonel Roger Morris in 1765 for himself and his wife, Mary Philipse, as an escape from the heat and smells of the New York summer. Greatly influenced by the designs of sixteenth-century Italian architect Palladio, Colonel Morris turned to a clean, austere form of classicism. This harkening back of design felt cutting edge in the 1700s, when architects were typically leaning into an overabundance of ornamentation.

Perched at one of the highest points of Manhattan, the colonel's country estate was named Mount Morris. As I walk around the two-story house, I imagine that if I lived in this mansion, I would open the windows on both floors to let the cool hilltop breezes waft through the rooms and enjoy the panoramic views.

These superb views helped General George Washington when he and his Continental officers took over the house in the autumn of 1776, after the colonel and his wife had to flee during the Revolutionary War. From this vantage point, they could effectively plan his army's strategy for the Battle of Harlem Heights, Washington's first victory during the Revolutionary War. (There is no documentation that Martha Washington was with the general at the mansion at this time.)

I walk to the front of the mansion and step up into the colonnade to knock on the front door. As I wait for a response, I admire an elaborate glass and wood fanlight over the entrance (one of my favorite features of classical houses, it beckons sunlight into the front foyer).

The heavy wood door opens, and I am greeted by an energetic young man who introduces himself as Vincent Carbone, the public relations director I spoke to on the phone. We shake hands and he proudly informs me that the Morris-Jumel Mansion, which operates as a historical house museum owned by the City of New York, holds the distinction of being Manhattan's oldest existing house.

I step inside the spacious front hall and Vincent takes me on a tour of the grand house's restored rooms, graced with crown moldings at the ceilings and painted portraits on the walls.

On the ground floor, Vincent guides me to the place I have come to see, the dining room. I step into the fifteen-by-fifteen-foot room next to the mansion's front door and realize that I am standing in one of the first dining rooms in the country. I find it a quietly elegant space, graciously lit by four large six-over-six windows that provide views out to the front and sides of the house.

I am welcomed by a stately tall case clock of walnut and pine that stands at attention in the corner of the room. With a long, slim body, classical details, and an arched clock face, it appears almost like a butler supervising the dining room proceedings.

I try to imagine General Washington entertaining guests here. Everyone would be seated around the wood dining table, which occupies the center of the room, with six chairs on the bare floorboards. Candles in crystal holders would have lit the room in the evenings, their flickering light bouncing off the table set with simple white plates and crystal glasses.

The entire space is wrapped in a majestic wallpaper called Draped Cone made by a French wallpaper company from the late eighteenth century, Zuber. This design was a popular one from that period: a light taupe and dark brown pattern of cones and stripes that delivers a liveliness to the room.

My eyes travel to the fireplace that sits along one wall and is framed by a massive mantel of simple wood moldings. Vincent tells me that the fireplace would have provided welcome light and warmth during the winter months.

"Good." I laugh with approval. "Dinner would have been more enjoyable if the general was not suffering from frostbite."

I am most delighted to find a recessed niche at the north end of the room that is decorated by a rounded arch: an early American serving alcove. Inside the alcove, Vincent reveals a secret door that leads to a passage to the basement kitchen, allowing servers to enter and leave the room with minimal detection. For me, finding hidden doors and panels is part of the fun of exploring historical houses. I will resist exploring any passageways, but I do investigate this alcove. Inside, I find a piece of furniture that would have been new for the time: a sideboard (or buffet) that showcases, on its counter, teacups, cutlery held in wood boxes, and a silver urn.

"Drinks were also kept on the sideboard," explains Vincent. "Diners indicated their drink preferences to servers, who would bring them a glass of wine, whiskey, or bourbon. The practice of placing wine bottles on the dinner table so diners could help themselves was to emerge in the early nineteenth century."

Morris-Jumel serving alcove

I sigh. "This might be the only drawback to enjoying dinner in the Morris-Jumel dining room," I say, shaking my head. "I would be mortified to ask the servers to bring me a third or even fourth glass of wine." I make an executive decision in my mind that for Franny's dinner, we will have the wine bottles on the dining table.

While it's not overly elaborate, I find that the Morris-Jumel Mansion dining room has an elegance and stateliness fitting for the determined general, a reward for his hard work to start building a nation. I am glad he could find comfort here.

And for all of its secret exits and newfangled design, I know that the most fascinating aspect of the Morris-Jumel Mansion is that it has a dining room at all.

The dining room came late to North American houses. The concept of a specific room set aside for dining had its beginnings in France in the mid-1600s, when Louis XIV introduced new culinary customs at his court. According to Louis, any respectable French house must include a dining room.

By the early eighteenth century, the English upper classes had adopted the dining room and used it to show off their expensive eating habits. Multiple platters of food would be served, using dozens of plates and plentiful staff to serve guests.

"Here in North America, settlers were too busy surviving, never mind making a separate room in their houses just for eating," says Vincent. "They had enough to worry about to just feed themselves."

Vincent explains that first-generation settlers in the New World built themselves one-room houses such as wood cottages or log cabins to secure shelter. The decor was basic, residents slept in any room, from the main room to the attic, and they stored farm equipment, grain, and building materials throughout the house.

"They ate all over the house," says Vincent. "Even the wealthy ate their meals in the hall, the parlor, or the bedroom, not in a dedicated dining room."

But by the mid-1700s, the English, like Colonel Morris, brought the idea of the dining room to North America, and eventually, as settlers gained more wealth, the dining room came into prominence. The gesture of separating eating in a dining room from cooking in a kitchen was a significant step in establishing the gentility of a household.

The unsightly clutter of the kitchen space could be hidden from the view of guests behind walls, while the gleaming dining room gave the impression of cleanliness, status, and sophisticated taste.

"It was all about showing off your wealth," says Vincent. "The elite developed rules governing just how the dining room should be decorated and furnished. Today we might park our fancy sports car in the driveway for prestige, but in 1790, it was the dining room that wowed the neighbors." He adds that such rooms were decorated with high-quality woods, like mahogany, cherry, and oak. With decorative moldings, paneling, and classical details, the dining room became the most stylish room in the house.

After we admire the quiet sophistication and polish of the Morris-Jumel Mansion dining room, Vincent takes me outside through the side door of the mansion. We step into the bright sunlight and the garden.

"There is no documentation on where the Washington dinner took place in the mansion," says Vincent. "It might have occurred in the dining room. However, the staff of the mansion believe that due to the buildup of summer heat inside the mansion, the dinner could have taken place outside—in the garden."

To my delight, Vincent announces that tonight, the dining room for this historical dinner will be the garden.

Ahead of me as I walk from the house, I see a huge white tent set up in the garden. Inside the tent are twenty tables replete with

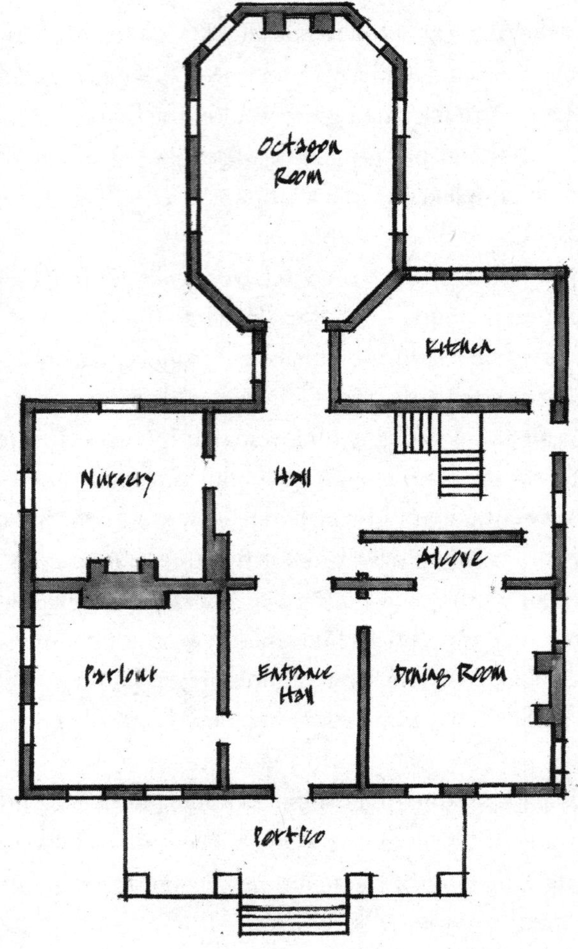

Morris-Jumel Mansion

crystal centerpieces of bountiful dahlia, lavender, and black-eyed Susan flower arrangements atop crisp tablecloths set with white linen napkins and white china plates. Ten chairs (white still) with upholstered cushions surround each table. I also notice that in the center of each is a place card naming it after a famous Founding Father, general, or one of their wives.

Tonight's cutlery is set in essentially the same way as it would have been in 1790: fork to the left, knife to the right, and—unlike our contemporary settings—the spoon is placed upside down, which was done in Washington's time to avoid a mishap with dangling lace cuffs. If I were here in 1790, I could easily picture myself awkwardly catching my lace cuffs on other utensils on the table, or worse, causing a glass of red wine to spill on my dinner partners.

I leave my historical haze behind as Vincent leads me to the colonial kitchen in the basement of the mansion. On the way down the rickety, winding basement stairs, I grab an apron off a hook and take my place alongside the other volunteer cooks, who have already begun prepping the food, chopping lettuce, pitting cherries, and whisking sauces in this historical kitchen. I am looking forward to cooking some of my favorite dishes just as they were served in 1790, using period-accurate recipes.

I take the lead on whisking a rémoulade that I hope will be the star of the menu, and then move on to other dishes. Three hours later, with my kitchen activity complete and happy with the results, I change from the apron into a light summer suit to join the other guests for dinner and give my keynote remarks. I stroll to the front of the house with Vincent, and we watch as arriving guests are greeted by the chair of the Morris-Jumel Mansion and an actor dressed as George Washington, complete with a powdered white wig, general's hat, and blue military uniform with brass buttons. I am amused to notice that as the general poses for photos, he keeps his mouth closed just like Washington was known to do—perhaps to hide his decayed teeth?

The mansion is the perfect backdrop for this historical occasion. Guests take selfies on the front steps with the costumed President Washington while servers offer silver platters of wine and hors d'oeuvres. The air is alive with the spritely melodies of a Mozart string quartet. I am surrounded by the sounds of laughter and happy conversation as guests of various ages and backgrounds mingle and shake hands. Suddenly, our President Washington announces that dinner will be served. The guests find their assigned seats according to the seating plan set on an easel at the entrance to the big tent.

I take my seat at the head table, named after General Washington, and Vincent slips into the seat to my left. My neighbor to the right, with her red hair coiffed in a stylish bob and a big smile, introduces herself as Lorraine Bell, the past regent of the Knickerbocker Chapter of the Daughters of the American Revolution (DAR). My first mental image of a knickerbocker is the New York basketball team, but then I recall that the term refers to the original Dutch settlers who came to New York. I know from my research that the DAR membership is limited to women who are descended from a person involved in the American Revolutionary War, and they played a key role in preserving the Morris-Jumel Mansion and converting it into a museum in 1904.

I am a little nervous to give my dinner remarks about the accomplishments of their ancestors. But Lorraine has an amiable nature and kindly introduces me to two other tables of DAR members. Amid much laughter, hugging, and selfies with President Washington, my nervousness vaporizes into the evening air.

Soon, it is time for me to open the festivities, and so I step up to the podium. I thank the guests for attending this celebration of Washington, the Founding Fathers, and the Morris-Jumel Mansion. I appeal to them to sit back, blur their eyes, and try to imagine themselves on this very site in the late seventeenth century. Instead of seeing an elegant twenty-first-century dinner party before them, with the skyscrapers of New York in the distance, everything but the classical house would disappear. This mountain would be covered in dense forest, and out from the trees along a dusty road, Thomas Jefferson would pull up at the front gate in a carriage. Regretfully, he would have been accompanied by enslaved people; the Washingtons also owned enslaved people who would have assisted with the dinner. They would be cleaning the front steps, carrying trays of food, setting up tables in preparation for the presidential cabinet dinner.

The enticing aroma of meat roasting and pies baking would waft from the hearth. Through one of the side windows, one might catch a glimpse of President Washington writing some last-minute notes at his desk.

After all, with the end of the Revolutionary War just seven years earlier—after key moments like President Washington and his troops scoring a turnaround victory crossing the icy Delaware River on Christmas Day 1776, the British surrendering at Yorktown in 1781, and the signing of the Treaty of Paris to tie it all up—the United States was now an independent country. And President George Washington would have had his hands full.

Washington had many questions to answer, things we take for granted today. For example: Who would pay back the country's large debt from the Revolutionary War? Washington had Alexander Hamilton establish the first bank of America to allow the federal government to assume the debts incurred by the states. Where could Washington build a new capital city—a cleaner, grander one that reflected a prosperous future and would garner respect for the new nation? That was where DC came in. And on a formal level, Washington wanted a presidential protocol. How should he be addressed: His Highness? His Excellency? Washington, of course, settled on Mr. President.

Members of the new cabinet had widely differing views on the future vision of the new country, including the practice of slavery, economics, and paying back the debt. Discussions grew heated. The infighting was fierce, especially between Alexander Hamilton and Thomas Jefferson, so Washington needed to unite his cabinet. If these issues were not resolved amicably, the entire experiment of a United States of America could fall apart.

So in that summer of 1790, Washington had the idea to host his colleagues in northern Manhattan. Today it would be called "team building." Washington took his cabinet for a sightseeing tour of the former Fort Washington to remind them of the fierce fighting and the lives lost in support of the revolution, then returned for dinner to the Morris-Jumel Mansion, which had been President Washington's headquarters during the war.

Joining the Washingtons were:

Thomas Jefferson: author of the Declaration of Independence, Washington's first secretary of state, as well as future third president

Alexander and Eliza Hamilton: Washington's first secretary of the treasury and his wife

John and Abigail Adams: Washington's vice president, who would be elected president himself upon Washington's retirement, and his legendary wife and future First Lady of the United States

Henry and Lucy Knox: Washington's initial secretary of war and namesake of Fort Knox and his devoted wife, who broke from her English family in favor of Henry and the new republic

Toward the conclusion of my talk, I look out at the crowd, and I can tell by their faces that they are deeply moved by the occasion and the people we are celebrating at this dinner. With that, I ask the guests to rise out of their seats, and I offer a toast to Washington and the Founding Fathers.

Then, I don't know what comes over me, but without thought, I offer a second toast.

"To the women of the revolution—Martha Washington! Eliza Hamilton! Abigail Adams! And Lucy Knox! They were at the dining table at this dinner, and they were dedicated patriots too!"

There is silence. And then, loud and passionate shouts throughout the tent, "To the women!"

I may have connected with the audience, I think, as the tent continues to echo, "To the women!"

There is enthusiastic applause for my remarks and toasts all around at each table. I return from the podium and, after toasting each of my tablemates, sit down next to my dinner partners and new friends, Vincent and Lorraine.

Lorraine, who specializes in genealogical research, after discovering that her ancestors had aided in the cause for independence in the Revolutionary War, joined the DAR when she and her husband moved from Canada to New York in 2007. For the next three hours, Lorraine, Vincent, and I talk about the Washingtons, New York, food, restaurants, architecture, and ice hockey—after all, Lorraine and I are Canadians at heart.

As we chat, servers flood the floor with steaming plates on silver trays and lay them in front of the guests. A wonderful scent of fresh herbs and sizzling butter swirls within the tent canopy. Recalling my cooking activities earlier today in the mansion's historical kitchen, I can hardly wait to taste the dishes, and I tell Lorraine about how tonight's menu came to be. There is no historical record of the menu from the Washington dinner of July 10, 1790, so for tonight, I proposed dishes of the period, including many from a cookbook

I purchased at the Washingtons' historical home in Mount Vernon titled *Dining with the Washingtons*, which shares a wealth of insight on their favorite meals.

The first dish is a salmon fillet. I think that the president would have enjoyed this: His favorite foods were fish and hoe cakes (corn bread). Washington was proud of his fishery in Mount Vernon. He considered himself a simple man with simple tastes, but felt that menus from the office of the president should have prestige to reflect the status of the country. Also, with his dental challenges, Washington would have appreciated the soft texture of fish.

I bite into my salmon and am pleased to discover that this is no slab of dry fish on a plate. Gently pan-fried in butter, the fillet is tender, the flesh delicate and flavorful, the middle moist, and the exterior crispy. It is accompanied by stalks of sautéed asparagus drizzled with more butter, and my contribution to the dish: an anchovy-tinted rémoulade sauce.

To make the creamy eighteenth-century French sauce, I blended together olive oil, mayonnaise, vinegar, nutmeg, horseradish, and a touch of anchovy until thick. I adorned the sauce with capers and chopped lemon pickle to enhance the delicate flavor of the salmon. The salmon, asparagus, and rémoulade are a luscious combination of complementary flavors and textures. I decide right away that this is a winning dish for Franny's birthday dinner.

As we dig into our salmon, we all agree how positive it is that Washington included the wives and children at his cabinet dinner—an indication of how different and equitable he saw the beginning of the new country compared to the male-dominated old-world traditions.

We gaze around the dining table and try to imagine what it would be like to eat with the Founding Fathers and their wives. As a continuation of the impromptu toast, we focus our discussion on the women and their contributions to the revolution.

All of us at the table compare notes on our knowledge of Martha Washington. Martha was a dedicated companion to her husband, traveling with the general and his troops during the severe winters of the Revolutionary War. Her presence at the Continental Army's winter encampments was a morale boost not only for her husband, but for the entire camp. The spouses of the other cabinet members (Eliza Hamilton, Abigail Adams, and Lucy Knox) were also patriots. They were their husbands' prime advisers, aided in writing their speeches, joined them at Washington's winter camps, and took care of family and homes while their husbands were away fighting the war. It was unacknowledged assistance that many women took on to show their support.

We gaze around the dining table and try to imagine what it would be like to eat with the Founding Fathers and their wives.

As we wait for our first round of dishes to be collected, Vincent notes that this manner of serving one course at a time is not how it would have been done at formal dinners in the Morris-Jumel House dining room. In the eighteenth century, meals were served in a method called *service à la française* (service in the French style), which is the practice of offering various dishes of a meal at the same time. Diners helped themselves from the serving platters, similarly to how we eat at a Chinese restaurant today, family style. Dinner, usually served at 3 p.m., was the most formal meal of the day and consisted of three courses.

Before guests entered the dining room, Vincent explains, the table would already be set for the first course—cauldrons of soups, fish, and a number of side dishes. The idea was that the dining room doors would be flung open and guests would be impressed by the amount of food, the fine furnishings, the numerous staff, and the impressive architecture.

After the first course was finished, the serving platters were immediately replaced with the second course. The second course had the largest dishes of the meal, including meats, poultry, and fish accompanied by vegetables and salads. This selection was accompanied by a series of smaller dishes of meats and vegetables, all arranged by size and symmetry around the main body of the meal. The table became an entire architectural construction of meats, seafood, and vegetables, all lavishly decorated to enhance the occasion.

"The aim was for the dinner and the entire room to overwhelm the guests with the wealth and opulence of the host," concludes Vincent.

I think, *Perfect for the eighteenth century, but that's not how I want our guests to feel at Franny's birthday dinner.*

I am so entranced with Vincent's dinner descriptions that I haven't even noticed our second course appearing: a colorful layered salad served in crystal glass bowls to increase the visual appeal by exhibiting the range of vibrant hues.

Thinking of the Washingtons' dinner guests, I prepared this salad of layered lettuce and beets in the Morris-Jumel Mansion basement kitchen with Thomas Jefferson in mind. From my previous book, *The Kitchen*, I knew Jefferson loved vegetables, eating meat only as a condiment. It is a dish of brilliant, curly leaves of Boston lettuce, layered with emerald broccoli florets and chunks of deep red pickled beets, along with peppery-flavored strands of grassy watercress. Indigo nasturtium and yellow calendula flowers speckle the bowl as elegant finishing touches. The salad is gently touched with a tangy dressing from a recipe that would have been made in Jefferson's own house, Monticello. Based on a French vinaigrette, the dressing's olive oil, Dijon mustard, mashed egg yolks, vinegar, and salt are whisked into a frothy cream, pulling all these flavors together into a burst of summer freshness.

When I take a bite, the textures in my mouth range from crunchy to creamy, the tastes of the individual ingredients playing off each other like a culinary ballet.

Once the salad dishes are taken away, the servers present us with a succulent roast of pork. This dish has a special place in my heart: My mom made a fabulous roast pork with stuffing, which is actually the same style that would have been served in Washington's time. For tonight, I prepared a stuffing of breadcrumbs, sage, marjoram, basil, butter, and egg and spread it thickly over the open surface of the pork. I then rolled up the loin and tied it together with kitchen twine. The final step was to slow-roast it in a Dutch oven. Now at the table, the roasted pork has been thickly sliced at a diagonal to expose a wonderful cross-section: the fat, the rib, the lean "eye" of the meat, and—a bonus—the crackling.

Crunchy, salty, and blistered, this ultra-crisp skin that sits above the layer of the pork's fat and meat is an indulgent, fatty textural pleasure. With the deep, rich flavor of the meat, stuffing, and fat crackling, I am launched into roast pork ecstasy, all accompanied by an apricot tart baked with a flaky crust and topped with cream.

The eighteenth-century final course was closest to the modern concept of dessert. Consisting of cheeses, pastries, and fruit, it could also include meat pâtés and other savory preparations. The word *dessert* evolved from the French *desservir*, meaning "to remove what has been served, to clear (the table)."

My recommendation for tonight's final dish was cherry pie and ice cream. Apple and cherry pies were favorites of the president, and ice cream was often on the Washingtons' menus. I announce to my dinner companions that the cherry pie that appears on our dining table is based on a historical Martha Washington recipe, developed by culinary historians at Mount Vernon. As we dig in, I know immediately that I have made the right choice.

It is an irresistible blend of three pleasurable tastes: the tang of Morello cherries, the mild saltiness of golden, flaky crust, and the sweet smoothness of vanilla ice cream. However, it is the cherries that deliver the magic. They have a tart burst—and while they do not dominate, the other flavors perfectly meld to give the cherries center stage. The heavenly creaminess of the ice cream is the finishing touch.

Washington enjoyed ice cream throughout his life—it was especially easy on his tender gums—and even had an early ice cream machine at his house in Mount Vernon.

After the final course in 1790, the servants and enslaved attendants would have left the table area so that the diners could enjoy a few glasses of wine together alone. Then, it would have been customary for Washington to raise a toast to the assembly before the guests separated by gender. Gentlemen would remain around the dining table to smoke, drink port or brandy, and discuss politics. Ladies would retire to the drawing room for coffee, tea, and civilized conversation. By custom, ladies did not smoke or drink heavily, and they were not supposed to have opinions on matters such as politics. However, with these savvy women at the dinner, there is little doubt that politics would have come up at least sometime in their discussion.

Tonight, as the sun sets and the watercolor skies turn to dusk, the surrounding gardens disappear into blackness. No matter: The white lights inside the dinner tent emit a soft glow that transforms the interior into a globe of warmth and camaraderie. A cool summer breeze off the Harlem River refreshes the guests, and the party continues with vigor.

The tables are now cleared of the plates, menus, silverware, and salt and pepper. The servers continue to diligently offer coffee and keep the guests' glasses replenished with wine. Instead of the energy level winding down, as one might expect at the end of a sumptuous dinner, increasingly boisterous conversation has taken over. With the bonding, relationship-building, and common experience of enjoying a great dinner together, the noise level grows stronger and stronger.

The Morris-Jumel Mansion dinner is a feast of making new friendships and reaffirming old ones. Many personal toasts are made into the evening. Contact details are exchanged. Hugs and handshakes. Invitations to come back to visit one another's homes.

Looking around the garden dining room, I realize that the Washingtons knew dinner was not just about the food. It was also a vehicle for bringing people together. The practice of dining together has a necessary function of nourishment, of course, but the hallmark of a great dinner is the hospitality of the host. Ideally, the host makes an extra effort to create a friendly and generous evening with food, drink, atmosphere—a display of hospitality to make visitors feel welcome. A shared experience that can lead to a bond of solidarity.

Reluctantly, we need to bring our evening to a close. Nobody wants to go home. I seek out Vincent and we shake hands. I thank him for his hospitality.

He is thrilled with the good cheer of the evening, as am I. "We love to share the house with people," says Vincent. "People come here to rediscover Washington and rekindle their patriotism. Presenting this dinner is a key role that the Morris-Jumel Mansion plays in our community."

Walking into the night, Vincent disappears into a spectacular flurry of bright yellow fireflies swirling, twirling, and dipping in circles in the mansion gardens.

Fireflies in Manhattan? Who could arrange this magic? The fireflies' ethereal blinking lights in the darkness astonish the dinner guests, who chase them like schoolchildren. Is this a special send-off for this celebratory dinner from President and Martha Washington?

As we set out into the evening, Lorraine tells me, "This dinner was not just about bringing the members of the first presidential cabinet together. It was also a conscious effort to have the wives at the table. While the women did not have official titles, their roles would have been as influencers, strategists, and sole trusted advisers to the Founding Fathers."

With their devotion to the republic, sharp intellect, and experience working together, it might have been the wives who were the real power inside Washington's first presidential cabinet. The Founding Fathers were having a hard time getting along. They needed to set out on the same foot. The Washingtons knew that getting everybody together for dinner would be a good idea.

Their hospitality might have changed history.

Morris-Jumel Mansion

65 Jumel Terrace, New York, New York, United States

morrisjumel.org | info@morrisjumel.org | (212) 923-8008

Dear Franny,

In the mid-eighteenth century, few houses were built with a room dedicated to dining. But Morris-Jumel Mansion's first resident, Col. Morris, was an architectural connoisseur, and he wanted to turn dinner into a showcase. Morris laid the groundwork for Washington, and whether his cabinet dinner took place within this boundary-pushing room or in the delightful garden, as I experienced, I gleaned many ideas for your birthday dinner.

Mrs. Washington was known for setting a relaxed mood for the dinner to come by welcoming guests with a refreshment at the front door. I would love to do the same.

There was no chandelier over the table. That's good with me—the lower the light, the fewer wrinkles on our faces. The lighting at the Washingtons' dinners would have been low—candles only. Candles set a romantic mood. That would help us slow down and linger over dinner.

I really liked the eighteenth-century wallpaper in the MJM dining room. Wallpaper is a decor element that we sometimes forget. Maybe we can find a vivacious wallpaper to visually rejuvenate our dining room.

The Washingtons made their home a center of hospitality. Taking the dining room outside was a way to create an informal atmosphere where people could relax and meet family. President and Martha Washington knew that bonds and teamwork are reinforced through dinner. They made the idea of a trusted cabinet work well, and it exists to the present day.

And those fireflies? I can try, my love, but I am sure the Washingtons consulted a much higher power to arrange that.

XOXO

J.

2

NOMURA SAMURAI HOUSE, 1860
Kanazawa, Japan

GROWING UP AS A third-generation Japanese Canadian, I felt an affinity at an early age for traditional Japanese architecture. Though my family lived in a conventional North American house, Japanese ceramics, screens, paintings, and bento boxes were scattered throughout. When people say traditional Japanese architecture, this typically refers to buildings built during the Edo period, between 1603 and 1867.

Over the years, I have collected dozens of books on Japanese gardens and traditional houses. Just leafing through the pages leaves me in a tranquil state—the serenity of the gardens, the clean lines of the wood structures, the modulating light through the shoji screens (translucent paper inserts inside natural wood frames).

My appreciation of the traditional Japanese house was a major factor in my decision to enter the architecture profession. But it wasn't until I attended architecture school that I came to understand how all the pieces fit together—the screens, the wood, the mats, the different approach to space. Then I really became besotted with traditional Japanese houses.

On top of it all, my favorite architect, Frank Lloyd Wright, once wrote that traditional Japanese architecture was a major influence on his work—the long horizontal lines, prominent roofs, deep eaves, and, most important, the spiritual connection to nature. He made repeated trips to Japan, traveling throughout the country.

A regret I've had is that I have never been to Japan, never mind inside a traditional Japanese house. My only contact with the country and its architecture was through books.

But I always dreamed of visiting Japan. So, when Franny buys me a surprise plane ticket to make the trip a reality, I am ecstatic. She encourages me to explore on my own, and says she'll come with me the next time.

I decide that priority one for me is to visit a traditional house in the country to learn firsthand about the history behind it all: the homes themselves, the dining room, the cuisine, and the unique, little-known aspects of the dining culture. Along the way, I hope to taste, smell, and create dishes to add to Franny's birthday dinner and experience the etiquette of eating in Japan.

As a follower of Frank Lloyd Wright, I want to see what he saw. I want to eat what he ate. The architect wrote that the country was "the most romantic, most beautiful on earth." I believe you, Mr. Wright. And now, thanks to Franny, I have a chance to see it for myself.

I don't speak Japanese.

I anticipate that this could be a problem for me in Japan. Having grown up and spent all my life in Canada, I speak only English. But I look Japanese, and in Japan, I know I will be expected to speak the language. Not only that, but I know there are many aspects to Japanese etiquette—the trouble is, I don't know exactly what they are. And surely, since I look the part, this will be another expectation of me that I'm not sure how to deliver.

So, when I hesitantly step through the arrival gate at Narita Airport in Tokyo, I am both relieved and elated to see my tour guide, Jun Hayashi, waiting for me with a big sign that says "OTA."

"Ota-san," he says to me with a big smile. "Welcome to Japan!"

Jun is well-known in Toronto for leading tours around Japan for both individuals and large groups from major corporations. He was recommended to me through friends as *the* expert guide of Japan, a combination historian, cultural expert, gourmet, and tour organizer. When I met Jun to plan the trip, I told him about my obsession with finding a traditional Japanese house and experiencing its dining room. I am also counting on him to teach me about the etiquette of Japanese dining. I don't think I could be in better hands than with Jun.

After a night's rest, my Japan odyssey begins. Jun and I happily board one of Japan's famous bullet trains at Tokyo Station, and he tells me we are headed to a city called Kanazawa, a few hours west of Tokyo. He has arranged to visit a traditional house that was once owned by a samurai in the nineteenth century.

Before we board, my tour guide warns me, "Ota-san. When you go through the doors of the train car, sit right down. Do not stand, look around, and block the doors. The doors close fast, and Japanese people will be angry if you block their way."

Of course, as soon as the doors open, Ota-san completely forgets Jun's lecture. I step into the train and stand in the middle of the door looking around—blocking everybody's way.

Jun groans. Yikes, it's only day one and I have already let down my etiquette mentor.

The rest of the train ride goes well and, somehow, I don't offend anybody. I don't know which I like better—the scenery of rice paddies, bamboo forests, and emerald mountains at 150 miles per hour or the variety of bento lunches complete with sake that

I scope out each time we pull into a station along the way. I sit back and admire the countryside: mountains, parks, and riversides covered in flowering sakura trees (Japanese cherry blossoms). It is April, which means that I'm fortunate enough to be visiting in the brief period that the sakura are in full bloom, filling the air with clouds of the most delicate pink.

When we pull into Kanazawa, excited about visiting a real samurai house, I leap off the train right over the portable steps. Jun rolls his eyes to the sky. I detect that he does not approve of my exuberance. Perhaps he had different expectations of me.

I am not annoyed with Jun's displeasure with me. In fact, I am very grateful to him. I know that Jun is trying to make me aware that there are many unspoken subtleties that are engrained in Japanese culture. For instance, I have already noticed that Japanese people are more quiet walking the streets or sitting on the train than Westerners. It is evident that there are many messages transmitted in Japanese nuance and body language that North Americans are not aware of. I am glad that Jun is teaching me these details of Japanese etiquette—I am especially looking forward to his coaching in the dining room.

We begin walking to find a hallowed place known as the Nomura Samurai House in one of the city's historical districts.

"There are not many places where one can see premodern Japan, such as in Kanazawa," says Jun. "They have worked hard to preserve the atmosphere of the long and rich history of the samurai."

I am in complete agreement with Jun's sentiments; I almost find myself traveling back in time, strolling traditional stone-paved streets and admiring the historical ocher clay earthen walls that enclose elegant houses. I imagine that this is how the area appeared in the nineteenth-century Edo era, with water rushing through cobbled canals and narrow streets lined with sakura trees that run between tile-topped walls. Around me, young girls in colorful kimonos preen for selfies in front of spectacular cherry blossom trees. Petals fall silently, like snowflakes.

Stepping through the vintage neighborhood, Jun tells me stories of the legendary samurai.

"The samurai were members of a warrior class who rose to power in Japan from the twelfth century," says Jun. "They were the 'enforcers' of the Japanese imperial court, halting rebellions and fighting for the emperor. Eventually the power of the samurai became so great that they took control of Japan." The samurai became the rulers of the land, culminating in a dictatorship run by a single samurai family (the Tokugawa clan) for more than 250 years.

Soon, we come to a rustic wooden gate with a tiled roof that is set into a stone wall. I am breathless as I peek through the gate opening and see that it leads into an enchanting courtyard of bamboo fences, moss-covered rock, and lush sculpted trees.

We are about to enter the Nomura Samurai Family House, Jun announces, built for the wealthy Nomura family. The date of construction could be as early as the sixteenth century, and while it went through numerous adaptations over the years, the 1860s stands out as the peak of samurai influence and power before it ended with the Meiji Restoration, when Japan modernized and the samurai were replaced by a national army in the 1870s.

Jun tells me that, as samurai, the job of the Nomura family was to protect their lord and his castle, which was built at the top of a hill. The samurai homes were built on the way up to the castle and acted as a line of defense. The Nomura clan were one of the most powerful and high-ranking samurai families during the Edo period.

Pointing to the gate, Jun says that samurai homes were typically modest dwellings, with the distinction that only samurai were allowed to have walls and gates to provide security. The front gate of the residence was where guards would hide and prepare to protect their leader against any assailants. In the world of Edo, the threat of violence was always present.

I try to picture myself as a samurai, hiding at the gate, ready to pounce like a panther on any enemies of my lord. My next thought (I must have dining rooms on the mind) is to wonder if samurai were allowed to eat any special Japanese pastries while they were on duty.

As Jun continues his tour, we are met by a polite staff member who welcomes us to the house. I give this person a very deep, low bow to express my gratitude. Out of the corner of my eye, I can see that Jun is shaking his head. I instinctively know I have done something else wrong; another etiquette lesson is coming my way.

Jun takes me aside and tells me he is disappointed at my bowing etiquette. He politely begins to give me a bowing lesson.

"Ota-san," he says sternly. "There are three positions for bowing." He demonstrates . . .

- *Bow #1:* This is a quick bow, with the head lowering only to the one o'clock position. This is a bow that your boss would give you at work in the morning.
- *Bow #2:* We hinge at the waist and the entire upper body lowers to the three o'clock position. This is appropriate for asking a father for his daughter's hand in marriage.
- *Bow #3:* The third is the deepest bow—to the four o'clock position, when the father grants you permission to marry his daughter.

Jun tells me that as the visitor and customer to this house, the proper protocol is for me to give the staff bow #1, the one o'clock bow. That person should be more than grateful enough to return the gesture to me with the three o'clock bow.

Thinking back, I realize that my bow had dipped far lower than what Jun would find acceptable—more like between the three and four o'clock positions. I am learning that in Japan, a bow is not just a bow. It also sends a message of understanding, protocol, and respect.

Arigato, Jun. I got that. I'll have to tell Franny this bowing story. She's going to love this one.

After my impromptu bowing class, I walk through the gate. Inside the outer walls, I enter a small courtyard of stepping stones. But I have to look down and place my feet carefully. The stones are purposely arranged in an irregular pattern that forces me to slow my walk. It is a way to slow my mind and leave the outside world behind. This design strategy perfectly addresses my guiding principle for dinner to be a place to slow down.

I stop on one large stone and look up, admiring the simple, undecorated style of the two-story samurai house. In shape, the walls are low in height, while the tile roof is more prominent. The structure consists of horizontal beams supported by vertical posts that allow for long, clear spans, resulting in a spacious, open interior. There is no need for interior walls to hold up the roof.

The origins of the traditional Japanese house design stem from the late 1500s, when Japanese architecture developed its own distinct style, influenced by the isolated mountain tea houses of Buddhist monks. The tea ceremony demonstrated the humble, simple, and plain. Japanese houses are modest on the exterior, trying to fit in with the surroundings.

Wood emerged as a preferred building material due to a plentiful supply of conifer trees. It's used in its natural form, left unpainted in an appreciation of the grain, carpentry, and joinery methods.

Though I am entranced by the architecture, Jun hurries me along to the front entrance of the house. The first space I walk into is called the *genkan*, an area behind the front door marked by a slight depression in the floor where guests are to take off their shoes. Wearing outdoor shoes in the house is a no-no in Japan:

Dirty shoes should never touch the rest of the floors of the house, and many hosts offer their visitors indoor slippers. The genkan is one of the features that has survived through the ages and is still present in almost all Japanese homes today.

I can see that Jun has quietly checked my feet to make sure I have removed my shoes. He is probably remembering an unfortunate episode last evening at our restaurant. I had returned to our dinner table from the bathroom, still wearing the communal bathroom slippers, having forgotten to switch them back with my personal pair. My slipper faux pas left many of the surrounding Japanese folks laughing, shaking their heads and pointing at the uncultured visitor from Canada. So today, I am on top of footwear etiquette.

We enter a narrow corridor with a series of shoji screens along either side. Behind these white paper panels is a length of spaces partitioned by still more screens. Straight ahead, I can make out one large area toward the rear of the house.

I love the peaceful, calm, and austere nature of this house's interior. Rather than separate walled-off rooms that we might see in Western homes, the Japanese house presents as a series of empty spaces that are functionally flexible, largely undecorated, and not designated for a specific purpose. The same room might be used for sleeping, entertaining, and eating.

I once learned that to understand the Japanese house aesthetic, one must have an appreciation of *ma*.

The Japanese concept of ma permeates many aspects of the culture. It is a pause in time or emptiness in space. It is silence, the opposite of sound. It is stillness, free of noise. It is present in religion, aesthetics, manners, film, even the slight pause in the middle of a bow.

In architecture, ma refers to the empty space throughout the interior of the house. Western architecture focuses on building walls, but Japanese house layouts are intentionally designed to create this emptiness. As I pass through the Nomura house, I notice that there are few decorative ornaments. Ma is about the life that occupies this space.

After slowly wandering through the interior, we come to the rear of the home. Jun slides open a shoji screen and we step through the door to enter the largest and most elegantly appointed space in the house.

After all these years of waiting, I am finally seeing a tatami room, the ceremonial dining room of a traditional Japanese house.

I am ecstatic. After all these years of waiting, I am finally seeing a tatami room, the ceremonial dining room of a traditional Japanese house. Jun explains to me that, as is the case for many rooms in a Japanese house, the tatami room was originally a multipurpose room. It often served as a study, as a sleeping area, and most importantly, as a banquet dining space for entertaining guests.

I gaze around the twenty-by-twenty-foot open space; it has a clean, humble feeling and is devoid of furniture. In this dining room, there is no Western-style table or chairs. The floor is entirely covered in tatami mats, thick, woven straw mats, each measuring about three by six feet. The side walls feature sliding shoji panels that diffuse sunlight into the room.

To my left is an alcove, or *tokonoma*, designed with a slightly raised plinth. Inside the tokonoma, a hand-painted scroll of a mountain landscape hangs on the wall, and beside it, an arrangement of flowers sits on a simple table. The altar-like presence of the tokonoma reminds me of a mantel in a Western house.

The most notable element in the room is a long shoji screen that stretches across the rear wall. As I wonder what could possibly be behind the screen, a staff person slides open the panel to reveal a magnificent garden just outside these walls.

The garden scene takes my breath away. It is one of the most beautiful landscapes that I have seen in my life—a secret walled garden that exudes a sense of peace.

I walk to the veranda at the edge of the house, where I am exposed to a wonderland of miniature shrubs, banks of irises, and mature maples with their branches sculpted to appear as though blowing in the wind. I can see stone features artfully carved into lanterns, step bridges, towers, and walkways that meander through

the green paradise and lead to a gracious pond of colorful koi carp, their long fins and tails dreamily swirling in the dappled water.

The natural world's views, smells, and sounds enter the home through the tatami room, uniting house and garden, to emit a feeling of serenity. All the while, the delicate pale sakura petals drift, twirl, and dip in the air, finally dropping to float on the running water.

After a few minutes of quiet contemplation together in the garden, Jun turns to me and explains that, since the tatami room was the place for formal banquets during the Edo period, he wishes that we could eat in it, to enjoy the full experience of the room. But the Nomura Samurai Family House is a museum, and we are not allowed to have a meal here.

However, Jun reveals that he has an alternate plan for lunch.

"Ota-san," he says. "I think it's time for you to eat like a samurai."

Jun and I leave the tranquility of the samurai home and saunter down the road to an adjacent traditional Japanese house built with a spacious tatami room. This house, though, has been converted into a restaurant.

Jun leads me into a large tatami room with mat floors and shoji screens, similar to the Nomura House's spacious room, but with less majesty or fine wood finishes. The tatami room dining aesthetic is basic. Except for the simple wood frames around the screens, there is little else in terms of furnishings and decoration.

The mat floor is set for a Japanese meal with two individual tray tables and two large cushions (*zabuton*). I can feel my appetite begin to stir.

Jun tells me that for formal dinners in the tatami room, the Japanese traditional dining customs call for diners to kneel on the floor with no chairs.

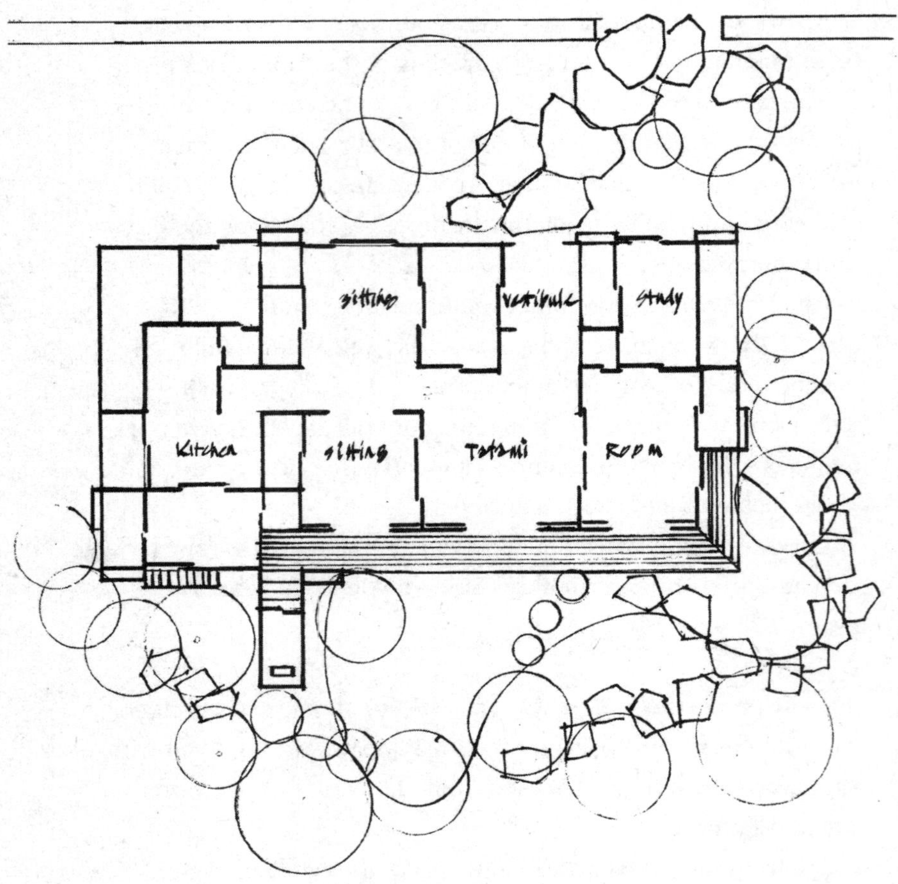

Traditional Japanese house

He demonstrates the proper form of kneeling: One knee at a time gracefully touches down on the tatami, with the tops of the feet flat on the floor and calves tucking under the thighs, so that Jun is sitting on his heels (no ankles crossed) with toes pointed to the rear. To finish, he lowers his bottom all the way down.

I follow Jun's kneeling lead—this is one etiquette piece from Jun that I can follow perfectly. I have done this many times during the martial arts classes I have taken over my life.

And thank goodness, Jun approves.

"*Jozu*, Ota-san," he praises me with a smile and a quick one o'clock bow.

I think we're bonding.

By the middle of the Edo period, it had become a convention for samurai to sit kneeling in this manner when meeting authority figures, such as their military leaders, as a symbol of obedience and loyalty. By the turn of the eighteenth century, all Japanese adopted this manner of sitting in their everyday lives, and it became established as the proper sitting posture.

But sitting on the floor when dining is not unique to Japan. This eating posture is practiced in many cultures around the world, including India, China, Vietnam, Korea, Persia, and Arab countries. Medical articles indicate that it offers health benefits such as improving posture, supporting digestion, and easing anxiety and stress.

But Jun tells me the main reason that the Japanese prefer kneeling on the floor to eat is tradition. "Japanese have a strong pride in their culture," he says. "Today, Japanese trend toward eating at a Western table and chair, but there are still many who continue to practice the kneeling tradition with strictness and pleasure." As an island nation, Japan was isolated from other countries for over two hundred years, and therefore Western-style chairs were not introduced in the country until the Meiji era in 1868.

My own observation of Japanese history is that the dedication to traditions derives from the Edo period, when relations and trade between Japan and other countries were severely limited. Foreign nationals were banned from entering Japan, while common Japanese people were kept from leaving the country. It was at this time that Japanese cultural practices such as Kabuki (traditional dramatic Japanese theater), ikebana (the art of flower arrangement), sumi-e painting (brush and black ink watercolor painting on rice paper), woodblock prints, and ceramics flourished into art forms.

Jun explains that at banquets during the Edo period, food was served to each diner with dishes on their own tray table. These trays were lacquered with vermilion on the inside and black on the outside, measuring about fifteen by nine inches, sitting four inches off the ground.

People of higher social standing ate off tray tables that were more ornate in design and sat higher off the floor. In today's more egalitarian Japanese society, most diners eat off a tray that sits directly on the floor.

My tray sits on the floor, and placed on it is a pair of black lacquer chopsticks positioned horizontally, the pointed ends facing the left. Chopsticks, first developed around 1200 BCE in China, became the eating utensil of Asia around AD 500. The popularity of the chopstick in China has often been attributed to the philosopher Confucius, who was against violence and disliked the presence of pointed objects when he was eating. He considered knives to evoke warfare, killing, and violence, which led him to prefer chopsticks.

They even had an influence on cooking techniques. Chefs realized that they could conserve fuel and cook food faster by cutting it into smaller pieces, and so food was cut up to cook quickly and evenly when steamed, grilled, or fried over the *kamado* (a stove powered by charcoal or wood). This method eliminated the need for knives at the dinner table and made the use of chopsticks more prevalent.

Traditionally, each component of the meal was placed on its own individual plate when served to diners. I think that when I serve a Japanese dish at Franny's dinner, we will use chopsticks. The guests can keep them as a souvenir of the dinner.

While we kneel and settle into our tatami room surroundings, Jun and I engage in an informative discussion about Japanese dinner etiquette. As a Japanese Canadian, I am aware of a good number of the conventions; however, he points out his top 5 dos and don'ts for me to keep in mind:

DO use the warm wet towels to wipe your hands—not your face.

DON'T touch the food on the communal plate with the end of your chopsticks that you ate from; instead, flip your chopsticks to use the opposite end.

DO lift rice bowls and soup bowls to your face.

DO slurp your noodles. It's thought this method of intake enhances a dish's flavor.

DON'T forget to leave the bathroom slippers in the bathroom when you leave—as I already learned the hard way.

Kneeling on the tatami in front of the lacquered tray tables, Jun tells me that the epitome of Japan's formal dinner experience is kaiseki dining, often considered to be the haute cuisine of Japan.

My ears perk up. Kaiseki dining? Given my obsession with culinary trends, I know kaiseki is an internationally recognized gourmet experience in Japan. Of course, Jun, a Japanese culinary expert, knows all of this. He informs me of the top 5 features of kaiseki:

Loving Care. Kaiseki food is actually quite ordinary; it includes soup, stewed vegetables, or grilled fish. It is the love and care that goes into its preparation and serving that makes kaiseki unique.

Quality Matters, Not Quantity. Kaiseki is a light meal. It is approximated to be 80 percent of what a person can eat. Diners are not to feel overly full. The priority is to have a harmonious experience focusing on the flavors and nuances of each dish.

Timing Is Everything. Kaiseki is serving in-season ingredients at their peak freshness. Dishes are presented simply to allow the true flavor of each ingredient to be expressed.

More Than Just a Meal. Kaiseki is a total art form. It is punctuated by the visual presentation of the food as well as the clothing of the server, the background music, and the architectural surroundings.

Purity Rules (this is the big one). Nothing is worse than over-ornamentation. The way kaiseki is displayed focuses attention on the ingredients' color and shape and the overall design of how things sit on the plate. But each dish is also properly displayed at the height of its natural beauty. The preference is to serve single ingredients on their own, rather than complex combinations of aroma, flavor, and texture.

Jun adds that the guests themselves also influence the meal. Age, profession, family background, interest, education—all are taken into account when deciding the flavors, colors, and mood of the meal. Guests are elements in the gathering's design, just as much as foods and utensils are.

Jun tells me that he has arranged a wonderful surprise for me.

"Ota-san," he announces with a huge smile. "You are very lucky to be in Japan during the sakura blooming season. As my guest, I am treating you to your own *hanami*, or sakura flower-viewing party. And for this special occasion, we will be eating kaiseki style."

With the shoji screens opened to view the blossoming sakura outside, Jun reveals that he has arranged for us to partake in a light lunch of kaiseki-inspired dishes to be served here in the tatami room.

I cannot believe Jun's generous gesture. I had not expected to dine in the tatami room at a traditional Japanese home, but now I know why it was set up for a formal dinner. I am overjoyed; this will give me the full experience of dining like a samurai.

Jun continues to explain that in Japan, the blooming of the sakura symbolizes a time of renewal, rebirth, and optimism. The appearance of pink marks the ending of winter and signifies the beginning of spring. Spring promises new life, so the blooming of cherry blossoms brings a sense of vitality and vibrancy. The Japanese love to celebrate and cherish the cherry blossom trees, and many people hold these hanami flower-watching parties.

However, there is also a fleeting aspect to these gorgeous flowers. While they fill the countryside with beauty, they disappear almost as quickly as they arrive. They symbolize both life and death.

"We celebrate the blossom's uplifting but impermanent nature," says Jun. "But the sakura also teaches us to embrace the grace of life while knowing its transience." Soon, the flowers will be gone with the wind.

"I get it," I say. "We must celebrate in the moment."

It is another lesson for my birthday dinner for Franny.

While the kaiseki dining experience can vary in the number of dishes and their order, there are usually six to nine courses served, and the chef decides their sequence. They might include an appetizer, clear soup, sashimi dish, sushi, grilled fish, a braised vegetable, rice dish, and dessert. Today, we will have an abbreviated version, just three courses, but it will be enough to convey the art and cuisine of kaiseki.

As we speak, a kimono-clad server gracefully emerges from a side-room kitchen and glides over to bring us hot towels. I wipe my hands with the towel and admire the floral patterns and the movement of the kimono's fabric. The kimono is Japan's traditional garment: a lapped-front garment with square sleeves and a rectangular body worn with a broad sash (an obi) and zori sandals. During the Edo period, kimono colors were based on seasons, gender, or sometimes political and familial ties.

The kimono fell out of fashion during the Meiji period (1868–1912), when the government encouraged people to adopt Western-style clothing. But the delicate patterns, sumptuous colors, and striking silhouette of the kimono continue to make it a popular robe to wear on special occasions to celebrate a traditional Japanese past.

Jun tells me that all traditional-style Japanese dinners in the tatami room would be accompanied by the national drink: sake. He stands and disappears behind a screen, reappearing with two handmade ceramic bottles and setting one on each of our trays.

Sake is a traditional alcoholic beverage made from fermented rice. Dating back more than two thousand years, sake was a sacred drink used in Shinto religious ceremonies. Because it is Japan's national drink, it is impossible to separate sake from the culture. It is consumed at personal milestones and ceremonies commemorating all occasions from birth to death. Sake holds an honored religious and sentimental place in Japanese culture, passed down through the generations.

Jun fills my sake cup (handleless, stemless, small enough to cradle in one hand) to the brim, then places it back on my tray. In turn, I pick up the second ceramic sake bottle on his tray and fill his cup. I know enough about sake to know that this is part of the fun: keeping your companion's cup full.

We toast each other with the phrase *kampai*, which roughly translates to "drink your cup dry."

Our sake is slightly cool and has a bright umami flavor with a hint of lemon and apple. But as I slowly sip it, I also detect a slight fizz. I tell Jun that I've never had a sake with fizz, but I like it. This must be something new; it's a fun and flavorful way to start a traditional Japanese dinner. It makes me think of starting a dinner with an apertif of prosecco.

Jun excuses himself and disappears behind the screen again. When he emerges, he is carrying a tray of food. He bows to me as he places it on my tray stand. I realize Jun is playing the kaiseki dinner host to me. A kaiseki meal, I have learned, begins with the host handing a tray to the principal guest. I, in turn, bow to him in thanks. Jun withdraws for a second tray for himself. (If we had more guests with us, Jun would fetch his own tray last, and once all the guests had received and set down their trays, he would invite the guests to begin eating.)

Unlike in Western dinners, where each food is typically served on a single dish, Japanese food is served on individual small plates that can have different shapes, sizes, colors, and decorative patterns. The small plates and bowls in kaiseki dining are carefully chosen and arranged to be visually appealing, with a sensitivity to enhance the presentation, flavor, and tactile and sensory quality of the food.

The art of Japanese dining presentation also emphasizes the season by celebrating the special ingredients that the time of year brings. From the patterns and textures on the dishes to the color schemes of the tray, every detail reflects the beauty found in each season. During the spring, pinks, greens, and sakura blossoms might appear as garnishes on servings of eggplant, bamboo shoots, clams, and bass. In winter, decorations of pine, bamboo, and plums could sit alongside dishes of snow crab, char, daikon radish, and sweet potato. Scarlets, golds, and red maple leaves highlight fall dishes of persimmon, chestnuts, matsutake mushrooms, and salted abalone. Finely sliced string beans, cucumber, and shiso basil leaves represent the lighter colors of summer to accentuate the flavors of grilled sea bream, prawns, tofu, light custards, and melon fruits.

The art of Japanese dining presentation also emphasizes the season by celebrating the special ingredients that the time of year brings.

Our first course, on a black ceramic platter, is a sumptuous display of three pieces of nigiri sushi, with thinly sliced strips of fish draped over a mound of rice. The first piece on the left is a slice of sea bream. It is next to a piece of succulent, fat orange shrimp with the head and red tail still attached. The last is a thick, delectable-looking slice of deep red tuna—simple but appealing. As a garnish: pink ginger sculpted into a sakura flower and a cucumber thinly sliced to resemble an unfolding fan.

In accordance with the kaiseki principles that Jun explained, the fish is always very fresh, and the rice is made with specially sourced water to give it the perfect flavor and texture.

I start with the sea bream's delicate flavor, picking up the white fish sushi with my chopsticks and turning it upside down to softly dip part of the fish topping in the soy sauce. I purposely do not touch the rice part in the soy sauce; I know the rice will absorb too much soy, making the sushi too salty.

The instant I place the piece into my mouth, the mild flavor of the fish touches my tongue; it tastes like it was freshly caught from the sea. I detect that the rice is perfectly soft, offering a hint of airiness. As the rice breaks into individual grains on my tongue, the seasoning of rice vinegar, sugar, and mirin blends with the thin layer of wasabi nestled within. All the flavors and textures come together in one bite.

After I finish the first piece of sushi, I take a quick taste of the pickled sweet ginger, erasing the flavor of the last morsel in my mouth so I can refresh my taste buds after the sea bream and ready myself for the next piece. With pleasure, I continue to enjoy the flavors and textures of the shrimp and savory tuna. Kneeling on my cushion, I contemplate how the taste of the sushi is as natural and pure as the cleanliness of the tatami room.

Franny loves sushi. Even more than I do. When we first started going out together, I thought she was exaggerating her love of sushi . . . maybe to find favor with me? But oh no. As I was to find out, Franny is a sushi-eating machine. I was very happy when it became clear that there would be many sushi dates to come. Sushi at her birthday dinner is a must.

I am surprised when Jun brings a second carafe of sake to our trays. While my usual experience is to enjoy one type of sake through an entire meal, I realize he is exposing me to different flavors. It is a reflection of how sake has become popular in recent years around the world and has morphed into different varieties.

We *kampai*, and I slowly bring the cup to my face, inhale the sweet aroma, and take a sip. This sake is warm, full-bodied, and bursting with floral flavors; it's the style that I am used to. I know that sake is carefully heated to just below the boiling point. I love the way it slowly warms my throat, then my stomach, finally acting as a balm for my whole body.

I notice that the sake is also having a warming effect on Jun. He is relaxing and getting a little louder. He comes out of the strict kneeling position and brings his legs around to sit with legs crossed. I am grateful that he has changed positions; I also bring my legs around to sit cross-legged.

A generous portion of black cod on an elongated lacquered board arrives next, the dark skin slightly singed by a charcoal burner (in traditional kaiseki preparation, skewered fish broils over the grill or charcoal and is then carefully deboned with tweezers). It is a minimalist, artistic presentation; the only embellishment is a dab of grated white daikon radish on a fresh shiso basil leaf.

I split the charred flesh open with my chopsticks and bring the fish to my mouth. I breathe in its aroma: slightly sweet with a hint of smoke. The moment the fish enters my mouth, I crunch down on the skin and the fatty oils ooze out of its tender flesh. As my tongue touches the firm fish, I fall in love with the delicate flavor and moist, meaty consistency of the cod.

I dip my chopsticks into a mixture of soy and daikon and barely touch it to my lips; that adds to the delicate combination of flavors. Black cod is one of my favorite fish to eat—slightly sweet, straightforward, grilled to perfection.

Two more bottles of sake emerge with Jun from the kitchen area. I am having trouble keeping up, but I will try. This sake has a distinctly cloudy appearance and a mellow, tart flavor appropriate for the dessert course, *mizumono*, with which we conclude our sample kaiseki meal.

The presentation of the final course is simple, yet it's the most colorful of the three. Green melon cut into bite-sized sections graces the top of the tray. Beside the melon is an exquisitely sculpted round pink sakura-flavored mochi bean cake garnished with a real sakura flower. But the dessert that appeals to me most is a square of pink *yokan*, a gelatin made with agar-agar and red bean paste. I used to eat yokan with my grandmother, although this one is garnished with gold leaf. As the jelly slowly melts in my mouth, its strawberry flavor—made rich with a condensed milk mixture—brings back memories of simpler times and makes me feel like I'm seven years old again.

None of the desserts are overpowering in their sweetness, and they are all reflective of the festive sakura season.

As we sip from our sake cups, Jun brings up the growing global popularity of Japan in the culinary world. He says that dinners such as kaiseki and settings like the traditional Japanese house offer a completely different approach to dining, beyond conventional Western culture.

From this tatami room experience, my opinion is that the most unique aspect of kaiseki, and the reason for its fame, is its connection to nature. In an increasingly digital world of texting, hacking, and annoying cell phone ringtones, we are searching for an experience of pure ingredients, pampering hospitality, and artistic presentation set in a gentle, meditative environment. The tatami room allows diners to become one with nature—with the seasons, the colors, and the tastes.

I mention to Jun that in 1905, when Frank Lloyd Wright returned from a two-month tour of Japan, he said that he had finally discovered a culture and a nation that treasured nature as much as he did. Now, after kneeling on the tatami floor and connecting with the magical garden and the purity of the dishes, I know what Wright meant.

As our meal comes to a close, I thank Jun profusely for bringing me to this tatami room and for his knowledge and generosity. I tell him that I could not have asked for a better Japanese dinner etiquette instructor and tour guide. We both laugh about my clumsiness over the past two days.

My dinner companion has taught me that the experience of kaiseki is a culinary treasure. But I find that it is not just the food that matters. It is also the clean and rich atmosphere of the tatami room itself, the appreciation of a traditional culture, and bonding with meal mates over a shared love of food.

But most of all, Jun has kindly demonstrated the emphasis that Japanese dinner etiquette places on hospitality, respect, and care of the guest.

We fill each other's cups and *kampai* again.

Oh yes. The sake also helps.

Nomura Samurai House

1-3-32 Nagamachi, Kanazawa, Ishikawa, Japan

Dear Franny,

Dining in the tatami room was so refreshingly different from Western eating practices in terms of architecture, dishware, and customs. Here are some ideas that we can use at your birthday dinner.

The concept of ma might be key in creating an enjoyable, slowed-down dining experience. At the Nomura house, it starts at the front walk of the house, with the irregular stepping stones, and continues with the spatial arrangements of the interiors. It exists within the careful arrangement of food on dishes, and even in dinner conversation.

The uncluttered appearance of the tatami room really appeals to me. Clean, peaceful, with few visual distractions. I liked how all focus during dinner was on the food.

I love the idea of a variety of small dishes served on a tray. Dishes are specially chosen to enhance the presentation of the food. Visual appearance is critical in Japanese dining.

We don't have a magnificent Japanese garden, but there could be other simple ways to bring nature into the dining room—wildflowers in a vase, colorful plantings in window boxes on an outside balcony, the sound of running water from a small fountain. I had a friend who once laid hundreds of flat black stones in her living room to allude to a river.

Most of all, I love the kaiseki practice of the host bringing the food trays into the tatami room, bowing, and then personally serving each guest one at a time. To me, this is the ultimate in demonstrating unconditional hospitality. The message is: I am here to feed you and satisfy your every need while you are in my dining room.

Oh yes. I have this unique dinner party idea. I could demonstrate the one o'clock to four o'clock bowing techniques to our guests.

Thanks to Jun, I've had a lot of practice!

XOXO

J.

3

EDITH WHARTON'S DINING ROOM AT THE MOUNT, 1904

Lenox, Massachusetts

I AM IN THE MIDDLE of rereading one of my favorite novels. Closing my eyes, I try to imagine myself in a Gilded Age dining room, softly lit by candelabra and jammed to the ceiling with furniture, paintings, statues, plants, feathers, and cushions. I would be seated in an oak chair, being served multiple courses of duck, salads, roasts of beef, fowl, and mutton, as well as elegant desserts and continuous glasses of wine and brandy, coming one after another. A glorious culinary experience.

But maybe not. Unfortunately, sitting among scrutinous peers, I might be bound up so tightly in a men's corset or a waistcoat and white tie that I could barely move, breathe, or swallow a morsel of food. The conversation stifling. The pressure to impress overwhelming.

Welcome to 1870s New York high society dining. Welcome to Edith Wharton's book *The Age of Innocence*.

Edith Wharton was one of America's greatest writers. She wrote over forty books in forty years; her masterpiece *The Age of*

Innocence is likely her best-known novel. Though the story is primarily about love, it also depicts magnificent dinners. As I read the book, I became fascinated with the food, the social etiquette, and, of course, the dining room. *The Age of Innocence* earned Wharton the Pulitzer Prize for fiction in 1921, making her the first woman to win the award.

The Gilded Age was a time when wealth and social class were at the forefront of everyone's minds, and so these themes are prominent in Wharton's novel. Though each era has its own distinct characteristics, there is a generalization that this was America's version of England's Victorian era, with their overlapping years in the late 1800s lending similarities in the display of personal wealth and influence. It is an era so different from ours today, a time when longing was kept excruciatingly repressed and sexual tension was enflamed by an illicit gaze across the room or an accidental brush of one hand against another.

In *The Age of Innocence*, Wharton evokes a time of calling cards, starched collars and corsets, paneled dining rooms with elaborate table settings of fine china and silver, gaslit streets, stately brownstones, and a society obsessed with possessions. As someone who is infatuated with the accoutrements of period cuisine, traditional furniture design, and historical architecture, I love reading it all.

But most of all, it was the food, dining room, and gastronomic experience that established the era's reputation for elaborate excess, which is made apparent in Wharton's novel. Food plays a central character in her books. The dining room in *The Age of Innocence* is more than just setting. The plot and character development are conveyed over teas, luncheons, and dinners. The posturing, scheming, and hypocrisy are played out in veiled dinner conversations amid platters of salmon served with crayfish, caviar-filled cucumbers, oysters, figs, floral-shaped sorbets, and gelatinous desserts—all presented with beauty and elegance.

Besides being a great author, Edith Wharton was also known for superb dinner parties, her love for food, and being a generous host who extended limitless hospitality to her friends.

To fully understand Wharton, I want to know about her house, her dining room, how she entertained, and the food that she ate. Most of all, I want to emulate this famous hospitality for Franny's dinner.

Like a mad, possessed character in one of Wharton's novels, I absolutely need to get to the source of it all.

To visit Edith Wharton's house, I drive through the emerald-green Berkshire Hills in Massachusetts to the town of Lenox. I am surprised that there is this dense forest, steep terrain, and rough wilderness only three hours from the concrete sidewalks and skyscrapers of Manhattan.

I turn off the main highway and drive along a back road of overgrown trees and ponds filled with bulrushes. I spy a small sign telling me I have reached The Mount—the name of Wharton's house. All I can hear are the chirping of crickets and the swish of long grasses blowing in the wind.

I pull my car into the parking lot and am met by a friendly staff person in a small wooden booth. She hands me a brochure with a map, points me to the path leading to the nearby woods, and says, "The house is at the end of the path. You won't miss it."

I am glad for her reassurance. I would hate to be lost in the wilds of the Berkshire highlands. I didn't bring provisions.

After a long drive from Toronto, I am glad to have a spirited walk in the fresh air. I set out along a shaded path that winds through mature trees and shrubbery and past outbuildings. The walk also gives me a chance to think about the research that I have done in preparation for my visit on Wharton's background and culinary life, consulting books, articles, images, and The Mount website.

I have learned that she was born as Edith Newbold Jones in 1862 into a New York family so wealthy that it inspired the phrase "keeping up with the Joneses." From 1866 to 1872, the Jones family traveled multiple times to Spain, Italy, France, and Germany—childhood trips that were responsible for the young Edith developing a knowledge of languages and a deep love of art, architecture, and literature.

Edith was a strong, self-reliant woman who rejected the conventions of her time. She was born into a world where women were expected to be only wives and mothers and were put on display at balls and parties. End of story. However, she defied these expectations and became one of America's greatest writers.

Writing was not considered a proper occupation for a society woman of her time. It was too "vulgar." It was thought that if women began writing fiction, it would lead to a lack of reality, chaos, and wild fantasies in their lives. Men claimed that they were discouraging women from writing for their own good. Those women who forged ahead and made a career out of writing were subject to scathing criticism.

In 1885, at the age of twenty-three, Edith married Teddy Wharton, an affluent sportsman, and her future appeared to be set for life. Yet, the restrictions placed on her only seem to have intensified her drive to learn more about reading and writing.

As I stroll in the bucolic scenery of the path leading to The Mount, I begin to feel some rumblings of hunger. I realize it is late afternoon and my mind turns to—what else?—dinner. Pulling out a chocolate chip cookie to quell my pangs, I consider Edith Wharton's culinary life.

With wealthy parents who loved to entertain, she grew up in an atmosphere of affluence and formal banquets. She would have been at the table for many elite dinners, which she later used as inspiration in which to immerse her readers.

These dinner parties—through etiquette, fashion, architecture, and food—were also a social transaction, an affirmation that you belonged in the upper classes. They were a reflection of who you were: more ceremony than celebration of food. I find Wharton's descriptions of these kinds of dinners in *The Age of Innocence* phenomenal. Her writing sits us right at the table with her characters as they navigate social graces to maintain their place in society.

But, alongside extravagant multicourse feasts—caviar starters, two kinds of soup, a parade of elaborately presented main courses (whole baked fish with caviar, roast game served with jellies and salads), and crepes or macarons for dessert—Wharton also enjoyed simple fare.

During her early years growing up with her family, Wharton also relished smaller, intimate dinners at home. There were no social games here: Her family's cooks made straightforward fare that she loved just as much (think fried chicken, smoked mackerel, corned beef, and boiled turkey, with simple sides and sweets like stewed celery and strawberry shortcake).

I am completely enjoying my casual walk, thinking about Wharton's culinary life, when I come to a slight curve on the sun-dappled path. Suddenly, between the tree branches, I am face to face with Edith Wharton's house: a gleaming classical château with a white stucco facade rising into a gracious four-story structure. It is stunning. It is also the exact opposite of what I was expecting.

Built on a high hill to take advantage of the views of the Berkshires and Laurel Lake in the distance, The Mount is part of a collection of mansions that has come to be known as the Berkshire Cottages. Being from the Gilded Age, these estates are known for their grandeur, but what fascinates me about The Mount is how very different its facade is from the surrounding Berkshire Cottages from that time. The others were designed in darker shades and have tall chimneys, turrets, conspicuous towers, irregular silhouettes, jutting elements, and finials. Wharton despised their opulent intricacy and ornamentation, and so, for her forty-two-room estate, Wharton turned to the classical architecture of ancient Greece and Rome.

Everything on the front facade is designed to be balanced and symmetrical: The evenly spaced windows are set off by elegant green shutters inspired by New England country houses, with minimal other embellishments. I have an affinity to classical architecture, so I greatly admire the proportions of Wharton's house, almost box-like in its elegant simplicity.

Standing in the front courtyard, I gladly join about a dozen other Wharton fans as part of a group tour. Our leader for the day introduces himself as Bob. He's a distinguished-looking gentleman, nattily dressed in a Havana-style straw hat that shades him from the sun and a fashionable summer jacket and tie. Bob, who has a gentle and knowledgeable demeanor, is one of the many volunteers who donate their time and intellect to The Mount. He tells us that he has been connected with the museum for years and that he never tires of giving tours to new people and introducing them to the wonders of Wharton's house and garden.

As we all admire the house's noble presence, our tour guide outlines the story of how The Mount came to be.

To pursue her interest in design, which was first sparked while traveling in Europe with her family, Wharton bought 113 acres of land near Lenox, Massachusetts, in 1901. Working closely with architects Ogden Codman Jr. and Francis L.V. Hoppin, she designed the home, including its gardens, architecture, and interiors, over the next year. Her inspiration was the classical architecture of Europe that she had come to admire during her travels: columns and pediments, structures based on symmetry and simplicity.

Tour guide Bob beckons us to The Mount's front door. He tells us that while Wharton was known for her prize-winning fiction, she was also an authority on architecture. In fact, her first book was on interior design.

"What?" I blurt out. "I had no idea!"

Bob explains that in 1897, Edith Wharton co-wrote a manifesto for early modern American interior design and architecture, *The Decoration of Houses*, with one of her collaborators on The Mount, Ogden Codman Jr. Published before any of her famous novels, it is still considered an important work in the field.

At sixteen thousand square feet, The Mount is smaller than its neighboring cottages, but that is part of Wharton's house design philosophy. In Wharton's mind, the design of houses had taken a turn for the worse in the second half of the nineteenth century: She tired of the ornate and heavy Victorian architecture and design, which seemed to have carried into the design of the surrounding Berkshire Cottages. She thought them vulgar, showy billboards of wealth, aggrandizing the owners around her. Wharton thought that a house should be livable for the owner, not simply a showcase. Victorians, in contrast, liked rooms full of ornate furniture, gilded mirrors, figurines, and framed portraits. To them, more was always better.

Stepping inside the front door, I immediately see that her interiors are the complete opposite of Victorian clutter. Her house is a clean, light living laboratory to put her design ideas from *The Decoration of Houses* into practice. Her rooms are based on classical simplicity and balance—a balance that grows from architectural function. Out with the Victorian knickknacks. With this, Wharton revolutionized interior design in America.

Looking around the softly lit entrance hall, I admire the arched ceilings, plaster-paneled walls with alcoves to display sculptures, and terra cotta floor tiles. It is an elegant, but not ostentatious, way to enter the house. I immediately feel welcome.

When her guests arrived, tired and dusty from their train journey, Wharton liked to meet them with champagne, so I try to imagine her approaching me with the same bubbly greeting. This is how I want to usher in guests at Franny's dinner.

I inform Bob about my love of kitchens, and he guides us to the end of the ground floor hall. We enter the room where the magic of Wharton's dinners happened.

The cheerful, light-filled space of white wainscoting and soft green walls has a display of glass-faced cupboards stocked with early-twentieth-century food products. Gleaming white subway tiles line the wall behind the giant stove. A window behind a deep porcelain sink offers a glimpse of the garden view that the eight to ten servants who worked in the kitchen during Wharton's time would have had.

We leave the kitchen and ascend a narrow, winding staircase with a wrought-iron railing that curves up to the second floor. (Wharton did not want a grand staircase.)

At the top of the stairs, we enter a sunlit arched hallway that stretches across the second-floor length of the house. The dramatic ornamental ceilings, with plaster reliefs, and terrazzo floors are reminders of the years she spent in Italy.

As we walk the corridor, I am anticipating a dining room similar to a scene in the film adaptation of *The Age of Innocence*: a long rectangular table at which twelve guests are seated, waiting to consume a multitude of courses; decor in dark wood-paneled walls, clad with portraits of family members to remind visitors of the wealth, power, and lineage of the homeowners. Painted in earthy tones, Gilded Age dining rooms were often a dark and intimidating affair. The stress of entering such a room, I imagine, might cause me to have indigestion before the meal even started.

But no. As soon as I step into Edith Wharton's dining room at The Mount, I realize she has thrown these Gilded Age conventions right out of her Palladian windows. She followed her own rules from her design book, *The Decoration of Houses*:

Edith Edict #1: Color. Walls should be sufficiently light in color to necessitate as little artificial light as possible.

Today, Wharton's dining room is painted a soft pink (the result of a 2002 renovation), but during her time at The Mount, Wharton had painted her walls an off-white. She wanted public rooms like these to be consistent with the classical aesthetic of the rest of her house's private quarters, bright and reflecting light. (Wharton disliked dark colors. She thought New York's brownstone townhouses ugly, referring to them as "chocolate-colored coating of the most hideous stone ever quarried.") Even the five French dining

chairs pulled up to the table are white with webbed backs, continuing the air of lightness. Wharton also used mirrors to create the illusion of more windows, making her grand hallways appear larger and bringing the outdoor landscape into the house.

Edith Edict #2: Furniture. At the table, there are no places of honor. Everybody is important.

At the center of the dining room is a round table that, both spiritually and architecturally, grounds the dining room—maybe even the entire house. Wharton rejected huge rectangular tables that seat a crowd of people. She designed The Mount expressly for small-scale entertaining and intimate conversation. I personally love round tables because they are conducive to conversation. Unlike the Victorian long tables, where a hierarchy is instilled by who sits next to whom, there is equality at Wharton's round table.

(Another example of inclusivity: I am delighted to see a large, soft cushion for Wharton's beloved dog at the foot of her chair. She even kept a glass jar filled with dog biscuits on the dining table. I've often thought I must have been a beagle in a previous life, so this detail makes me like Wharton even more.)

Edith Edict #3: Table setting. Make it fanciful.

The table is set with crisp white linen napkins at the ready for diners. At the center is a bountiful floral bouquet of white roses, and in front of each diner, there is a vase holding a single rose. The table gleams with silverware, glassware, and four silver candleholders. Each place setting—featuring a white bone china dinner plate, designed with a Hampton Court pattern of magenta vine leaves and a twenty-four-karat gold border—has a handwritten place card in front of it. The entire table ensemble is a lively display that would stimulate passionate eating and conversation.

Edith Edict #4: Lighting. Candles only.

Wharton used candlelight for illumination, but also to create ambience and beauty. She disliked the way overhead chandeliers and electric lights altered a woman's complexion and didn't flatter food, so at The Mount, the dining room does not feature an overhead chandelier. Wharton wrote that candlelight could transform a room, preventing it from feeling like a railway station or restaurant.

Edith Edict #5: Walls. Art becomes tiresome.

Wharton once wrote that art on the walls should be kept to a minimum to allow the architecture to be appreciated. She even wanted to show the detailing designed into each of the windows—which Victorian style often hid behind layers of heavy drapes and blinds.

Instead, Wharton's dining room walls are clad with white plaster sculptures that not only break up the light, but also add a sense of delight. They are sculpted to nod to the room's culinary purpose: a duck and other birds, fish, fruits, and nuts, with garlands for a festive touch.

Edith Wharton's strongly held edicts about architecture are prominently on display at The Mount, perhaps all for the benefit of her house guests. She lived for visitors. Wharton preferred only two or three guests at a time, for a mix of long stays (a few days) and short (a few hours).

Wharton made a point of spending as much time as possible with like-minded people, many of them editors, publishers,

academics, and fellow writers. Henry James, for instance, was a frequent favorite guest.

A typical day for Edith Wharton entertaining guests:

6 a.m.: Rise and shine. Writing and sitting in bed reading newspapers.
11 a.m.: End of her workday. Walking the grounds with her gardener.
12 p.m.: Lunch with guests on the expansive terrace, an Italian element requested by Wharton. The Mount's location on a ledge offers dramatic views of the gardens and Laurel Lake.
Early afternoon: A walk around the grounds with guests or a drive in the country.
Late afternoon: Reading in the library, literary critiques. Tea from China with honey and scones.
7 p.m.: Dinner in the dining room.
After dinner: Literary critiques in the drawing room.
Before bed: Stargazing.

Everything led up to dinner at the end of the day. Dinner was when Wharton deepened her relationships with selected childhood friends and made new ones.

Earlier in my life, it was my mother who created a convivial dining atmosphere. She did it with humor, unobtrusively steering the flow of chatter around our dinner table. Maybe at Franny's dinner I can channel her ease to encourage lively, revealing, meaningful exchanges between friends and family, much like there would have been around Wharton's table.

Edith Wharton loved the company of men. Although she was married to Teddy Wharton, there were many other men in her life. In the evenings, Wharton entertained the cream of American literary society, as well as figures like childhood friend Teddy Roosevelt and painter Maxfield Parrish.

She once said, "The core of my life was under my roof, among my books and my intimate friends."

Unlike other women of the time who were preoccupied with social climbing, Wharton had a community that gave her companionship, support, and intelligent conversation. These men, some of whom were outstanding authors, gave her insights into different lifestyles: Many were homosexuals or engaging in unconventional relationships. There was complete freedom among Wharton and her friends to say what they pleased, to listen and learn from one another.

When Wharton entertained, conversation was key, but food, of course, also played a central role. Despite her wealthy upbringing, Wharton was a meat and potatoes person; at her dinner parties, she would serve substantial and hearty dishes rather than ostentatious ones.

One such party at The Mount took place on July 8, 1911. It would prove to be a turning point in her life. With her husband,

Teddy, away on a fishing trip, Wharton relaxed and entertained three of her closest friends: Henry James, historian Gaillard Lapsley, and banker John Hugh Smith. They stayed for days, with roasts, wine, and wit filling the dining room.

Although Wharton favored familiar fare, dinner parties at The Mount were nonetheless lavish affairs, requiring a staff of ten to prepare the elaborate menus. Everyone who visited raved over the food.

The meal was prepared in the kitchen on the ground floor, then transferred onto a serving tray and sent up the dumbwaiter to the butler's pantry one floor above, where it was plated. It was then served in the grand dining room, where Wharton would already have been making wine plentiful.

One dish that might have been on the dining table during the July 1911 dinner is mock turtle soup, an imitation of the more ostentatious green turtle soup that was a favorite of the Wharton house. According to an article by writer Shoshi Parks for National Public Radio on turtle soup and the decline of diamondback terrapins, there was no other dish more associated with Gilded Age dinners than green turtle soup (or simply, turtle soup). The dish was an opulent display of wealth, prestige, and power, although it hadn't always been that way.

The soup's star ingredient, diamondback terrapin, started off as common food for Indigenous Peoples for centuries, and for sailors in the 1700s. But between the mid-1800s and the 1920s, North Americans went culinary crazy for the terrapin. Turtle soup became synonymous with prestigious dining in America.

This was not great news for the terrapins. By the turn of the twentieth century, overharvesting had left the terrapin population an endangered species, though it was thankfully saved by an unlikely phenomenon in North American history: Prohibition. Sherry gave terrapin soup its rich and unique flavor, but with no sherry for sale in the United States between 1920 and 1933 (in

Canada, throughout the 1920s, depending on the province), the popularity of the soup declined. The terrapin was saved.

But the prestige of turtle soup was not in its taste; it was in the expense. The dish was a status symbol, and guests would ooh and ahh over it, with its coveted ingredients.

Less wealthy families opted instead for mock turtle soup, an imitation created in response to the overhunting of the turtles needed for the original dish. By the late nineteenth century, most cookbooks gave housewives a recipe for the "mock" version (my first exposure was from the classic 1887 *White House Cook Book*, which also includes an additional recipe for green turtle soup that uses real turtle meat).

In the United States, mock turtle soup eventually became more popular than the original dish. Versions were served at restaurants across the country, while commercial soup companies marketed canned mock turtle soups to consumers right into the 1960s. Today, it is a forgotten dish.

Given my obsession with historical cuisine, I have long heard about turtle soup being served at elite dining rooms during the nineteenth century, and it has always piqued my curiosity. If mock turtle soup was a favorite dish served in Wharton's dining room, I have to make it. I want to inhale the aromas, taste the broth, experience the texture in the same way Wharton and her guests did in her elegant dining room.

I have long heard about turtle soup being served at elite dining rooms during the nineteenth century, and it has always piqued my curiosity.

First of all, I want to be sure to communicate that no turtles are harmed in the making of my soup.

Once I return to my own kitchen in Toronto, I commence my mock turtle soup–making adventure by opening *The White House Cook Book*. But when my eyes land on the text, I can hardly believe what I am reading. The opening lines give these directions:

First: Scald a calf's head.
Second: Remove the brain.
Third: Chop the brain into small pieces.

Yikes! Never in my life have I cooked a calf's head or cut up calf brains. But these (or other organ meats) were the nineteenth-century substitution for the texture and flavor of green turtle meat. The recipe also suggests meatballs, ham, and hard-boiled eggs. I go with meatballs and also decide to use stewing beef.

As I chop the meat, I remind myself how lucky I am to be cooking in the present day. If I were a nineteenth-century cook, I would be hauling the turtle up onto a cutting board, slicing it open, removing the inner organs and blood, cutting off the fins, sorting the tough sections of meat, cutting away the fat, and sorting the turtle eggs.

Instead, I plop my faux turtle meat into a soup pot with beef broth, sweet herbs, onions, pepper, and salt and let it stew for hours, thickening it with flour. When I add a quarter bottle of sherry to the soup, the room fills with the magnificent aroma of wine melding with meat and herbs.

I gaze into my pot. The soup has transformed into a shimmering deep brown broth with meat and caramelized onion bits peeking up through the liquid. As instructed in the recipe, I garnish it with hard-boiled eggs to mimic turtle eggs. My mock turtle soup is ready to eat.

When I dip my spoon into a bowl of the thick soup, I am not expecting much—the ingredients are so simple. But as I bring the hot soup to my mouth, I breathe in a heavenly aroma of beef fat and wine, wafting deep into my nostrils. The initial taste on my tongue is a deep beefy flavor that fills my mouth with pleasure, a taste made complex by the influence of chopped onion, lemon juice, and shades of tarragon, parsley, rosemary, oregano, and thyme. The boiled egg yolks instill a rich creaminess and fullness to the soup.

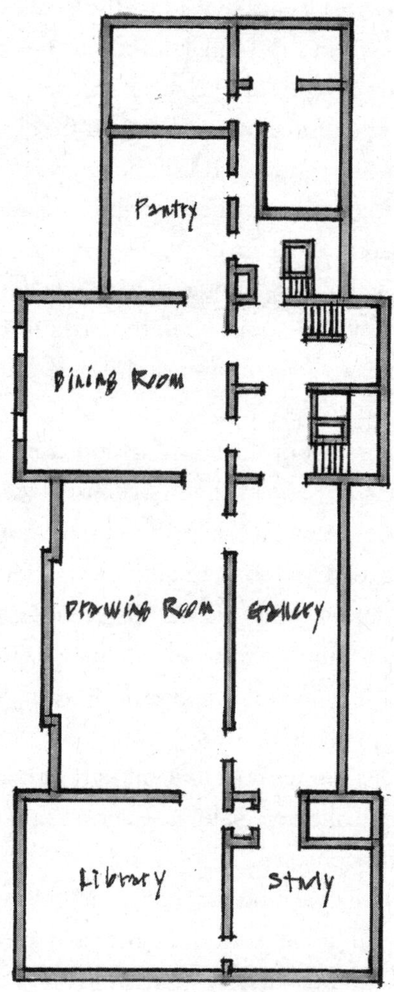

The Mount, second floor

However, the knockout punch is the sherry, which gives a kick and leaves a sweet alcohol flavor to linger on my taste buds. I can understand how this is the signature ingredient of the dish, giving it a unique and prestigious flavor. To me, the mock turtle soup is reminiscent of the French beef bourguignon, with fortified sherry wine substituting for the Burgundian red wine.

As I savor the tastes, I find that I like the mock turtle soup very much. Rich, meaty, and substantial, it is a satisfying soup that gives me a culinary insight into Wharton's dinner parties and the dining room in her classical house. I'm glad that I cooked and tasted this historically significant dish; however, I don't think I will include it on the menu for Franny's birthday dinner. Guests might be disturbed at the weirdness of comparing the ingredients to real turtle meat. A more hospitable option would be to serve a succulent Wharton-style roast beef, the main dish at the momentous dinner with Henry James, Gaillard Lapsley, and John Hugh Smith.

There is no transcript of the conversation around the table at this 1911 dinner, but one of the things that struck me from my tour of The Mount was learning about what a good friend Henry James was to Wharton. A good conversationalist is always appreciated at a dinner party, but on this evening, James must also have been a good listener. Taking an active interest in Wharton's life, he must have focused on key questions, expressed concern about her welfare, and then offered advice.

Because perhaps the most significant part of that dinner was one particular topic of conversation: Wharton's marriage. It was not bringing her happiness.

Teddy Wharton had symptoms that we might now diagnose as bipolar disorder. Edith had suffered emotional and psychological stress because of her husband for some time, and there had been no improvement in his condition. The Mount had been their home for nine years, but it had also been the scene of infidelities and financial problems. At the urging of Henry James, who convinced Edith that it was an unacceptable situation, she left the marriage.

The couple separated that September, and Edith left The Mount to travel to France. Regretfully for her, the couple sold the house later that year and the contents were auctioned off. In 1913, Edith and Teddy divorced, and Edith remained in Paris, where she lived for the rest of her life. She never returned to The Mount.

Despite these hardships, it was hard to keep Wharton down. When World War I broke out, she organized hostels for refugees, worked as a fundraiser, and wrote for American publications from battlefield front lines. She was awarded the French Legion of Honor for her courage and distinguished work.

In her later years, Wharton spent her time with artists and intellectuals, and achieved great literary success in Paris. Over the next twenty-four years, she published eleven collections of stories and sixteen novels, including *Ethan Frome* in 1911 and *The Age of Innocence* in 1920.

Edith Wharton's legacy is her writing, certainly, but she is also known for the limitless hospitality she showed at The Mount.

A guiding principle for me in designing Franny's dinner is to make my dining room a center of hospitality. But what exactly is hospitality? What am I to learn from The Mount?

The *Cambridge Dictionary* defines *hospitality* as "the act of being friendly and welcoming to guests and visitors." According to Henry James, Wharton went far beyond this definition. About one of his stays at The Mount, he wrote to a friend that he was "treated with a benevolence that brings tears to my eyes."

Standing in Edith Wharton's dining room, I notice that the afternoon shadows are growing longer against the paneled walls.

I check my watch and realize it is closing time for the museum. I take a long last look across the splendidly designed dining room where Wharton and her dinner guests indulged in wine, roast beef, and lively conversation.

In my mind, I can almost hear muffled snippets of conversation and glasses tinkling, and could that be the aroma of gravy, browned potatoes, and baked pies?

I do believe that houses have memories and personalities. And I believe that Wharton's offerings of unbounded food, wine, accommodation, conversation, and companionship are so strong that they might be embedded in these dining room walls forever.

Some people might dismiss me as being overly zealous, but there is no doubt in my mind that I can feel the soul of the dining room around me, the good feelings that that were once experienced here. I can almost hear the house coaxing me to stay a bit longer, to savor these last moments with Wharton's welcoming personality all around me.

If you visit The Mount, I invite you to stand in the dining room, overlook the round dining table set with her sparkling dishes, breathe in the scent from her fresh-cut flowers, and be enchanted by the view out the windows to her lush garden.

You might be entranced by her hospitality too.

The Mount
2 Plunkett Street, Lenox, Massachusetts, United States
edithwharton.org | (413) 551-5111

Dear Franny,

The dining room was the spiritual center of Edith Wharton's house. Unlike other dining rooms in its time, this was not a room where host or guests were expected to impress each other with their wealth, but instead, a vehicle for socializing and frank conversation. Here are some things I learned from Wharton's amazing dining room and her approach to hospitality.

Wharton wanted to create an Italian villa vibe: light and breezy, with views to the sensational garden. Dining while looking out to her fountains, flowers, and grotto would be calming and serene. Are we outside or inside? I don't know, but "we ought to open another bottle of wine." (That's a Wharton quote.)

Guests like Henry James raved about Wharton's generosity with food, and he wrote that snacks and refreshments were available all day. She served substantial, filling food. Wharton wanted her friends to feel pampered at her house. I think we might consider an Edith Wharton roast beef for your birthday dinner.

For Wharton, the point of being around other people was to indulge in the long, wide-ranging discussions that are only possible in intimate groups—her dining room was also her salon. Her round table allowed her to see and hear everyone at dinner and not to miss out on any conversation.

Wharton knew that a way to slow down for dinner and enjoy the ambience was candlelight. Somehow, candlelight and intimate conversation seem to go together.

Would you like a dog? We don't have one right now, but we might have one in our next life. I'll keep a place for the dog biscuits on the dining table—just in case.

XOXO

J.

4

CLAUDE MONET'S DINING ROOM, 1905

Giverny, France

THE PAINTINGS OF THE French Impressionists fill me with optimism and hope. Overflowing with color and shimmering light, they make me feel like the world is a good place. And my favorite artist of the movement is Claude Monet.

In the 1870s, traditional art consisted of paintings with meticulous, accurate depictions, clear outlines, and smooth surfaces—art that exactly replicated, and sometimes idealized, what you saw. However, Monet was a rebel. He was a leading figure of the avant-garde painters who broke away from these conventional ideas of art. He sought to capture the essence of the natural world by using dappled colors, capturing light in new ways, and painting in the outside air. He used thick paint application, bright color, and loose brush strokes to give only the impression of his subjects.

I always knew that the great artist spent the last forty or so years of his life in the small town of Giverny, in a house painted in his signature pastel palette and surrounded by the incredible flower-filled gardens, lakes, canals, and bridges that inspired his work. But it was a surprise to me to learn that Monet also often welcomed his artist friends for gourmet lunches to this house. On top of it all, he designed his own dining room that was the heartbeat of the house.

As I search for culinary inspiration for Franny's significant birthday dinner, I find myself daydreaming about what it would've been like to dine with this exceptional French painter and be joined by his artist friends. A visit to Monet's dining room might be the closest I could ever come to having lunch with the magnificent Impressionists who changed the art world forever.

When I arrive in Paris in September, the atmosphere is electric. Sidewalk cafés are packed with crowds laughing, drinking, eating, enjoying a balmy extended summer. The entire city is a festival. With so many people milling around the streets, it appears as though nobody is staying at home.

But I can't get too caught up in the metropolitan atmosphere. I am, after all, en route to Claude Monet's country house and garden in Giverny. Monet's abode has been on my bucket list for decades, and I am so happy to have my younger brother, Chris, with me on this trip. Chris is looking for ideas as he starts a new garden at his house in Los Angeles. To help him out, I have invited him along to visit the famous garden that Monet kept. He may as well start at the top.

With this goal in mind, we are both happy to leave the frenetic busyness of central Paris and drive the narrow, winding country roads of the French countryside. I am filled with excitement as we zoom past fields of lavender and herds of dairy cows in green pastures, and through hamlets of sepia-colored stone houses.

It is still early morning when we arrive in the tiny village of Giverny, about an hour west of Paris, pulling into the parking lot in front of a stone house with two tricolor French flags gently fluttering in the breeze. We are thrilled to have arrived at the artist's house and garden.

As we get out of the car, the aromas of sage, dahlias, asters, cosmos, and black-eyed Susans welcome us from the garden before I can even see the plants. We approach the garden entrance and I spot our guide, Marie Lalonde, a spirited, dark-haired woman with a warm smile.

"Monsieur John! Monsieur Chris!" says Marie with an exuberant greeting. "Welcome to Monet's house and garden."

I stick out my hand for a formal Canadian handshake, but Marie will have none of that. She greets us with a hug and a kiss on both cheeks. "As a guide and lecturer on Claude Monet's home, I am so happy to meet you and share my love for his garden."

Chris and I are glad to be led on this private tour by our effervescent host. Marie, who is equipped with a graduate degree in fine arts from the Sorbonne, shares that she has a personal interest in visual arts and photography.

"My brother and I like to eat," replies Chris with a laugh. "We are looking forward to seeing Monet's dining room and hearing about his food."

"Monet also loved to eat," says Marie. "He preferred local, rustic French food, much of which came from this garden. You have come to the right place."

Local, rustic French food sounds like a good starting point for some inspiration for Franny's birthday menu. With the amber sun breaking over the tops of the surrounding trees and tile rooftops, Marie takes us by the arm, anxious to introduce us to the wonders beyond. But first, Chris puts his hands up. "Whoa! Please, dear Marie," he insists. "*Je prends un café.*"

So Chris, Marie, and I wander over to a lovely little coffee shop near the entrance to the Giverny garden and order three

Americanos steaming with warm milk. For Chris, coffee in the morning is priority number one—even over Monet.

As we sit and savor the dark roast, Marie begins to describe Monet's early life.

"Claude Monet is one of our most famous artists—but he was lucky to become an artist," says Marie. "In the early 1860s, his father was a merchant and he wanted his son to go into the family's grocery business. I am sure he would have been a very good grocer, but instead, Monet followed his passion and became one of the founders of the Impressionist painting movement."

Marie tells us that other founders were Auguste Renoir, Edgar Degas, and Paul Cézanne. Monet came to know these painters in Paris, and they became lifelong friends.

Born in Paris on November 14, 1840, Monet liked the outdoors and loved to paint the world around him: beaches, boats, landscapes, ladies with parasols, family picnics, and small-town life. But plein air (or open-air) painting was not taken seriously as "real art" at the time. It was thought that true artists painted their subjects in the controlled light of an indoor studio. Monet, nevertheless, did it his way.

Eager to see what grew from Monet's creativity, I glance over at my brother. Looking rejuvenated from this coffee fix, he gives me a nod.

"All right, let's go," he shouts. "I need some ideas for my garden in LA!"

I laugh. Chris owns an adorable Spanish bungalow in West Hollywood that I love, but his garden plot is tiny. Still, I'm glad he's raring to go.

Marie leads us through the brick entrance building, and we step through a narrow door into the garden. Immediately, I am stunned by the beauty that surrounds us. It is September, and the gardens, especially the dahlias, are awash with vibrant, late-summer color.

Everywhere I turn my head, there is another explosion of color and scent. It is a floral masterpiece. Sprawling, sweet-smelling flowers trail over archways of climbing plants entwined around vibrant shrubs.

As I float through the lush garden, I am overcome with the beauty of the magnificent paradise—cascades of flowers, blooms tumbling over hedges, fruit trees, ornamental trees, climbing roses, and long-stemmed hollyhocks in riotous color combinations of hot reds, yellows, oranges, and pinks that pop and contrast against a backdrop of cool greens, blues, purples, and mauves.

Chris is equally amazed. "This garden is one of the wonders of the world," he declares. "How can a place be so beautiful?"

Marie could not be more charming. She breezes through the flowers, imparting knowledge as she goes. It's obvious she loves this place and finds interest here each day. I can't help but be drawn in.

"This is not an organized or manicured garden," says Marie. "Everything grows freely. Monet planted bunches of flowers of different heights to create volume and arranged others by colors to create harmonies. He spread and mixed the simple flowers with rare varieties."

Chris's face is a picture of astonishment. I am sure he is thinking about employing some of these techniques in his own garden.

I can also see that the lush floral compositions Monet created are like his paintings: bright patches of color and light. Flowers patter across the garden like his dappled brushstrokes.

We continue our slow stroll along twisted paths under a lush vegetation of bamboos and weeping willows. As we round one corner, we find a peaceful pond of water lilies, wisterias, and azaleas. It is Monet's paradise, complete with a Japanese garden, footbridge, and a pond full of floating lilies.

"Look at that," remarks Chris, pointing to a deteriorating wood boat on the opposite shore. "Even his old rowboat is like an Impressionist painting."

To me, it seems impossible to imagine a more perfect, soothing life than to be in the garden of Giverny, with its poppy-splashed meadows and sun-dappled autumn afternoons. Taking in the sense of delight in Monet's paintings and his garden paradise, I say to Marie, "Claude Monet—what a happy person. He must not have had a care in the world."

Marie gives me a serious look. Nothing could be farther from the truth, she informs me.

"The great irony is that Monet was a tortured artist," Marie says. "He committed acts of violence against his paintings—slashing, burning, stomping on them. He had a tempestuous personality. When work did not go well, he fell into a rage or depression. Tragedies filled his life."

Monet, she goes on, watched his first wife, Camille, die in 1879 at the age of thirty-two. His stepdaughter died in 1899, and then in 1911, his second wife, Alice, passed, followed by his son three years later.

Throughout his early years, Monet also had serious financial problems, to the point that at the age of twenty-eight, he tried to take his own life by drowning himself in the Seine River. Only when his work began to sell to American collectors was he able to purchase a home in Giverny and live a self-sufficient life. In 1883, middle-aged Claude, Alice, and the eight children from their blended family settled into the Giverny farmhouse. Everything Monet earned went into taking care of his family, whether to find the greatest ingredients for their food or to improve the house.

Monet struggled with depression all his life. He was moody and unsociable, and when people wanted things from him, he could be contemptuous. He often said that painting was torture for him, and he would go into uncontrollable tirades before exhibitions, lashing out at his artwork. He ranted at art critics and the public who bought his paintings, calling them stupid, idiots, and snobs. When he would return home from his painting sessions, his family waited in fear, gauging his mood by the sound of his footsteps.

"It is unfortunate that an artist so focused on bright landscapes could be so difficult," says Chris.

"But we have to thank him for his incredible art," says Marie. "Monet wanted the joy and tranquility of his paintings to be a source of peaceful meditation for his admirers."

As though emerging from the dream of the magnificent garden, I remind our group that I came particularly to see the Monet dining room. What spirit and energy will Monet's house inspire for Franny's birthday dinner?

Beyond the landscape of riotous pinks, violets, and brilliant yellows, my eyes can vaguely make out the roofline of a house. We start heading toward it, along a meandering path. As we get closer, I realize that it is no wonder I'm having trouble seeing the house—it is painted in gorgeous pastel colors that blend into the surrounding garden, beckoning like something out of a fairy tale.

Soon we find ourselves standing in front of the two-story farmhouse. Its stunningly long facade stretches over one hundred feet. As impressive as this is, the most breathtaking feature of the exterior is the color—the walls are in a cheerful pink stucco, with shutters and trim in contrasting emerald green. The house colors act as a perfect backdrop for the display of pink roses and blue forget-me-nots. I notice it is the same green that is used on all the benches, trellises, and fences in the garden, as well as the bridge spanning the pond in his Japanese garden.

Standing under a rose-covered canopy at the front door, Marie explains how Monet first noticed the village of Giverny while looking out of the window of a train traveling between Paris and Normandy. It was the eccentricity of the house and its overgrown orchard garden that caught his eye. (The house was already pink, although its trim at the time was gray; he later painted it to its current signature green.) Monet immediately knew he wanted to move there one day. In 1883 he rented the house and then eventually bought it.

Marie leads us through the front door at the center of the front facade. Her tour of the house starts with the little blue sitting room where Monet and his family would gather after meals to talk, read, play cards, and listen to music. This room is the first interior reveal of Monet's love of color—the wood trim and furniture are painted a pale blue and teal that harmonize with the Japanese woodblock prints hanging on the walls.

Marie shows us around the house, and then we return to the ground floor to see the kitchen. It is like entering a blue wonderland: The walls are lined with ceramic tiles from Rouen, France, that are white and a soft royal blue, along with cupboards painted white and a robin's-egg tone. Shades of muted blue continue on the gingham curtains and woodwork. Monet combined the cool blue walls with the warm sheen of his copper saucepan collection to bring a cozy, old-fashioned farm kitchen atmosphere to the house.

As impressive as this blue oasis of a kitchen is, it is the dining room that I have particularly come to see. A doorway connects the two rooms, and I can feel my eyes become as big as saucers when I step into Monet's dining room.

Engulfed in a glorious space, with walls awash in a glowing yellow, I feel as though I am being bathed in morning light. The soft hue brings me a feeling of joy that I can actually feel on my skin and inside my chest. It is entirely uplifting, the most stunning room in the house.

Looking around, I find that the vibrant yellow does not stop on the walls, but continues to the ceiling beams, armoires, wood trim, and chairs. Light pours in from a pair of south-facing windows that offer a stunning view of the Monet garden.

It is evident from its large size and luminous decoration that Monet considered the dining room to be the focus of his home. I can see that it was not meant for grand parties, but rather a private room for the family and visiting friends: It's spacious but made intimate with elegant wood paneling and delicate wood molding that add accents and texture to the walls. I am thrilled to be in the room where Monet shared these moments, dining with his children and entertaining his guests.

Although he was a private, moody man, Monet nevertheless enjoyed entertaining. Marie tells us that lunch at Monet's house was a coveted invitation, and he welcomed artists such as Renoir, Cézanne, Degas, Auguste Rodin, Édouard Manet, Camille Pissarro, Vincent van Gogh, and James McNeill Whistler. (How I wish I could sit at that table with them.)

Lunch was served promptly at 11:30 a.m. (the time the family always dined, enabling Monet to make the most of the afternoon light) and dinner sharply at 5:30 p.m.—although guests were never invited to dinner because Monet went to bed early so that he could rise at dawn. Any guests to the house were familiar with Monet's rigid schedule.

Monet's cook, Marguerite, would produce a dish that honored the guest: Renoir is known to have liked a particular kind of bouillabaisse, and Cézanne once provided one of his favorite cod recipes. It would have given Monet great pleasure to serve vegetables that he had grown in his own kitchen garden. Meat came from the prize chickens, ducks, and turkeys that he raised next to his house. He fished for pike from his own river.

Dishes included pot-au-feu (a rich classic French soup of tender beef, root vegetables, and marrow), roast chicken, duck, pigeon, pike, salads, tomatoes, eggplants, artichokes, onions, pears, and his beloved apples. Monet was particular about the way his food was prepared: vegetables only steamed briefly (asparagus almost raw), two salads—one for the family and a separate identical salad for Monet with extra pepper.

Today, the table is set with fourteen wood-frame chairs (I imagine them occupied) with wicker seats topped with blue gingham cushions and backs with curving spines painted chrome yellow.

A true artist in every way, Monet enjoyed impressing company with his table decor. He had two china sets. For everyday meals, Monet used Japanese-inspired blue and white Creil-Montereau faience dishware decorated with cherry blossoms and little fans. On special occasions, the table was set with Limoges Ahrenfeldt dinnerware in a vibrant yellow with blue edges.

Silver cutlery, white linen tablecloths, and delicate crystal glasses would complete the layout. The table was always decorated with flowers from his bountiful garden. This makes me want to have generous bouquets of flowers on the table for Franny's birthday dinner. She loves flowers, especially pink lilies. She'd be right at home in Monet's dining room.

Chris and I are especially impressed with the vast collection of seventeenth-, eighteenth-, and nineteenth-century Japanese block prints that line the walls of the dining room; they were great sources of inspiration for Monet. Beginning in the 1860s, Japanese woodblock prints became greatly admired by many Western artists—especially the Impressionists, who were intrigued by the unique use of vivid color, transparency, and composition in these works. These colorful prints depicted scenes from everyday Japan, including landscapes, actors, courtesans, and other aspects of daily life. It was a new aesthetic approach for the Impressionists, an inspiration to a break from Western traditional art techniques, compositions, and themes.

Deeply admiring the central role that nature played in Japanese culture, Monet came to fuse Japanese motifs with his own palette of yellow, white, blue, and green brushstrokes to develop his own distinct artistic style by concentrating on light and nature.

Marie explains that this fascination with all things Japanese was soon the rage among other artists like van Gogh, Manet, and Pissarro. I can only imagine the intense discussion of Japanese art that would have taken place between bites of bread, soup, and cheese as these Impressionist masters gathered in Monet's glowing yellow dining room.

For all of the amazing details in the dining room, its brilliant color is still its most striking quality. It is no accident that Monet chose yellow for the center of his house. For Monet and the other Impressionists, yellow was more than a pretty color. It was a connection to nature, light, and the sun. It was a color that meant a lot to Monet, as his work was a celebration of these themes. Throughout his life, Monet was fascinated with shifts in light and color.

He immersed himself in yellow, including in many of his paintings like his *Grainstacks* series, a collection of twenty-five canvases that repeated the same subject to show the differing light and color at different times of day and seasons. The works are a form of meditation to explore paths into the natural world. He also made use of the color yellow, and everything it evokes, in his *Poplars* series and the paintings *Irises* and *Water-Lilies, Setting Sun*.

With this color, Monet wanted to elicit a contemplative response, appreciate the color harmonies, and find peace. So I think that yellow would be a perfect color for any dining room to meet my goal of slowing down for dinner, leaving the outside world behind to relax over food.

Yellow has been called the color of happiness. With his own demons tormenting him, it is no wonder that Monet made his dining room into a sunlit sanctuary. For me, standing in the dining room is like being soothed by a warm golden balm.

A Day in the Life of Claude Monet:

5 a.m.: Rise before dawn. Take a cold bath. Explore the countryside, looking for painting subjects.

7 a.m.: Eat a hearty breakfast of eggs from his chickens, Dutch or Stilton cheese, cold meats, local cured bacon and pork sausage, toast, marmalade, dark-roast coffee, and croissants with homemade black currant or gooseberry jam.

9 a.m.: Out the door, usually accompanied by his oldest stepdaughter, Blanche, who helped him with his easel, canvases, and other painting equipment.

11 a.m.: Monet returned to the house for lunch. He was often impatient to sit down to lunch. He valued punctuality.

11:30 a.m. (on the dot): Lunch—the main meal in the house. He adored fish, especially the pike from his own pond, though he never lingered over food. Service was quick, and he disliked slow eaters. Desserts were baked peaches, pound cake, apple doughnuts, and tarte Tatin.

After lunch: Monet used the afternoon light to work on his afternoon subject in the outside air.

5:30 p.m. (no later): Dinner with family, beginning with soup. Monet sat at the head of the table and carved game, roasts, and poultry at the table himself.

7 p.m.: Evening with family in the salon to read and talk.

9:30 p.m.: Bed, to be ready for the next day. No compromising on bedtime.

Luncheons hosted by Monet were more than a display of hospitality. For the other Impressionist artists, the dining room

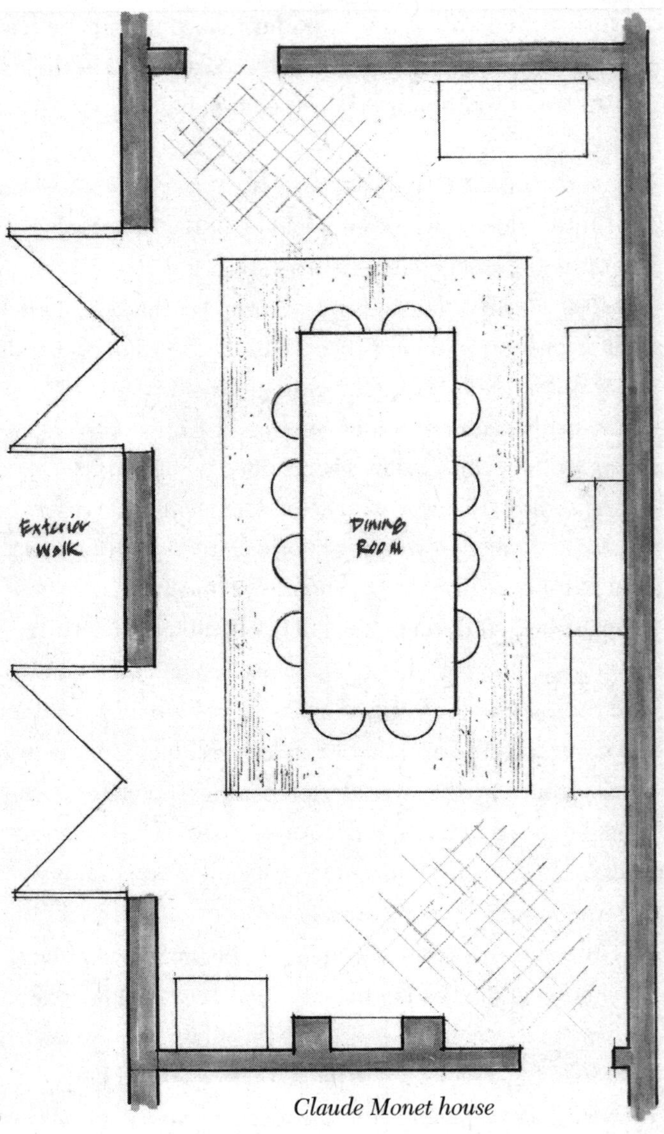

Claude Monet house

would have been a salon of lively and influential discussion. They likely would have raved about the fabulous food that came out of Monet's natural gardens and rivers. Surely they would have talked about his Japanese prints on the walls and their impact on the international art world. As the revolutionary painters of their time, they most certainly would have debated their role as artists and their place in the world.

As Marie, Chris, and I leave Monet's magnificent house and garden, I thank her for her informative tour and her contagious enthusiasm for Monet. I feel grateful to have gained a more intimate knowledge of the famed artist from this day.

Taking a last look at the house and garden, I mention to Marie that I am surprised at the number of fruit trees in Monet's garden. She smiles broadly and says that Monet especially liked apples. One of his favorite desserts was tarte Tatin.

"Really!" I exclaim. "I love tarte Tatin too."

I explain to Chris that tarte Tatin is a delicious French apple cake that was invented in the region. It's made with a crisp, buttery crust and sliced apple, caramelized in butter and sugar, and served upside down.

Marie tells us that Monet and Alice brought back the recipe from their stays at Hôtel Tatin in Lamotte-Beuvron, about a hundred miles south of Paris. Monet even painted a seductive version of an apple tart in a famous canvas titled *Les Galettes* (*The Cakes*).

Ping! This culinary tidbit from Marie gives me an idea for Franny's dinner. To honor Claude Monet, a classic French artist, I plan to make a tarte Tatin, a classic French dessert. If he loved the cake enough to create a painting of it, I have to give this baking challenge a try.

C'est bon!

Chris and I return to Paris and I am intoxicated. But not on French wine. My light-headedness derives from our exhilarating experience at Monet's garden, house, and sun-filled dining room.

In addition, I am completely focused on making a tarte Tatin with Normandy apples—the same type of apples that Monet grew in his glorious garden.

I love to cook when I travel, so to follow through with my obsession, I have arranged for the two of us to take a baking class to make a Claude Monet–inspired tarte Tatin with Lisa Arielle Allen, a fully trained pastry chef from the esteemed Ferrandi école de gastronomie. She went on to additional training at the five-starred Prince de Galles hotel pastry kitchen and now, along with her partner, runs her culinary business, named Tarts & Truffles Paris.

To meet Chef Allen, Chris and I hop onto a Metro subway train and ride to the Daumesnil neighborhood in the eastern section of Paris.

We gingerly make our way to an upper-floor apartment and ring the bell on the door. As it swings open, we are enthusiastically greeted by a young woman dressed in a crisp white chef smock with "Ferrandi" stitched in black letters across the front. Our tarte Tatin baking instructor has a big smile, an infectious laugh, and long dark hair pulled back in a ponytail.

"*Bienvenue à Paris!*" Lisa exclaims as she welcomes us into her home with a light Paris-style smooch on both cheeks.

"I was so excited when you called me to make a tarte Tatin," Lisa enthuses. "I've loved Monet and his use of light and color since I was a child."

Magnifique. A Paris-based *chef pâtissière* who loves Monet as much as I do. This only confirms that I am in the right place.

Lisa escorts me and Chris into her apartment, and I see that the dining room table is laid out with folded aprons, cutting boards, rolling pins, bowls of flour, baskets of apples, and other materials and ingredients we will need to make our tart come to life. Later we'll also be using the stovetop and oven in her compact kitchen.

The first task in preparing a tarte Tatin, Lisa says, is to make the dough, so Chris and I dutifully take our places at our prep stations at the dining room table. She tells us there are different ways to make a crust for a tarte Tatin, but today we'll be making a short crust with flour and butter.

As we start to organize the ingredients laid out on the wooden board, I am impressed with Chef Lisa's intense attention to the exact measuring of the ingredients. She has equipped us with an electronic scale to measure the precise amount of flour, butter, and sugar to the second decimal point.

"Be focused, John," she warns me. "French baking is a precise art."

Even though Lisa is a good combination of serious culinary teacher along with a warm, likable personality, there is no nonsense. Yikes, I feel like I'm back in my Bloor Collegiate high school chemistry class.

As Chris and I sift our flour, Lisa reveals the history of the tarte Tatin, first made (by accident) by sisters Stéphanie and Caroline Tatin. They ran the Hôtel Tatin, an establishment in front of a train station that was frequented by many hunters. Legend has it that one Sunday after the opening of the hunting season, while preparing an apple pie for a hunters' meal, Stéphanie, in the heat of the moment, forgot to line the pan with the pastry; the pan only held apples when she put it in the oven. Quickly realizing her mistake, she decided to drape the pastry on top of the apples and continue baking the pie. By the end of the nineteenth century, the pie made by the sisters was famous throughout the area.

"I wish all my mistakes in life turned into a classic French dish," Chris says to Lisa.

With that, our pastry instructor hands me and Chris each a metal scraper, and we follow her example in cutting cold butter into small chunks and blending it with the flour. The room fills with the sound of rapid *chop chop chop* as we all slice through the butter on the cutting board. I find chopping is a good fit with my rambunctious personality. Soon enough, the little pieces of butter become coated with flour until it all becomes a crumbly sand-colored mixture.

We gather up the crumbled butter and flour mixture on the wooden board and form a small well in the center. Lisa explains that the well is a depression that will hold a liquid solution of water, salt, and sugar to complete the dough.

Unfortunately, when I pour the liquid into the well, I pour too fast, and the water runs out over the edges of the well and onto the table. Some spills on the floor. It is a flour and water fiasco.

I look over at Chris and he is bent over laughing at my incompetence. He almost has tears in his eyes. He proudly points to his perfectly managed flour well filled with liquid.

"Here, let me take a selfie of this," he says.

It is another good-natured brotherly episode that I will probably hear about for years.

I am grateful when Lisa quietly cleans up my mess and, with a big smile on her face, picks up where we left off, folding the ingredients together into a dough. I realize that I have a long way to go before I can attend Ferrandi.

Finally, Lisa reaches over and gathers up handfuls of red apples.

She explains, "Good apples are key to a great tarte Tatin. It's really all about the apples."

For the next twenty minutes, Chris and I peel, core, and chop apples into perfect quarters as she continues. "The French are obsessed with apples. Different apples grow in different regions of France, and the French are very proud of their apples. Each has a unique flavor, and they name their apples after the region they come from. They are very proud of the dish that comes from their part of France. An example is champagne—a name only permitted for the sparkling wine made from grapes grown in the Champagne region."

Our French baking teacher tells me that to make a tarte Tatin, you need apples with firm flesh that holds up well to cooking. Monet grew Reine de Reinettes in his garden. At this time of year they're not available in France, so we are using Normandy Gala apples, which are a close cousin to the Reinettes.

The room fills with the sounds of my knife cutting through the crisp apples. When I pop a chunk into my mouth, the white flesh has crunch and a tart, sweet flavor.

"We are about to begin the most important process of making tarte Tatin—the making of the caramel," announces Lisa.

This is great news. I love anything caramel. I feel like I was born with butter and sugar in my veins.

Chef Lisa escorts us into her kitchen, where she pours sugar into a small saucepan along with water and turns the burner up to high. It doesn't take long before the clear solution comes to a rolling boil. And then, in a few short minutes, the water thickens into a dark brown syrup, which Lisa transfers into a cake pan, swirling it around so that the bottom of the pan is coated in toffee.

Our *chef pâtissière* looks at me and then looks at the apples. I get it. Chris and I lay our chunks of apple in a circular pattern in the pan and then slide it into the oven. After forty-five minutes, we remove the apples from the oven and prepare for the final step—adding the crust that we so lovingly prepared earlier.

As the tarte bakes and the aroma of apple and pastry fills the room, Lisa, Chris, and I continue to talk about Claude Monet and his love of tarte Tatin.

I tell Lisa that during our visit to Giverny, we noticed that Monet grew a variety of fruit trees, including apple, pear, peach, apricot, cherry, plum, and fig. We could see that Monet grew these orchard fruits espaliered (flattened) against the walls of his garden.

"It looked like he was trying to train the branches of his fruit trees to spread like a fan," says Chris.

Lisa tells us that by growing this way, Monet's fruit trees were able to catch the reflected sunlight and heat from the garden walls to promote early ripening and heavy yields. I wonder to myself if I'll see apple trees spread like a fan during my next visit to Chris's house in LA.

Finally, the timer goes off. "It's time for the flip," says Lisa. This is the trickiest part: Since tarte Tatin is an upside-down cake, the flip is necessary to show off the apples on top. Chef Lisa removes the pan from the oven. To release the upside-down tarte, she firmly sandwiches a plate over the top of the pie and, with professional confidence, flips them. She puts the plate on the kitchen counter and slowly lifts the pan.

Wisps of steam rise. Will the pastry stick to the pan? Will the apples fall apart? We hold our breath . . .

Et voilà!

Like magic, a clean sculpture of bubbling caramelized apples is revealed atop the crisp pastry base. It is a perfect tarte Tatin.

There are ecstatic cheers from Chris and me. *Magnifique!*

With a radiant smile, Lisa slices narrow pieces of tarte Tatin and slides them onto crystal plates. The tarte slices come to the table with a simple dollop of crème fraîche on the side. It is a thing of culinary beauty.

Really. I am so happy, I can practically hear thousands singing "La Marseillaise," the French national anthem, in my head.

The first forkful that greets my tongue tastes of tender warm apples, and pleasure radiates through my body. It is all about the flavor of the Normandy fruit—sweet but still with some zing. The Gala apples hold up. The crisp structure cooks to a softened texture but isn't mushy.

Next, I taste the glorious, sticky, sweet yet smoky caramel. It is sensational. The toffee completely soaks the apples in a deep, rich sauce. It also brings to mind the burnt sugar on the top of a crème caramel.

My teeth break into the crust of sturdy pastry. The taste is of a decadent buttery, salty exterior. The combination of rich caramel, tart apples, and satisfying crust creates a symphony of pleasurable flavors. With the morsel of tarte in my mouth, I begin to chew, and I am in ecstasy with waves of sugar . . . apple . . . butter . . . caramel . . . pastry . . . over and over again. The crème fraîche is a perfect complement. It counteracts the tartness of the apple—like a sour cream, but not as sour.

I thank Chef Lisa for a wonderful French baking experience and tell her I've never enjoyed apples so much before. I thank my brother Chris for sharing this Claude Monet experience with me and for being such a convivial garden and baking companion. He is a great brother.

Looking down at my plate, I notice that the tarte Tatin is the opposite of the flawless French desserts that are in fashion today. To me, tarte Tatin is abstract enough that the crust can crumble, the caramel can drip, a few apples can fall out of line. No problemo. Tarte Tatin will always look appetizing and taste fantastic. As a simple upside-down apple tart, it is modest but with a sophisticated taste.

Tarte Tatin, like Monet's garden, doesn't have to be perfect.

In Monet's garden, tall flowers cascade over low-lying flowers to make a gorgeous bouquet of color. Rather than having a perfect appearance, the intention is to evoke happiness, pleasure, good feelings. Giverny lacks the militaristic precision and geometry of a formal garden such as Versailles. It's friendly and welcoming rather than trying to impress.

That's what I like about Monet's house and garden. And that's what I like about tarte Tatin.

They're both a little messy.

Claude Monet's house and gardens
84 rue Claude Monet, Giverny, France
claudemonetgiverny.fr | (0) 2 32 51 28 21

Dear Franny,

What surprised me about Monet was that his life was not just art—it was a holistic existence that connected with everything around him. Art, dining room, nature, food, and family all became one. Here are some thoughts from Monet's dining room.

For Monet, everything emanated from the sun. His glorious yellow color scheme radiates throughout the dining room from the walls to the wood beams to the dish cupboards to the patterns on the plates. It is like sunbathing on a warm summer day.

The location and design of Monet's dining room says everything about his approach to hospitality. With the largest room in the house, he brought friends and family together at midday, sharing the vegetables from his garden, the fish from his river, the fruit from his trees, and the chickens from his yard. Lunch in his dining room was the centerpiece of his day.

For his fellow Impressionists and guests, the Japanese prints on the dining room walls would have been great conversation starters. I can only imagine that lunch with Monet would have been full of insights, exchanges, and new ideas. If he were here today, I doubt anyone would be checking their phones at the table.

Tarte Tatin is the perfect metaphor for Monet's food: rustic, basic, and made from his garden. This is a dish that I am definitely making for your birthday dinner.

If we have a Monet-inspired yellow dining room, we might never have another cloudy day.

XOXO

J.

5

HIGHCLERE CASTLE'S "DOWNTON ABBEY" DINING ROOM, 1912

Hampshire, England

IT WAS LOVE AT first sight.

I'm not talking about my spouse—although that did happen.

While watching the first episode of the television series *Downton Abbey*, I became transfixed by the images of the castle. The architectural grandeur entranced me: its glorious towers, massive brown sugar walls carved with intricate moldings, arches, balustrades, and gargoyles, as if from an Old English legend involving dragons and knights. Later I learned that it was the magnificent Highclere Castle, an English country house that has since gained fame around the world.

I became infatuated with everything that transpired at "Downton Abbey." How could I not?

The series, which takes place between 1912 and 1926, post–Edwardian era, is filled with images of sumptuous food and luxurious castle interiors, and portrays the complicated relationship between the aristocratic family and their servants. It is everything I live for.

And if it wasn't the castle at large drawing my affections, it was certainly the dining room. So many discussions, flirtations, squabbles, put-downs, decisions, and pivotal moments in the series happen in the dining room. I was dying to sit at the table where diners dressed in white ties, tails, and corseted dresses are served multiple courses by attentive footmen. And what are they eating, anyways?

One day, while researching famous dinners and dining rooms, I discover that I can actually visit Downton Abbey.

Faster than you can say "Maggie Smith," I am already mentally planning my trip to London: There might be valuable lessons to be learned for Franny's dinner.

In my excitement, I book the first tour I can find without digging through details. But then I ask myself, "Am I crazy? Where even is this place?"

I have no idea where exactly this tour will take me, or if a "Downton Abbey" really exists. My fear is that the castle might be an ersatz television set inside a studio building, and the images I've so admired are pumped-up special effects. If this is true, then my bubble will be burst and I will have wasted a lot of time.

The first step in my quest to find the Edwardian dining room at Downton Abbey starts in London, England, one of my favorite cities to visit. Friendly, cheerful, polite people fill the sidewalks. The city, even on a chilly December day, has a joyful ambience.

I am thrilled to be here at this time of year, because the best time to visit an Edwardian house is at Christmas. From the sumptuous feasts to the handcrafted charm of festive cards and decorations, the Edwardians were masters of celebration, infusing every aspect of the Christmas season with artistry and sophistication.

In Britain, the Edwardian period spanned the reign of King Edward VII from 1901 to 1910; the period is sometimes extended to the start of World War I. Characterized by an eclectic blend of Baroque, Arts and Crafts, and Tudor influences, Edwardian houses featured symmetrical facades with balanced and evenly spaced windows and doors. A perfect description of the stately Downton Abbey castle—or at least the one I know from television.

To help me connect with Downton Abbey, I meet my London tour guide, Frank Burgess, at Victoria Coach Station (about a ten-minute walk from Buckingham Palace) to board a bus that will whisk us out of the city and deposit us somewhere in the English countryside. Frank is an instantly likable person about six feet tall, with a shock of salt-and-pepper hair and a fair complexion. We shake hands and I am immediately impressed by the eloquent manner with which he speaks, all with a gently authoritative English accent. As a native Londoner, a historian, and a former television editor, Frank is, in my mind, the perfect person to help me discover the world of Edwardian England. It is early in the morning, but I am caffeined up and ready to visit what might currently be the most iconic house in the country.

I plop down in my seat next to Frank and we are off. On our way out of London, Frank assures me that yes, the Downton Abbey castle really does exist and that's where we are headed. At least my quest is heading in the right direction.

During the two-hour drive west, Frank explains that the program is filmed at a place called Highclere Castle in Hampshire. The origins of the building date back to the 1830s, when a gentleman named Henry Herbert, the third Earl of Carnarvon, renovated an existing country house to construct a grand castle for himself.

To make his dream palace come true, Herbert called on Sir Charles Barry, the most famous architect of the era, to remodel Highclere Castle into a truly grand mansion with over three hundred rooms, including a double library, a grand staircase, about thirty baths, and of course, a superb Edwardian dining room for nightly grand banquets.

Today, the castle is still owned by an Earl of Carnarvon: the eighth, who had it passed down to him fifty-five years ago, when he was a very young man.

With the enormous house in deteriorating condition, the earl almost had to sell the mansion in the early 2000s. Thankfully, his spouse, the Countess of Carnarvon—or Lady Fiona, as she is known—invited screenwriter Julian Fellowes, best known at the time for his *Gosford Park* screenplay, to the castle. Fellowes fell in love with the ambience and found it an inspiration for the *Downton Abbey* series.

When our bus turns off the motorway, we follow a narrow road that winds through grass-covered hills and then over a picturesque stone bridge. My anticipation grows; I can almost hear the dramatic violins of the *Downton Abbey* theme music over the drone of the bus.

The bus drives down a slight dip in the road, we take a wide turn through the trees—and there it is. Dominant in the landscape, the castle is stunning, golden, and radiant in the sun. It is even more majestic in real life than onscreen.

As Frank and I step off the bus, I am immediately besotted by architect Barry's masterpiece: enormous, monumental, soaring to the sky on an open landscape of snow-dusted hills, valleys, and Lebanon cedar trees. I am breathless.

The facade, I can see, is made up of two distinct architectural styles. The most prominent feature of the castle is the square base of the three-story structure, in a classical Renaissance style with regularly spaced windows that wrap around the building. Then, the delightful flourish of the facade comes from the flamboyant neo-Gothic spires, pinnacles, and finials that rise on the central and corner towers. I realize that it is these pointed neo-Gothic elements that deliver the vertical height and emotional thrill of viewing the castle.

A quick vocabulary note: In the Edwardian era, *house* and *castle* were interchangeable terms. Back in medieval times, kings built their castles with stone to repel attacks from spear-throwing invaders, but when gunpowder later became a threat, cannonballs demolished the stone walls, destroying them and leading to forts being designed low to the ground to avoid their fire. Then, in the nineteenth century, wealthy royalty wanted to regain their status, so in England and North America, they built ersatz "castles" to reflect their status (think Canadian Pacific hotels). Highclere follows this tradition of calling its (quite grand) home a castle.

As Frank and I walk up to the historical entrance of the castle, I am surprised that Carson, the Downton butler, is not outside to greet me. Just as well, I think. He would probably direct me to enter by the side servants' entrance (in such a case, I am prepared to fib and tell him that I am the ambassador from Canada, and I must enter by the front door).

Without further delay, I push against one of the massive double wooden doors adorned with a stunning Christmas wreath. Stepping over the threshold, I am immediately enveloped in a world of decadence and intrigue. Marble columns and Gothic pointed arches that expand out across the ceiling like a flower bursting in spring give the entrance hall a feeling of royalty and stature. The entire interior is decorated for Christmas with holly, ivy, yew, laurel, mistletoe, and flickering candles.

Straight ahead is the saloon, a jaw-dropping party space that soars to a height of fifty feet, where a skylight spreads across the ceiling and floods the room with natural light. The saloon is dominated by a towering, majestic Christmas tree decorated with strings of glass beads, gold balls, and glass ornaments. Assorted gorgeously wrapped gold and black boxes glitter under the tree, waiting for Christmas morning.

On the second level, we walk through bedrooms luxuriously furnished with king-sized beds, soft duvets, and thick curtains that cloak tall windows.

Last on the tour is the dining room—the place I have especially come to see. I am eager to enter the space where so much of Edwardian life and manners took place.

As we step into the dining room, I am greeted by holly, ivy, and mistletoe garlands that adorn the door frames and mantelpieces. Red berries add festive color to the decorations.

I notice right away that the grand, spacious room appears exactly as it does in the television show. I am glad to know that it is not just a set, but a real dining room where the Earl and Countess of Carnarvon have their meals with friends and family.

I know from my research that the most important function of the Edwardian dining room was to impress. I look around to see that this dining room has more than done its job: I am totally engulfed by the rich, gilded atmosphere of the era—a thirty-by-forty-foot room that checks all the boxes for tradition, beauty, and decadence:

Tradition ✔

I turn around and am overwhelmed by an enormous painting of King Charles I on horseback on the east wall. It turns out that the earl's family are descendants of royalty. This painting at the head of the table is a not-so-subtle message that you are dining with some immensely important people. The other walls in the room are covered with portraits in heavy gilded frames that tell further stories about family's lineage and their roles through English history.

Beauty ✔

The backdrops for the paintings are walls wrapped in rich yellow and gold fabric with an intricate floral pattern that gives a warm feeling to the dining room. As I walk around the dining room, there is no clickety-clack noise from my feet; the fabric-wrapped walls and hanging tapestries have the dual purpose of decoration and muffling unwanted sounds. In addition, the dining room furniture rests on an expansive multicolored Caucasian rug of bold geometric patterns that covers the entire floor.

Decadence ✔

Below an impressive portrait of the first Earl of Carnarvon is an ornately carved fireplace of twisted columns from two logs of coromandel wood. The focus of the south wall is a grand and opulent hearth, which would have been a welcome enhancement for dinner guests during cold winter nights. Overlooking the dining room is an eighteenth-century longcase clock that adds even more stateliness to the space and reminds me of the clock I saw in the Morris-Jumel Mansion's dining room.

Against the east and west walls I see massive wood sideboards with marble tops, where, back in the day, the butler would lay out morning breakfast for the family. Underneath these sideboards are magnificent carved wood boxes called wine chests or cellarettes. Found in affluent homes from the eighteenth to twentieth centuries, they were filled with ice and used for easy access to chilled wine bottles. The genius of the design was that they were built on small wheels and could be pushed around the table for guests to refill their glasses. This alternative method of serving wine makes sense to me in an opulent dining room; refilling from bottles sitting atop sideboards at more modest houses such as the Morris-Jumel Mansion felt too exposed.

With the introduction of refrigeration, the use of wine chests decreased, but I am surprised that they have not made a twenty-first-century comeback. I think the convenience, beauty, and fun of the wine chest would be a perfect addition to Franny's birthday dinner.

Three large and elegant windows stretch across the north wall; they are framed with interior wood shutters and long drapes that filter sunlight and allow for gentle breezes into the dining room. A heavy wood-paneled ceiling tops off the cavernous eighteen-foot height of the room.

Dinner, the climax of the day, was when the atmosphere of the room would be at its most elegant.

Frank tells me that the dining room would be used by the family for breakfast and lunch, but dinner, the climax of the day, was when the atmosphere of the room would be at its most elegant.

The most impressive feature is the 1870 dining table at the center of the room. Custom built for the castle, Highclere's dining table includes a Victorian mechanism that can contract and expand the tabletop. With twelve extensions, the table can lengthen to allow thirty guests to sit around it. A closet at the servery end of the dining room holds the leaves of the table, and I notice that they are sequentially numbered to ensure that they fit together with ease.

For Edwardians, like in the houses of the Washingtons, Edith Wharton, and Claude Monet, the dining table was the spiritual unifier—the center of the house. A common surface that all the guests would sit around to eat and share secret codes, manners, and rituals. It is the most important piece of furniture in the entire mansion, where everyone comes to gather.

In fact, when the extravagant candelabras are lit, shining on the faces of the family and guests in their formal wear, everything else in the room fades into darkness. Even the portraits of the proud ancestors become dim—but they are watching. The lighting acts as a cocoon around the guests and emphasizes the closed society of the family and friends at the table. The dining table becomes an intimate room within a room.

"The presentation of the table was a statement of elegance and good taste," says Frank. "The aim of the lady of the house was to impress."

For the evening meal, the dining room table is a spectacular display of flowers, place settings, cut glass, sparkling china, shiny cutlery, and name cards—all resplendent with festive Christmas decor. There are natural elements such as pine cones, nuts, and berries. Color and texture are added using bright red napkins, ribbons, and bows.

The table is also set with a menu card in front of each place setting so that guests could pace themselves during the evening, and to keep track of which wine was to be drunk with each course. I see that these menu cards are written in French.

"Darn, I wish I had been a better student during my high

school French classes," I mention to Frank. "Maybe if we had studied menu cards, I might have paid more attention."

The cutlery, plates, and glassware have been precisely positioned on the table by the butler, using a measuring stick. Even the distance of the chairback to the dining table has been calculated and put in place. (Although, a word of warning: The chairback is not for leaning on; these graceful, delicate Hepplewhite chairs, straight legs tapering at the bottom, were embellished with intricately curved carvings in their backs, which were meant only for decoration and for gentlemen to carefully pull back to assist a lady sitting down.)

As we walk around the dining room, Frank points out that the lord and lady would sit across from each other at the center of the table. The lady of the house would strategically arrange the guest seating plan around her according to hierarchy or to facilitate her goals for the dinner, which might include social climbing, requesting a donation for her favorite charity, or examining the dinner manners of a new acquaintance.

"No surprise," he whispers to me with a wicked smile. "Even the Neanderthals had a strict hierarchy for who sat where at dinner."

Everywhere I turn, I am astonished at the level of detail that goes into the need to impress. The table is set with traditional Spode Stafford dinnerware, plain white with a small fillet of gold and the family crest on the flat rim of the plates and dishes. I immediately have family crest envy. I want to design one as soon as I return home.

At the southwest corner of the dining room, I notice a screen shielding a small space from the diners' view. I walk over to take a peek behind it and find a small room. I realize I have found the servery, the place where dishes receive their finishing touches of garnishes and seasoning before the footmen usher them to the guests in the dining room.

The appearance of the six-by-eight-foot servery is a real surprise. Just steps away from the opulence of the marble and wood-carved dining room, the servery is shockingly plain. It is a place that would not be seen by family and guests, so there was no need for decoration. I try to picture the butler and the footmen bustling about the servery as they move in and out of the dining room, carrying steaming tureens, platters, and dishes.

I turn around and find a staircase that leads down to the basement. As I descend into dimness, I can see that, unlike the rest of the house, the walls on the sides of the stairs are devoid of any ornamentation. I have to watch my step on the well-worn treads, and I feel as though I am descending into another world—the underworld of the servants.

As my feet reach the bottom of the stairs, I stand on a scuffed linoleum floor and look around the basement. There is very little light emitted from only a few electrical fixtures, and a complete absence of daylight. Ahead is a narrow hall leading to an assortment of closed-off rooms. There are no family shields, painted portraits, or tapestries down here—just rough plaster walls painted a mint green and exposed water pipes running below the low, arched ceilings. Compared to the lofty heights in the public spaces upstairs, the cellar ceiling seems oppressively low.

I wander the stark halls looking for the all-important kitchen. But it is nowhere to be seen; it must be in one of the rooms that is closed off. I am disappointed when Frank tells me that the Edwardian-era basement kitchen seen in *Downton Abbey* is a period set located off-site. A servant call-board on a wall is the only kitchen remnant from an earlier time.

Even though the kitchen is not accessible, I get a taste of the servants' lives downstairs by reviewing historical photos on the basement walls. The fifteen-by-thirty-foot staff dining room is a stark, austere space with unfinished walls. An unadorned fireplace centers the room, while an adjacent wall clock would remind staff when it was time to get back to work. Meals were served to staff at a long, surprisingly narrow, wooden table. Floors covered in flagstone for easy maintenance and durability finish the spartan dining room.

The seating arrangement at the staff dining table followed the pecking order of the servants: The butler, in charge of all the staff, would sit at the center of the table, with the head housekeeper directly across from him. To the right of the butler would be the maid of the lady of the house. To the right of the housekeeper would sit the earl's valet.

Food for servants was plain but plentiful—poached meats, casseroles, lamb stew, beef stew, and steak and kidney pie. Although these dishes were not fancy, they were filling. They had to be: Awake before 6 a.m., the servants would need to eat

Servant's dining hall

enough to carry them through their seventeen-hour workday of cooking meals, boiling water for baths, sweeping floors, dusting chandeliers, and being at the immediate call of the family.

As I study the photographs, I reflect that the bare staff dining room has the complete opposite appearance of the elaborate family dining room only one floor above. I cannot help but think it would be depressing to serve meals to my employers in magnificent luxury upstairs and then return downstairs to eat in a dank, dark basement.

As the afternoon fades to dusk, Frank tells me that our tour is coming to a close. With regret, we head toward the door, but I take one last look at the Downton dining room. I become entranced by the candlelight shimmering off the gold fabric walls, creating a dance of reflection, light, and shadow. I make a note that something gold could rejuvenate our dining area at home. It adds magic and sparkle to the ambience.

On our way out of the castle, Frank asks me how I enjoyed my visit. I reply that visually, I loved being in the legendary space. Its grandeur was even more impressive than I had anticipated. And the gold walls completely captivated me.

But I confess to him that some other aspects of the dining room gave me a feeling of stress: It was not comfortable. While other rooms in the house, with their plush beds and cushy sofas, exude softness and comfort, the dining room seems to be more about making grand impressions. It has a hard edge to it. Even though the prescribed purpose of the room is hospitality, the messages from the portraits of illustrious descendants, the hard, polished surfaces on exotic woods, and the regimentation of the plates and crystal say otherwise. Even the backs of the dining room chairs are not to be leaned on.

"I feel like if I were living in the Edwardian period, the purpose of the surroundings would be to put me in my place."

My travel guide's eyes become as round as full moons, and then he cracks up with uproarious laughter. He seems delighted at my critical viewpoint of the dining room.

I tell him that really, today, it's no problem. With our more informal, egalitarian twenty-first-century attitude toward dinner parties, the presence of a few paintings of illustrious ancestors would have no impact on my appetite. In fact, I would find it highly informative to see the family lineage laid out in portraits. I cannot think of anything more fun than indulging in roasts, homegrown vegetables, and wine while conversing with the Earl and Countess of Carnarvon about what it's like to live in a three-hundred-room castle. I would love it. But sitting down to dinner in 1912 might have been a different experience. It might have felt more like business than pleasure.

Frank shares with me that the Edwardian dining room was indeed a social conference center for the house. It brought the family and their friends together.

As we board the bus to take us back to London, Frank leans over and suggests that one element of the dining room we have not discussed is manners.

"Edwardians loved to eat fabulous meals, and the flavor of the food was important," says Frank. "But dinner was not completely about the food. For the elite, manners were everything. And it was in the dining room where manners were most on display."

As Frank explains, Edwardian life was synonymous with manners—a strange set of rules that led to strict formality. Only the upper class had access to the rule book on appropriate dress, posture, speech, and dining. The etiquette was set by the elite, who wanted to continue to wield power and to control the introduction of new upwardly mobile people seeking to rise to power. Displaying proper manners was crucial in gaining acceptance with the right people. The way that the new people presented themselves at dinner was the red or green light into the aristocracy.

"Today, our informal dining habits are thousands of miles away from the Edwardians," he says. "But in turn-of-the-century Downton Abbey, the rules of the dining room were used to weed out the undesirables. It ensured that those in power stayed on top."

"Really?" I say.

This gives me an idea. I love to write about culinary history in a lively manner. On the drive home, Frank and I excitedly discuss manners—who they were made for, who actually made them, and why.

By the time the bus gets back to the center of London and we drive past the famous Harrods department store, I have started a draft of my own rule book on etiquette and manners at an Edwardian dinner. I am looking forward to tweaking the details from my adventure in the Downton Abbey dining room on my flight home.

On my return to Toronto, I contact a highly respected historian named Samantha George, who is one of the most knowledgeable people I know concerning Edwardian life. As the curator of the Parkwood Estate mansion (an opulent fifty-five-room 1920s house in Oshawa, Ontario), Samantha is the perfect person to consult about Edwardian table manners.

To indoctrinate me in Downton-type etiquette, Samantha invites me to the glittering Parkwood Estate dining room and proceeds to introduce me to her course, Edwardian Dining 101, where I learn all the ins and outs of what to wear, what to say at dinner, how to accept food, proper use of cutlery, after-dinner conventions, and how to speak to the servants.

For inspired twenty-first-century readers, or anyone unsure about where to start or just hopelessly in love with *Downton*, I present: the top 5 rules for dining with Edwardians.

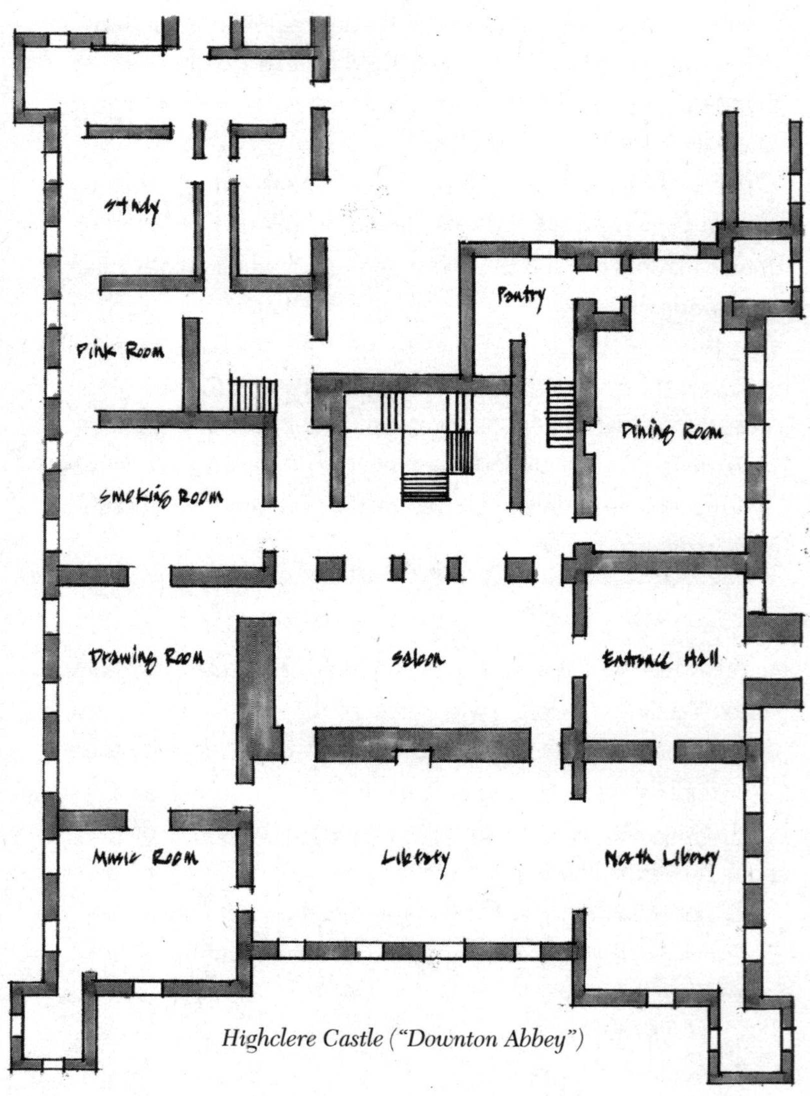

Highclere Castle ("Downton Abbey")

Imagine it's 1912, and you've received an invitation to dine with the wealthy Earl and Countess of Grantham. With their power and influence, your social standing could be raised a hundred rungs up the ladder. This is your lucky day. Or is it?

Not to worry. I have distilled the countless dos and don'ts of Edwardian dining room manners to five simple rules. Trust me, following these will get you through the evening with minimum embarrassment. Now, somebody please get me my corset.

Rule #1: The Woman of the House Is in Charge.

Women at the turn of the century had little power—except in the dining room. The golden rule you must know is that here, she was in control.

To give a large, successful dinner party with every detail in good form is perhaps the severest test of a lady's talents and social experiences. The woman of the house oversaw the guest list, the menu, the invitations, the seating plan—everything, right down to the flower selection. With the assistance of the butler, she controlled the dining room. A blink of an eye or an imperceptible rise of her eyebrow directed the butler to bring out the next course, pour more wine, or quietly sidle up to a dinner guest and advise them to change their topic of conversation.

Dinner conversation is instructed by the lady of the house. She turns to her left or right to speak with other people at the table. During the first course, the hostess talks to the guest on the right. During the second course, she turns left. For the third course, it's back to the right. Everyone follows. It's called "the turn of the chair." To help with the agreeable flow of dinner conversation, children would not be present.

Rule #2: Dressing for Dinner (Oxygen Is Overrated).

In the early twentieth century, the ideal female silhouette emerged from Paris design houses, with long gowns featuring an hourglass figure with a pronounced bust and hips. To achieve this look, women would wear an S-shaped corset, an undergarment that molded their bodies by tightening laces. By restricting breathing, mobility, and comfort, the corset also reinforced the female stereotype of being helpless and weak. Oh, but don't worry—the entire evening might only last eight or nine hours.

Clothing for Edwardian men in the dining room was the uniform of black pants, waistcoat, and jacket, with white tie, sharp collar, and starched shirt (ouch)—also highly uncomfortable. Gentlemen, such as *Downton Abbey*'s Lord Grantham, had their own valet to screw the men into these suits of armor. The dinner uniform was a statement that they had money and power, and could afford to pay another person to dress them them.

Rule #3: A New Way to Be Served—Know Your Cutlery.

By the mid-nineteenth century, diners grew tired of the existing French style of dining, where all the food was arranged at once on a table and everyone helped themselves. This usually meant that people only ate whatever was in reach, not wanting to bother their neighbors to pass a dish from down the table. During the Edwardian period in England and other parts of the Western world, a new serving method from Russia would radically alter dinner timing and etiquette.

Service à la russe (in the Russian style) involves courses being brought to the table one at a time. There might be twelve to thirteen courses; each would have to be consumed before the next was presented to the table (more on this below). Diners preferred the new Russian style because it gave everyone a chance to taste every dish, without putting anyone out. Hosts liked the system, as it allowed them to flaunt their wealth by showing that they could afford increased staff and dining utensils for the multiple courses.

Understanding your cutlery was, of course, crucial. By convention, forks are placed to the left of the plate, knives and spoons to the right. And there are multiples of each. Not knowing which knife or fork to use at each course could be your downfall. Begin eating a meal by using the flatware at the outside left and right, and then work your way in toward the plate as the meal proceeds.

Rule #4: Dinner Is a Marathon, Not a Sprint.

The number of courses could range from a modest eight to a filling thirteen. An example of *service à la russe* would consist of:

Hors d'oeuvres (often oysters or caviar)
Soup #1 (clear, such as consommé)
Soup #2 (thick, such as cream of mushroom)
Fish #1 (boiled, such as poached cod in a white wine sauce)
Fish #2 (fried, such as sole, fish cakes, or smoked haddock)
Entrée (lobster thermidor, duck confit, or seafood Newburg)
Joint (leg of lamb, filet mignon Lili, or beef Wellington)
Roast (at Christmas it would be roast goose or turkey with chestnut dressing)
Salad (artichoke and asparagus, watercress and scallions, or a winter vegetable)
Vegetables (Lyonnaise potatoes, creamed carrots, or braised red cabbage)
A hot dessert (Christmas pudding, mincemeat tarts, apple Charlotte, chocolate cake, Parisian éclairs, crêpes Suzette, English trifle, meringue pie, or bread pudding)

Ice cream and wafers
Fresh and dried fruits, coffee and liqueurs

The butler leads the way around the table with a decanter, from which he pours the wine. The footmen then follow to serve the food. Serving is carefully choreographed, as the footmen dip in and out between the guests together. They wait, lean in together, and move off at same time, like graceful swans on the pond. Guests would use the spoon and fork provided to remove the portion they desired—if any at all. The idea was to taste each course. Overeating was frowned upon: Take only a small serving, do not ask for seconds. (Don't worry, much more is on the way.)

Rule #5: The Staff—Just Ignore Them.

After dinner, the guests move to the drawing room for drinks and relaxed conversation, at which point, the staff begin to clean the dining room. Partying in the drawing room could go to 3 a.m. The staff would then have until 4 a.m. to clean the room, going to bed soon after to get up at 6 a.m. to light the fires and clean the house. This would be their regimen up to five times a week.

Looks counted. Butlers and footmen had to be tall and handsome. Maids were attractive and compliant, with "beautiful" hair (red hair was a no-no). But the service people were never acknowledged or thanked, because they did everything for the family, all the time, and it would have been monotonous for their masters to thank them hundreds of times a day. Their job was to be invisible. Acknowledgment was silent.

A positive aspect of Christmas in the Edwardian house was that it was one of the few times the family would say thank you to the servants. The family would present gifts to the servants that in some cases might include cash. The servants would enjoy their own festive dinner of roast meats, punch, and steamed sponge pudding on Boxing Day (December 26) after the main family meal. Another tradition that servants would enjoy at Christmas was the servants' ball, a party where servants could mix with their employing family as equals, enjoying dancing and refreshments together.

However, that period of thanks would be short-lived. After a day of rest on December 26, it would be back to the usual grind of catering to the family and guests for the next year, and the staff would resume their roles as invisible people. Depending on the household, servants might have half a day off per week or one day off per month.

Similarly to today, dessert at the Edwardian Christmas dinner would have been the crowning finale to a spectacular meal. Edwardian festive desserts included Christmas plum pudding, trifle, fruit cake, and Yule log. But the dessert that I always look forward to at this time of year is mincemeat tarts. I love the combination of sweet dried fruits with spices and distilled spirit enveloped in a short pastry crust and then drenched in a hard sauce.

Without a kitchen available in the mansion these days, I was not able to sample any Christmas cuisine in Highclere. On my return to Toronto, I decide that I want to get the full experience of an Edwardian Christmas, especially mincemeat pie.

To achieve the goal of an era-accurate mincemeat pie, I call on Mya Sangster and Sherry Murphy, who are the best bakers I know and are also members of the Culinary Historians of Canada.

"Of course we'll help you, John," says Sherry. "But be ready. We'll make mincemeat like it's 1912." I am not sure what Sherry is getting at, but never mind. To get the full period atmosphere, we agree to meet at a historical kitchen in Toronto, at a heritage home called Campbell House Museum.

At Campbell House the kitchen is in the basement, just like at Highclere. As I reach the bottom of the basement stairs, I have to let my eyes adjust to the dim light and smoky air, just the kind of place that Downton's cook, Mrs. Patmore, would work in. Mya and Sherry have already built a roaring fire in the hearth and have prepped all the ingredients. I hug my mincemeat instructors, who are both wearing historical long skirts that reach the floor, aprons, and baking hats. Even though I am back in Canada, the atmosphere around me is full-on Downton.

Looking around, I see that a long table in front of the fireplace acts as the prep counter, and my instructors have already laid out bowls, cutting boards, knives, and wooden spoons. They have even rolled out the dough and laid it in a pie plate and multiple tart tins. I thank Mya and Sherry for doing so much prep work.

"We're happy that you are so enthusiastic to bake," says Mya. "But these tarts aren't what you might expect. These are real mincemeat tarts, made with real mincemeat."

"Oh, that's nice," I say. "What exactly do you mean, 'real' mincemeat?"

"Well, it's not a simple answer," chimes in Sherry, as she hands me a knife and cutting board. "Why don't you start chopping some raisins and we'll explain."

For the next hour I become a nineteenth-century chopping machine, *chop, chop, chopping* raisins, currants, apples, and orange peel. I try to picture Daisy, the lowly Downton kitchen maid, standing next to me, also chopping in the castle's kitchen.

"Today we're going to make authentic, historical mincemeat," says Mya. "Unfortunately, the authentic way of making mincemeat has been largely lost in the last century."

Mya and Sherry explain that the current-day mincemeat pie originates from the medieval thirteenth century, when preparing meat with fruit and spices was, like smoking or salting, a form of preservation. Cooks would make large batches of mincemeat and store it in crocks sealed with a layer of lard for use over many months.

Mincemeat was enjoyed by commoners as well as kings. King Henry VIII was a huge fan of mince pies in his dining room at London's Hampton Court, often eating it as a main course. Thinking about his large girth, I imagine that Henry must have liked his mincemeat a lot.

The reason mincemeat includes the word *meat* is because that's exactly what it used to be: most often mutton, but also beef, rabbit, pork, or game. The pies were filled with a mixture of finely minced meat and chopped-up fruit, with a preserving liquid such as sherry or brandy.

After what seems like an endless time of chopping, I step back and admire the colorful mixture in my bowl. Mya and Sherry direct me to add white sugar, mace, cloves, nutmeg, and then a generous amount of brandy and sherry to the bowl.

Great, it seems to me that we are ready to start filling the pies! I am about to spoon the mixture into the pie plate and tart pans when Sherry stops me.

"Not so fast, John," she says with caution. "There are two more ingredients that have to go into the mix."

Firmly disappointed, I watch as Mya unwraps a brown paper package and pulls out a ten-inch-long cylinder of what appears to be animal fat. She places the roll on my cutting board and introduces me to my first encounter with suet.

"Suet is the hard muscle that protects the kidneys in the cow," explains Mya. "It's a part of the animal that used to be in mincemeat pie, but has disappeared over the years. In the

Edwardian period, cooks used all parts of the animal. Waste not, want not," she says.

I get it. I can deduce that I'm supposed to chop the suet into small pieces; it's a crusty white fat that requires more manual labor. No problemo, I go at it all out.

After I finish chopping the suet, both Mya and Sherry smile at me as Mya reaches over for a second, larger brown paper package. She opens up the parcel and slowly rolls the contents in front of me.

"What is that?!" I shriek.

I find myself staring at a sinister hunk of meat that scares the jeepers out of me. It must be around fourteen inches in length—a gray and sickly-looking beast that I can barely look at. I can see that it has a long, twisting point at one end and then a thick, muscular base at the other. It reminds me of a lizard or a small alligator or some sort of serpent.

Mya laughs at my horrified reaction. As it sits on my cutting board, she announces that it is beef tongue, another historical ingredient.

Wow. A beef tongue? I spontaneously jump back from the table. I didn't expect to use a beef tongue in a mince tart recipe.

I look down, very hesitant about even touching the tongue. I really feel sorry for the animal.

When I build up the courage, I grab it and can feel little bumps from the rough membrane rubbing my hands. Ugh. I have to look away as I slice through the lean meat (*phhht, phhht*—a squishy sound) and chop it into tiny mince.

As I chop, Sherry tells me that beef tongue was a valued delicacy at the end of the nineteenth century, but like suet, it has also faded from our tables.

No kidding. I can't imagine why, I think.

Finally, I plop the tiny pieces of suet and tongue into the bowl with the fruit and brandy and mix it all together. The final task is to spoon the mixture into the pie plate and tart shells lined with pastry dough.

But for these bakers, the pie and tarts are art pieces. Mya decorates the pie by cutting out intricate floral patterns of dough, placing them on the top crust, and then brushing it with an egg wash, while Sherry adorns the tarts with dough cut into stars and sprinkles crystallized sugar on top as a final touch. My mincemeat instructors slide our pie and tarts into the hot oven. Within minutes, the room fills with the aroma of home baking and cooked fruit and sugar.

And when they come out of the oven after thirty minutes, I am delighted. Mya's pie is magnificent: With dewdrop cutouts and leaf patterns, this pie should be on display at the Art Gallery of Ontario. Similarly beautiful, Sherry's tarts glisten, the sugared star-patterned tops catching the light.

I can't help but dive in. Cutting myself an enormous piece of mincemeat pie, I notice that the filling looks thicker and chunkier than what I am used to with today's mincemeat. As I bite into the first morsel, my teeth crunch into the crisp, ultra-flaky crust, which is full of butter flavor.

The next sensation is the taste of the warm, sweet mixture of raisins, currants, orange peel, and apple, surrounded by a blend of sugar, mace, cloves, and allspice. I delight in the notes of citrus and the tang of brandy that swirl in my mouth.

But after a second, the meat kicks in. Instead of the super-sweet flavor of contemporary mincemeat, the suet and tongue add a savory component that cuts the sugar. The meat does not dominate, though, having melted down and melded with the fruit and brandy to give the pie a heavy substance. I can easily understand how

King Henry VIII and the like loved it as a main course. The meat adds flavor and heft to the historical mincemeat pie.

Sherry's tarts are equally superb. Wrapped in buttery, flaky crust, the individually sized tarts are perfectly aromatic and festive.

I love trying new dishes, and the taste of this true Edwardian mincemeat pie is a delight. The ever-so-slight sweetness with a savory aftertaste is a thick and spicy treat. As Mya, Sherry, and I indulge, I try to imagine myself sitting in the Downton dining room, surrounded by the Crawley family, bathed in candlelight, amidst glimmering crystal glasses and giant portrait paintings.

Warming ourselves by the oven, my baking instructors and I help ourselves to more mincemeat pie. I bring a morsel into my mouth and let the sweet and savory flavor slowly roll around before taking another fantastic bite.

With this mincemeat pie, I feel like I'm getting a real taste of Edwardian Christmas.

Tongue and all.

Highclere Castle

Highclere Park, Newbury, United Kingdom

highclerecastle.co.uk | theoffice@highclerecastle.co.uk | (0)1635 253210

Dear Franny,

Even though participating in an Edwardian dinner was fraught with social potholes, I completely loved my visit to Highclere Castle. The Edwardian dining room is designed to impress—not a priority for us. But there are some aspects of this early-twentieth-century space that we can incorporate into a perfect dining room.

I loved the warm and uplifting gold fabric on the walls in the Highclere dining room. Muted light from the windows during the day and flickering candlelight at night reflects off these walls and makes the room shimmer. I would love to rejuvenate our dining room with something gold.

The wine chests filled with ice and wine bottles are a great idea that time has forgotten. We could move this wine on wheels around the table for guests to choose their favorite beverage. That could be our trademark of unconditional hospitality.

As the dining table is the house's central piece of furniture and a symbol of hospitality, it would be wonderful to have one that we love. It's not just a piece of wood—it's a place for dining, sharing, learning, laughing, and meaningful discussion. It would be great to find something that would reflect our personalities. Maybe it could be made with old hockey sticks . . . no, just joking, just joking . . .

I want to have multiple desserts at your birthday dinner—but I think I'll pass on the Edwardian mincemeat tarts. The ingredient list of tongue and suet might be a little too "historically authentic" for our guests.

While the dining room has been purposely designed to be overwhelming, I think you might fall in love with Highclere on the whole, with all its "cozy splendor," as the Countess of Carnarvon describes the castle.

I know you like cozy.

XOXO

J.

6

LUCY MAUD MONTGOMERY'S MANSE DINING ROOM, 1912

Leaskdale, Ontario

I FEEL LIKE I'VE FOUND a kindred spirit.

Right now, I am on the phone with Melanie Whitfield, president of the Lucy Maud Montgomery Society of Ontario, and as we discuss our common affection for the engaging stories Montgomery wrote, I'm reminded of a line from *Anne of Green Gables*: "Kindred spirits are not so scarce as I used to think. It's splendid to find out there are so many of them in the world."

Melanie manages the Leaskdale Manse National Historic site, a historical house museum in Leaskdale Ontario, outside of Toronto, where Montgomery lived between 1911 and 1926. As a great admirer of Montgomery's writing, I've always wanted to visit this house.

I've long been captivated by the writing of Lucy Maud Montgomery, Canada's best-known author of the early twentieth century and the creator of the beloved *Anne of Green Gables* series. From childhood to the present day, I've read the first Anne book over and over—it never fails to move and delight me. I have such admiration for the way that Montgomery sensitively portrays moments of happiness and disappointment in Anne's life. I completely identify with her ups and downs.

In my eagerness to see the house, I have offered to cook a dinner of Montgomery's recipes in the historical house's kitchen and serve it to Melanie in the dining room. My hope is that by offering dinner, I can explore Montgomery's dining room: sit at her table, eat from her dishes, use her cutlery, drink from her teacups, and of course, absorb any ideas to incorporate into Franny's dinner.

I didn't expect Melanie to accept my offer. I didn't even think she would answer my call.

But now, Melanie is on the other end of my phone.

"I'd love for you to cook and eat in Montgomery's dining room," she says enthusiastically. "I'm really excited about tasting some of her recipes."

My head spinning, I click off my phone.

"Oh my goodness, now I've done it," I say to myself. "I'd better start looking up those Montgomery recipes from 1911. I don't even own a jelly mold."

Montgomery's best-known work is *Anne of Green Gables*, a novel published in 1908 and set in the late nineteenth century that describes the life of Anne, an eleven-year-old orphan girl, red-haired, freckled, and full of imagination and integrity. The adventures begin after she is mistakenly sent to Matthew and Marilla Cuthbert, a middle-aged brother and sister who were expecting to adopt a boy to work on their farm.

The setting is the farm country of Prince Edward Island in Atlantic Canada, the same region where the author grew up. Anne is a sensitive, positive, independent-minded young woman making her way in a culturally restrictive world. It is a story of optimism, hope, character, and resiliency that has sold over fifty million copies.

I have always enjoyed reading *Anne of Green Gables*, but my deep interest in Lucy Maud Montgomery started when I began reading her diaries. While novels can, of course, provide insight into a writer's mind, there is nothing so important in telling a person's story as the raw thoughts, feelings, and quality of life that diaries share. What struck me most was how unashamedly she expressed her emotions for the world to see. Since *Anne* had been published to great success, Montgomery herself had gained fame and knew her diaries would be widely read, so she wrote and rewrote them to tell the story of her life.

To me, learning about a person's emotions is so important in understanding that person's life. Montgomery was dealing with many issues, including her marriage, her neighbors, her publisher, and deaths in her family. Her diary entries range from joyous to heartbreaking, dramatic to triumphant. But each entry gives an insight into her amazing life.

Even more so than today, to be a female at the turn of the twentieth century was not easy. It was a man's world, and women were expected to be subservient to men. Their financial security was dependent on their husband's salary, and if they did not marry young, they risked the prospect of being desperately poor in their senior years.

Montgomery was a prolific writer. Despite social conventions, which looked down on women writers, she published over twenty books, more than five hundred short stories, and five hundred poems during her life. She had an international cultural impact, and she continues to gain recognition more than half a century after her death.

From 1911 to 1926, Montgomery lived in Leaskdale, Ontario. My reading of her diaries reveals that as a recognized novelist, she was an active and central person in her community. I can only imagine that her dining room played an important role in entertaining guests at her house and cultivating her image as a woman. Plus, I am intrigued by the chance to cook in her kitchen. I love to discover ingredients and recipes from a bygone time and bring the dishes back to life. If there are early-twentieth-century delicacies that Lucy Maud Montgomery enjoyed in her dining room, I want to try them too.

To find Montgomery's house, I jump into my car on a sunny summer morning and drive an hour northeast of Toronto. It's great to be out of the city, and I feel rejuvenated as I drive up and down rolling hills, past fields of cornstalks blowing in the wind and enormous Holstein cows with doleful eyes.

Before I've even finished the coffee in my travel mug, the highway dips into a shallow valley and the hamlet of Leaskdale unfolds in front of me. I halt at the one stop sign in town and drive along the quiet main street, which includes a general store, a chip shop, and a historical church with a tall steeple. I glance at the address in my notes and soon find, nestled among a scattering of elm trees, the one-time home of Lucy Maud Montgomery.

I pull up in front of the two-story, buff-colored brick cottage with a cheerful front porch. It's a typical late-nineteenth-century farmhouse in the Victorian Gothic style, like so many in the region. I like its vernacular elements: a steep-pitched gable rising above the entrance, a cedar shingle roof, and simple four-panel wood-framed windows with a flattened arch.

I know from my research that Montgomery was married to Ewen (or Ewan, as she spelled his name in her diaries) Macdonald, a Presbyterian minister, who was the minister of St. Paul's Presbyterian Church in Leaskdale. The house that I am admiring was the manse, provided by the church.

I imagine myself sitting on the wide front veranda, graced with turned-wood posts and gingerbread roof brackets. I am especially drawn to the Victorian screen door of spindles and squiggly patterns, painted dark green. If I lived here, I would be stretched out on a hammock during the summer months, sipping homemade lemonade and waving to neighbors as they walked by.

Melanie Whitfield meets me on the front walk. She has been involved with the house from the beginning of its restoration in 2009 to the present. I have such admiration for volunteers like Melanie who put their passion and commitment into preserving historical houses. This one in particular is in immaculate condition.

As we stand in front of the house, built in 1886, I mention to Melanie that I find it enchanting in its simplicity and rural charm. To me, it appears a happy, ideal place to live.

But Melanie tells me that Montgomery had a different opinion. Of the manse, Montgomery wrote in her journal:

> *[The manse] is quite prettily situated. It is not an ideal house by any means, but it will do, and it is certainly much more comfortable and convenient than my old home. It is built of white brick in the ugly "L" design so common among country houses. My greatest disappointment in connection with it is that it has no bathroom or toilet. I had hoped that I might have a home with these at least. But what is to be will be! It is Allah! We must submit.* (September 24, 1911)

As we admire the colorful front garden of day lilies and pachysandra, Melanie recaps some highlights of Montgomery's story.

Lucy Maud Montgomery was born on November 30, 1874, in Clifton (now New London), Prince Edward Island, the province where she set her Anne books. Her mother died of tuberculosis when Montgomery was less than two years old. Montgomery's early life in PEI was lonely. Living with grandparents who were very stern with her, she spent much of her childhood by herself and created imaginary friends to help her cope. Later in life, she claimed this helped to develop her literary creativity.

In 1908, Montgomery published her first book, *Anne of Green Gables*. An immediate success, it established Montgomery's literary career. Montgomery described Prince Edward Island as a picturesque part of Canada where life moved at a gradual pace and people maintained local traditions.

Even though she was a successful writer, she was then still a single woman. Montgomery knew that when her grandmother passed, she would be left without a home, since the male heirs would take ownership of the house. It was a situation many unmarried women faced at the time. So it became socially and economically important for Montgomery to get married.

After her grandmother's death, Montgomery married Rev. Macdonald in 1911, who had accepted the position of minister in Leaskdale, Ontario. The newly married couple moved into the manse and lived there for fifteen years.

Unfortunately, Montgomery suffered from depression. She had severe mood swings. In her journals, she expressed pain at the death of her infant son Hugh, the horrors of World War I, and the death of her beloved cousin Frederica (Frede) Campbell. In 1918, Montgomery contracted the Spanish flu, and it drew physical and emotional energy from her for months. Despite these problems, she continued to write stories and poems, expressing her love of life, nature, and beauty.

I tell Melanie that reading Montgomery's journals is like reading passages from *Anne of Green Gables*. Anne Shirley is portrayed as an optimistic, happy, bouncy child who perseveres and never compromises her principles.

Melanie responds that in her diaries, Montgomery expressed the joy of walking to the general store for the newspaper, enjoying the sunlight filtering through leaves on the trees and the breeze on her face, writing, "What I live for are the high moments."

Nice. But if we turn to the Anne novel, a closer read reveals an insecure girl who is afraid of never having friends, is constantly questioning the injustices of the world, and has her own emotional ups and downs. Anne is in a constant search for a kindred spirit, a bosom friend.

I believe that Anne is Lucy Maud Montgomery. And Montgomery is Anne.

As the wife of a Presbyterian minister, Montgomery was responsible for giving multiple dinners and church luncheons. Her house in Leaskdale had no electricity, no running water, and, instead of indoor plumbing, an outhouse, which made entertaining a challenge. In addition, she had to find time to write. For many years, Montgomery had a maid to address domestic duties, although she often did the cooking for social events herself, as even her maids caused her unhappiness; her journals reveal constant complaining about the maids' disagreeable moods and incompetence.

On top of her own challenges, Montgomery also supported her husband through his mental illness, which was referred to as "religious melancholy." At the time, this kind of information stayed behind closed doors, so it fell to Montgomery to keep her husband going, motivate him to preach, and help him finish his sermons.

Unfortunately, Rev. Macdonald was not as interested in literature and nature as Montgomery was. Montgomery wrote in her diary: "I was never in love with Ewan—never been in love with him. But I was—have been—and am very fond of him" (January 5, 1917).

Montgomery was extremely disciplined, writing eleven of her twenty-two novels in Leaskdale while caring for her two sons, Chester and Stuart. Her other tasks included playing the organ at church, entertaining the congregation at socials, teaching Sunday school, leading various groups, and helping to write sermons for her frequently ill husband.

"People don't know what a strong woman she was," Melanie tells me, after listing off all of these duties. The great increase in Montgomery's writings in the 1910s and 1920s is the result of her need to escape the hardships of life, Melanie adds.

"But eventually, she came to like her house in Leaskdale," says Melanie. "It was the first house that Montgomery lived in where she had some independence and control."

Melanie escorts me up to the front porch of the house and we step into the hallway, a narrow two-story space with yellow floral wallpaper and a finely detailed wooden staircase and balustrade that leads to the second-floor bedrooms. It is a comfortable, homey space.

I am honored to enter the parlor, a large, comfortable room where, in a chair in the northwest corner, Montgomery wrote her stories and poems. She owned a typewriter, but all of her original compositions were done in longhand. The room is beautifully lit by tall windows with white lace curtains framed by olive drapes. Melanie points out items that Montgomery loved, including an upholstered couch, an organ that she played regularly, and a gramophone that she would drag out onto the porch to play records on into the night.

Melanie guides me farther inside the house and we step into the Montgomery dining room. Positioned behind the parlor and in front of the kitchen, it's a handsome, modestly sized room with cheerful sunlight pouring in from a south-facing window.

I can see that the twelve-by-fourteen-foot space is anchored by a round wooden table in the middle, covered in a white tablecloth and surrounded by four matching mission-style oak chairs. Over the table, a circular porcelain lamp hangs from the ceiling on decorative metal chains, ornamented with glass beads that reflect light.

I admire the table setting. It is elegant and simple; I genuinely feel a closer, more intimate connection with Montgomery by seeing her dishware and utensils. Melanie tells me that Montgomery was proud of her delicately attractive Bridal Rose by Limoges series that was the family's everyday china service. Decorated with pink roses, lavender flowers, and gold bordering on a bone white base, it was a popular design of its time. I especially like the platter in the center of the table, with a matching cover crafted with small holes in the lid to allow excess steam to escape and not overcook the food.

I am delighted to find that the modest dining room, lined with wood wainscoting and beige wallpaper dotted with pink diamonds, has a welcoming ambience. My eyes are drawn to the wooden doors, window frames, and wide floorboards painted shades of olive green. I feel like I would be very happy to dine here.

But Montgomery disagreed. She hated the dining room. She complained that the small size of the room added to the challenge of a minister's wife who was expected to entertain. She wrote:

> *The dining room is my most unsatisfactory room, having almost every vice a room can have. It is too small; it is the only way of getting from the kitchen to the other part of the house and so cannot be kept clean easily. It opens into the kitchen and gets too warm and too smelly. The furnace pipe goes up through it and is not decorative. It has five doors and only one window which gives a view of several ugly back yards including our own. Fortunately, these things do not affect the flavor of our food! (October 24, 1911)*

As we chat, Melanie reaches up into Montgomery's tall china cabinet, against the south wall, to fetch more dishes and teacups. Built in dark walnut, the cabinet adds elegance to her dining room, while its cathedral-style glass doors draw special attention to the intricate patterns on her cups, plates, bowls, and glasses. The cabinet also performs the extra functions of protection of the china and storage, reducing the need for shelves in the kitchen. I express my admiration to Melanie.

"Montgomery would have liked that, John," replies Melanie. "Having her own income from book sales, she was able to buy the entire set of Bridal Rose Limoges at one time. That would be a luxury not enjoyed by her neighbors, who would have preciously bought each butter dish or salad bowl, one piece at a time."

The largest and most impressive piece of furniture in Montgomery's dining room is her dark wooden sideboard,

also called a buffet. Sideboards were placed off against a wall in dining rooms, giving the origin of the name: at the side of the room.

Melanie invites me to slide open the built-in drawer to reveal Montgomery's cutlery. I then swing open the cabinet doors to find her serving platters and bowls. Topped by a counter surface, the sideboard assisted Montgomery in serving food and became a display place for her silver and other valued possessions, including a glistening silver tea set with matching sugar bowl and cream pitcher. A mirror built into the back of the buffet reflects light and gives the illusion of a larger room.

Despite her initial reservations about the dining room, Montgomery became accustomed to it, especially after her sons were born. Next to the parlor, it became her second-favorite place to write; her sons could sit in their high chairs while she wrote at the dining table. Eventually she derived pleasure from placing hand-embroidered doilies, vases of scented flowers, and paintings throughout the space.

Her dining room was frequently the setting for afternoon luncheons and dinners. Because of Ewan's professional obligations and Montgomery's large circle of friends, it became the center of entertainment in the Leaskdale community.

What is less well-known than her sterling reputation as a writer is Montgomery's talent in the kitchen. She was an excellent cook who took great interest in good food. She once wrote that if she had not been "a poor devil of an author," she thought she "would have made an excellent cook."

As the wife of the minister, she was responsible for providing food for countless church luncheons, Sunday school picnics, and potluck affairs. There were times when, if a young couple came to the manse to be married, it fell to Montgomery to make the wedding meal.

She even wrote a remarkable cookbook in longhand in a business ledger. In rounded, swirling cursive, she provides 440 recipes for hamburger steaks, canned chicken, pancakes, spareribs, scalloped fish, jelly rolls, cookies, cherry pies, and more.

The cookbook, published as *Aunt Maud's Recipe Book* by Elaine Crawford and Kelly Crawford, is a historical journey celebrating Canadian cuisine, specifically in rural Ontario, in the early part of the twentieth century. The simplicity of the recipes is a reflection of the seasonality of ingredients, the need for culinary innovation, and the absence, at the time, of outside cultural influences. What I find most fascinating is Montgomery's meticulous handwriting and her consciousness that future generations would be reading her recipes. The cookbook illuminates Montgomery's commitment to passing her recipes down in time.

In one of her journal entries, Montgomery wrote:

> *Frankly, I'm very fond of a good table. I keep one myself and I like to sit down to one. It is an old Montgomery tradition and when I hear anyone say, I don't care what I have to eat, I conclude that individual is either lying or is a pale anemic creature of very little use and no charm or force in the world. And I have mostly found that this conclusion was borne out by the facts of the case.*

In honor of the author, her cookbook, and her dining room, I am preparing a Lucy Maud Montgomery–inspired dinner to enjoy with Melanie in Montgomery's own dining room. I have researched and tested recipes from the cookbook, and today Melanie and I will sit down to enjoy them.

On July 7, 1912, baby Chester Cameron Macdonald was born, a fine happy baby. Motherhood brought Montgomery a new kind of joy, a pleasure beyond anything she had experienced. She once said, "I am a mother. I cannot realize it. It seems so incredible—so wonderful—so utterly impossible as happening to me!"

Part of her joy over her new baby was sharing this exciting time with her first cousin Frederica Elmanstine Campbell. "Frede," as she was known, had come to Leaskdale to help Montgomery after Chester's birth, and she was the most valued and cherished companion of the famous author. Just like Anne found her bosom friend in Diana, Montgomery found an emotional and intellectual bond with Frede.

Cousin Frede stayed through the summer and shared in the baby worship with Montgomery. There was much laughter, poetry reading, and fascination with newborn Chester. The house was in high spirits.

These happy moments were captured in a photograph from a dinner that shows Frede, Maud, Ewan, and Chester all looking joyous in the dining room. There is no date on the photo, but the occasion might be the evening of the christening of her son on September 8, 1912. A newborn baby, her favorite cousin in the house, a new life of motherhood—it was a great dinner to celebrate several happy occasions.

A typical menu served in the dining room of the manse might include:

Salmon pie (canned salmon baked in layers of onion, potatoes, and white sauce of butter, flour, and milk)
Buttered green beans (boiled and tossed with butter)
Browned potatoes (browned in bacon drippings)
Sunshine Salad (more on this later)
Watermelon rind pickles (more on this later)
Mrs. MacPherson's Gingersnap Cookies (made with brown sugar, drippings, and molasses)
Tea

I love Jell-O. There, I admit it. So it is no surprise that when I leafed through the Montgomery cookbook, I was attracted first to a positive and bright gelatin recipe called Sunshine Salad. Sunshine Salad—to me, it epitomizes the happy moments in *Anne of Green Gables*.

To really experience the Montgomery dining room vibe, I have brought gelatin powder, along with containers of orange juice, pineapple juice, white vinegar, orange sections, pineapple bits, and slivered carrot with me to Leaskdale.

Stepping into the ten-by-ten-foot kitchen at the rear of the house, I can see it is overflowing with knickknacks, kitchen utensils, and shelves filled with early-twentieth-century food products including Quaker puffed rice, White Swan coffee, and canned shortening. It has an informal and cluttered appearance—a place for someone who loves to cook.

The first thing I focus on is the baking table, built of dark wood with a butcher block counter and four drawers for storing utensils and baking sheets. I plop all my ingredients on the table and get ready to cook.

On the wall above the baking table is a shelf holding a clock, a hand chopper, china dishes, and a variety of oil lamps. Across the kitchen is the cookstove that Montgomery and her maids used for baking and preparing daily meals.

The wallpaper on the kitchen walls is a floral pattern of muted yellow, green, and red inspired by the early-twentieth-century Arts and Crafts movement, which promoted earthy colors and simple, natural shapes. Wood wainscoting is painted a muted red, as are the frames on the four doors in the kitchen.

I look for a sink with water faucets, but it is nowhere to be found. To get water in 1912 Leaskdale, Montgomery had to grab a bucket and go outside to use the pump.

Over the next hour, I buzz around Montgomery's kitchen with Melanie, chopping, mixing, and spreading out to prepare the Sunshine Salad, salmon pie, and vegetables.

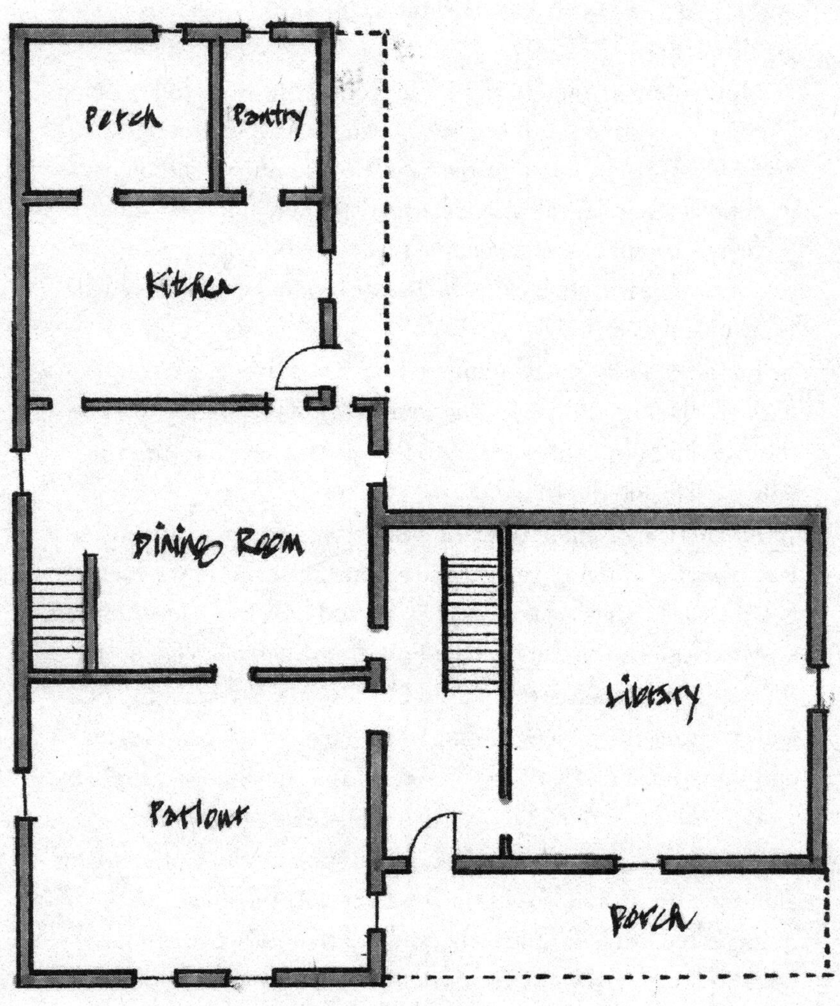

Lucy Maud Montgomery manse

To make the salad, the first step is to empty my envelope of powdered gelatin into a bowl and add water. As I stir, the gelatin mixture appears gray, viscous, and not terribly appealing.

Next into the bowl go the orange juice, pineapple juice, and vinegar, and I combine. The bowl is a swimming pool of orange, and I ladle the liquid into muffin tins to make individual Sunshine Salads.

Montgomery would have had an icebox, but since today the kitchen is a museum exhibit, my muffin tin with the orange juice mixture goes into a refrigerator for an hour. Montgomery's directions are to let the salads partially harden and then add the carrot, orange, and pineapple pieces to the salad molds. I am apprehensive. It's hard to believe this liquid concoction will transform into firm jelly.

But after about thirty minutes, I open the fridge, and sure enough, the liquid is beginning to firm up. Delighted, I sprinkle the fruit and vegetable slices into the salad molds. I return the jelly back inside the fridge.

Finally, the moment of truth is upon us. I remove the muffin tray from the fridge. I run a knife around the edge of one of the gelatin salads, then take a large spoon and coax it out of its mold.

Miraculously, the small cylinder of Sunshine Salad keeps its form as it slides out of the muffin tin. It gently drops on top of a leaf of lettuce that I have arranged on a plate. Success! Melanie and I give a cheer. Our Sunshine Salad is a sunshine success!

Before I plate the food, we lay a lace covering over the tablecloth and then place knives, forks, spoons, and cloth napkins alongside the Bridal Rose Limoges plates. At the center of the dining table, Melanie adds a bouquet of daffodils, Montgomery's favorite flower grown in the garden.

Just as we are about to sit down for dinner, I pause and take a quick gaze at the historical photograph on the sideboard of

Montgomery, her cousin Frede, husband Ewan, and son Chester. The picture captures them smiling broadly at this very dining room table during dinner. There is no doubt they are having a fun time together.

The image seems to convey opposite feelings to the complaints about the dining room expressed in Montgomery's diary. As I look at the photograph, I wonder what is causing Montgomery and the group to enjoy themselves. To me, it seems that they like being together and are enjoying the food.

But then I see something else. It's in their faces. They are smiling, animated, joyous—but they are also beautifully lit. In the photograph, the feeling of the entire room is enhanced by a source of dramatic light.

In Montgomery's house, with no electricity, lighting was provided by oil lamps, which gave off a low light that would cast dramatic shadows and reflections around the room. The muted light is especially evident in the reflection from the mirror behind the buffet.

Without electricity, the lamps were essential for light at night and to guide family and visitors to Montgomery's rear-yard outhouse in the dark. By providing a brighter light than candles, these lamps also provided a dramatic light around the dinner table.

In the photo, there is a softness in the skin tone of Montgomery and her diners from the modulated light in the room. It causes their faces to have a glow and softens their features. And then I notice that all around them, the features of the room's architecture and furnishings are enhanced in the shadow and light.

I can see that walls and ceilings are no longer flat, blank surfaces. The lamps create highlights and shadows around the room, including in the folds in the tablecloth, and patterns from flowers in vases and glassware on the table. Light shimmers and reflects off the buffet mirror, the polished silver tea set, silverware on the table, and the etched edges of the crystal bowls. The dining room glitters and light dances; happiness is brought to light, dreariness hides in the shadows.

I am not considering oil lamps in our dining room for Franny's dinner, but I can see how modulated lighting can dramatically change the mood of a dinner. I am reminded of Edith Wharton's dining room, where she was insistent on soft evening light, which she thought was more conducive to intimacy, honesty, and relaxed conversation.

All of the Montgomery-inspired dishes I have made are enjoyable, but the star of the show is the Sunshine Salad. Shimmering and bright, the gelatin and fruit chunks stand out on the plate like an orange jewel on a sunny day. The shiny translucence of the gelatin reflects gradations of light in streaks of yellow and orange, like a stained-glass window. The happy color truly brings a cheerful "Anne with an E" happiness to the plate.

I place a morsel of the jiggly gelatin into my mouth. It is as if I have stepped backward in time. The cool, solid texture turns to liquid on my tongue, and immediately I'm hit with a citrusy taste with overtones of orange and pineapple sweetness—but a second later, the sweetness is cut by a welcome hint of acidity from the vinegar. I had expected a dull, tasteless liquid, so the bright flavor brings a big grin to my face.

I indulge in the crunchy texture of the carrot, orange, and pineapple that provide the fruit and vegetable contribution to the salad. The experience is surprisingly refreshing and energizing, and as I dig into the straightforward salmon pie, I find that the Sunshine Salad is a zesty complement.

"The Sunshine Salad would have been a happy conversation piece at dinner," says Melanie. "It was so different and unique from other dishes of the time. Fun to look at, tasty to eat, and an impressive creation of the hostess, it might have been the delight of the party."

One big surprise is the Montgomery watermelon rind pickles—I had no idea that you could eat the rind of a watermelon. As I bite into the hard skin, I am delighted at the enormous crunch in my mouth. The watermelon rind is the crispiest pickle I have ever eaten. Magnificently sweet and sour at the same time, it provides a refreshing complement to the saltiness of the salmon pie. This unusual condiment epitomizes the no-waste approach to cooking in the early twentieth century.

Soon it is time for dessert, and I bring out a plate of Montgomery ginger cookies, jam sandwich butter cookies, and cherry tarts. Melanie gives me a big smile and pours steaming tea into Montgomery's exquisite Limoges teacups.

As we sip and enjoy the coziness of the room, Melanie reflects that even Montgomery, a hugely successful author, felt like she had to have a husband to validate her life. But if she had lived in our world today, she could have led an independent and fulfilled life as a single person.

Melanie tells me that Montgomery believed it was her duty as a woman to make her marriage work, once quipping to a reporter, "Those women whom God wanted to destroy, he would make into the wives of ministers."

"She made the best of it," says Melanie. "And that's what a lot of women did. At first, she disliked the dining room. But she loved to eat, cook, and entertain. It became the center of her house."

I once again suspect that Montgomery has put a bit of herself into Anne, as I recall a quote from the book: "It's been my experience that you can nearly always enjoy things if you make up your mind firmly that you will."

In 1925, Montgomery's husband, Ewan Macdonald, was offered a position as minister in Norval, Ontario, about thirty miles west of Toronto. The manse in Norval had numerous advantages that the Leaskdale manse didn't, including the modern conveniences of electric light and an indoor bathroom. It also had a larger dining room with dark wood trim and a bay window. At the turn of the century, dark-stained woodwork communicated to guests that the owners had refined taste and wealth enough to afford it.

Montgomery felt ambivalent about leaving Leaskdale. She had begun to feel sentimental about the manse and realized she had put down deep roots in the community, but the move would give Ewan a fresh start. It could alleviate his melancholia.

In a November 5, 1925, diary entry she wrote: "Norval manse is well designed and situated. And yet, how I love this old manse, where my children were born and where I have tasted such rapturous happiness and endured so much hideous agony."

However, Ewan looked forward to living in a more stately house in Norval. It is a striking illustration of the difference in emotional temperament between the two.

The Leaskdale community was sad to see the couple go. Montgomery brought intellectual input into the women's meetings and did outstanding work with young people. In the end, Montgomery found parting bittersweet.

On Christmas Eve 1925, she wrote:

> *How I hate the idea of leaving! And the thought of new places and people. I paused for a moment at the front gate as I came in. Will I have such a pretty view from my gate in Norval? The beautiful woods behind Mr. Leask's, the leaf hung corner of the side-road, the lovely hill field beyond with the elms on its crest. I love these things and grieve to leave them. But what has my life been but a succession of leaving things I loved?*

Once Montgomery made the move to Norval, she did for a time find happiness and adventure as a central person in her new community: leading the theater group, teaching Sunday school, playing the organ, giving literary talks, and organizing church picnics.

But in a way, she is still in Leaskdale. It is in Leaskdale where her "ugly" L-shaped house still lies proud, immaculate, and filled with her personal belongings as though she has just stepped out to the general store. It is in Leaskdale where her china cabinet holds stacks of her Bridal Rose Limoges china, silverware, and a silver tea set, ready to entertain another new bride. And it is in Leaskdale where her spirit still sits at the dining room table, leaning back in a dark oak chair and laughing quietly to herself as she writes and rewrites sections of her endearingly acerbic memoirs.

The Leaskdale Manse

11850 Regional Road 1, Leaskdale, Ontario, Canada

lucymaudmontgomery.ca/tours/the-manse | lmmontgomery.on@gmail.com | (905) 862-0808

Dear Franny,

I was thrilled to cook Lucy Maud Montgomery recipes and eat in her dining room. I truly felt her presence as I drank from her teacups and dined from her fine china plates. I feel like I understand her writing much better by visiting her house and discovering the ups and downs of her life. After being immersed in Montgomery's literary, social, and culinary life, here are some ideas I picked up for your dinner party.

The mirror behind Montgomery's buffet breaks up the light, reflecting it around the room, creating shadows and highlights, and making the space feel bigger. A simple way to rejuvenate our dining room could be by adding a strategically placed mirror and furnishings with brilliant, reflective surfaces.

Montgomery's dishes are made with basic available ingredients. Not everything has to be A5 Japanese Wagyu beef or foie gras from the French Dordogne Valley. I'm going to make Montgomery's Sunshine Salad for your birthday dinner. I've got a feeling it could be a big hit.

The watermelon rind pickles were crunchy, tart, and fabulous. I might make those for your dinner too.

Although Montgomery complained about her dining room, I quite like it. It's a cozy, intimate space. Montgomery's intimacy was created with muted light, trusted company, and unpretentious food. For her dinner with cousin Frede, Montgomery's dining room was a place to share food, thoughts, and happy feelings.

Lucy Maud Montgomery knew the importance of having someone who knew your very soul.

I'm glad we're kindred spirits.

XOXO

J.

7

DR. MARTIN LUTHER KING JR.'S CHILDHOOD DINING ROOM, 1936

Atlanta, Georgia

AMERICAN HISTORY IS FILLED with examples of passionate, rousing speeches. The Gettysburg Address by Abraham Lincoln was a poignant message to heal the wounds of a nation during the Civil War. John F. Kennedy's 1961 inauguration speech set the tone for a decade when he asked citizens to consider, "Ask not what your country can do for you, ask what you can do for your country."

But my favorite speech is the "I Have a Dream" speech that Martin Luther King Jr. gave, in a rousing and passionate voice, from the steps of the Lincoln Memorial in Washington in 1963. I get overwhelmed every time I hear it.

It is a lengthy speech in its entirety, but for me, the most powerful messages that King delivers are that he dreams that his four little children will live in a nation where they will be judged by their character, not the color of their skin. He dreams that children, both white and black, will join together as sisters and brothers. And he dreams that people of all religions across the country will join hands together and sing the traditional African American spiritual, "Free at last. Thank God almighty, we are free at last."

Inspiring, powerful, hopeful, his words ignited a civil rights movement. The speech continues to act as a torch in the struggle to achieve equality and a better future.

When I learn that I can visit the childhood home of Martin Luther King Jr. in Atlanta, Georgia, I am thrilled. The dinner table is still set just as it would have been when the King family sat down to dinner. I will be able to see the dining room where King sat with his family, where he was transformed from a young boy into one of the most important figures of the twentieth century.

In my opinion, Martin Luther King Jr. is one of the most important people to ever walk this earth.

I *have* to go to Atlanta.

Although it is a long walk from my hotel to find Auburn Avenue in the downtown of Atlanta, I feel no fatigue—only jubilation. I don't think I have ever felt more determined to find a historical house. My mission, of course, is to visit the birthplace of Martin Luther King Jr.

From my research, I know that Atlanta, like other cities in the South in the twentieth century, was segregated, meaning that white and African American people ("colored," as it was commonly put) could not typically use the same parks, schools, restaurants, and stores. African American men and women were often treated, at best, with disrespect.

However, the vibrant African American community on Auburn Avenue had come into its own during the 1890s, when businesses took advantage of the street's proximity to the railroad. During the early twentieth century, the neighborhood continued to prosper, with banks, insurance companies, churches, and music venues located on one stretch earning it the nickname "Sweet Auburn."

As I walk the neighborhood today, I can see some of the historical houses and storefronts of that buoyant Sweet Auburn heyday. The downtown neighborhood fell into decline after World War II and slid into a bad state by the 1970s, the victim of depopulation, crime, and the construction of Interstate 75/85, which split the district in two. But today, I can see vibrant restaurants, bed and breakfasts, and bakeries that have popped up, with new residents moving into spruced-up houses. Sweet Auburn, with its National Historic Landmark designation, is looking sweet again.

The King family lived on Auburn, a neighborhood in transition of handsome one- and two-story wood-frame houses. I start to count down the house numbers and soon arrive at 501—an attractive two-story house with a broad front lawn surrounded by a neat hedge and shrubs. I have made it to King's childhood home.

I step back to admire the large house; it looks to have been built in the 1890s. The exterior walls are clad with wooden clapboard painted a warm ocher, while rectangular windows equipped with brown shutters look out onto Auburn Avenue. The roofline has a peaked front gable that is decorated with shingles, and a fan-shaped arch tops off the house. As I add up the elements, I realize it's a Queen Anne style—or what most people would call a Victorian home.

Queen Annes were all the rage in America in the last decades of the nineteenth century. For Americans, the style seemed to arise from a romantic longing for home. It was a time when people were abandoning industrialized cities for the seaside and the imagined comforts of an earlier time. The asymmetrical informality of a Queen Anne home, with its eclectic mix of forms and building materials, had great appeal.

At the ground level, wide wooden stairs lead from the sidewalk up to a sweeping full-width porch that stretches across the front facade. The porch is framed and supported by turned-wood posts, wood trim, and gingerbread brackets, giving the house a welcoming and casual feeling.

I am met on the front walk by Diane Burgoon, a park ranger at the national historic site. Dressed in her crisp khaki uniform, including a round-brimmed ranger hat, Diane welcomes me to King's childhood home, the six-bedroom house where he grew up. She tells me that King was born in a room upstairs and lived here until he was twelve years old.

My tour guide is one of the many ranger guides at the Martin Luther King, Jr. National Historic Park, of which the Auburn Avenue birth home is the centerpiece. The thirty-four-acre park includes the Ebenezer Baptist Church Museum, where three generations of the King family preached, and the Martin Luther King, Jr. Center for Nonviolent Social Change. The park is also the site of Freedom Plaza, the resting place of Dr. King and his wife, Coretta Scott King.

"He was an ordinary child, a prankster known as M.L.," says Diane of the great reverend. "He enjoyed playing football and baseball. Martin was a paper boy and wanted to be a fireman when he grew up. It was not apparent from his childhood, but eventually that prankster would become America's foremost leader of the 1950s and '60s struggle for civil rights."

List of M.L. pranks:

- He popped the heads off his sister's dolls—to use them as baseballs.
- He scared neighbors by tying one of his mother's fox furs to a stick and poking it through a bush, pretending it was an animal.

- When it came time to do the dishes, he was suddenly nowhere to be found.
- To get out of piano lessons, Martin and his younger brother tried to harass their instructor, tinkering with their piano stool so it collapsed when the music teacher sat down.
- He once took the keys to the family car and drove it right through the rear wall of the garage.

"The community into which Martin Luther King Jr. was born in the 1930s was quite ordinary in terms of social status," says Diane. "No one in Sweet Auburn had attained any great wealth. It was a mixed community of average and low-income households. Most of the neighbors were deeply religious."

As Diane tells me this, I think about how impressive it is that a person who became *Time* magazine's Man of the Year for 1963 and the Nobel Peace Prize winner in 1964 for leading nonviolent resistance against racism in the US came from a modest background.

As we walk up the stairs to the house, I stop and try to imagine the King family seated in folding chairs around the porch. It is the kind of long porch where children congregate to play games and where adults might relax on a warm Georgia evening, drinking lemonade and waving to passersby.

As my park ranger invites me into the house, I gently push the front screen door and listen for the *bonk*, *bonk* sound of the door bouncing closed. King, decades ago, would have heard this sound thousands of times growing up in this house. I am glad to share that experience today.

I step into the vestibule and immediately notice a family photo hanging in the entryway. It includes King's mother and father (Alberta Williams King and the Rev. Martin Luther King Sr.), his maternal grandmother (Jennie Williams), and King with his younger brother (Alfred Daniel or A.D.) and older sister (Christine).

I move my attention to the rest of the house interior, characterized by ten-foot-high ceilings and dark wooden doors, window frames, and wainscoting on the lower walls. In 1909, King's maternal grandfather, the Rev. Adam Daniel Williams, bought this house for $3,500; it was in an average neighborhood, where no one was extremely rich or extremely poor.

Alberta Williams grew up in the house, and when she married the reverend, her new husband moved in with Alberta and her parents. All three of the couple's children were born here.

Diane tells me that King and his siblings were born into a financially secure middle-class family, and they received better educations than other children in the neighborhood. I wonder to myself whether that might have influenced the way King led his life. He didn't just help those less fortunate, he was a warrior for racial justice, and it would cost him his life.

We walk into the next room, the parlor that was used as a family and community gathering place. It's where the senior Martin Luther King conducted political and church meetings and where Alberta, who was the choir director at Ebenezer Baptist Church, held rehearsals, with Christine helping to serve choir members cookies and hot chocolate.

Standing in the parlor, Diane tells me the story of King's childhood growing up on Auburn.

In an upstairs bedroom on January 15, 1929, a boy was born to minister Michael Luther King and his wife, Alberta Christine. They named the child Michael Jr. Later, the father would change both his and his son's names to Martin Luther, in honor of the German theologian.

The reverend was a pastor at the Ebenezer Baptist Church, which was right down the street from his home. The boy had a happy upbringing, guided by spiritual teachings from his dad and grandfather. He felt fortunate in his parents and, in his public life, would express gratitude to them.

Ranger Diane takes me upstairs to the boys' bedroom. I step inside a room of rumpled beds and toys on the floor. M.L. and A.D. shared their upstairs bedroom with an uncle, and the room, Diane tells me, was always in a "great disarray." "Martin was known to be a very good Monopoly player," she says, with a smile. I find this an ironic childhood fact, since the aim of the game is to accumulate as much individual monetary wealth as possible from real estate speculation.

I follow Diane back down the stairs to the main floor, turning a corner into the King family dining room. A twelve-by-eighteen-foot room, this is the largest space in the house and the focus for parties and dinners with the extended family. Sitting between the parlor and the kitchen, the dining room is filled with sunlight from two tall windows with dark wooden window frames. The size and prominence of the room in the floor plan reflects the value of the times that dining, celebration, and being together should take place in the grandest room in the house.

Covered in a white tablecloth, the wooden dinner table is the centerpiece of the room. Anchored by a crystal vase filled with cheerful pink and yellow anemone flowers, the table is set for a dinner of seven with the King family's original dishes, cutlery, and water glasses. Arranged around the table are matching Sheraton-style wooden dining chairs.

Beyond the table, the walls are covered in a beige wallpaper with a light pink floral pattern that gives the room a cheerful ambience. A painted border near the top of the wall is painted a beige that enhances the lightness of the white ceiling.

The windows are decorated with embroidered lace curtains that gracefully fall onto a floral-patterned linoleum floor.

At the head of the room, a carved wooden mantel with red tile surrounds a fireplace. A mirror above the mantel reflects light and further brightens the room. To the left of the fireplace is a built-in wooden cabinet with glass doors to display the family's delicate glassware and drawers below to store dishes.

The doorway to the kitchen is also on this wall; it was through here that King's grandmother would bring in her home-cooked specialties for dinner.

King's mother sat at one head of the table, closest to the kitchen; his father sat at the other. The two place settings closest to the windows belonged to King's grandmother and Aunt Ida, who both also lived in the house. (I'm not told where the uncle sat.) Opposite them sat young King and his two siblings.

With several covered bowls, a serving platter, gravy boat, water goblets, and cloth napkins on the table, the Kings ate family style, with the meat, vegetables, and bread passed around the table. It strikes me as a simple and elegant table setting.

The reverend wanted his family to gather for a formal dinner in the dining room every night. No doubt good manners and proper dress would be even more important in the presence of the guests who would frequently join them. The children had to be well dressed.

Meals began with the children reciting a Bible verse before eating. Diane reveals that for several years young King's favorite was the shortest, simplest verse he could find—John 11:35, "Jesus wept."

The children were encouraged to talk about their school day and to take part in adult conversations about current events. King's father even quizzed the children on politics during the meals.

The dining room was the site of many of the family discussions about the existence of a racial problem in the South. King's initial

The dining room was the site of many of the family discussions about the existence of a racial problem in the South.

experience with prejudice that affected his development occurred when he started elementary school: His white playmates were to attend a different school than him. In addition, the father of one of these friends forbade the two of them playing together any longer.

It was at the dinner table that King brought up that incident with his parents, who then explained the history of slavery, the Civil War, and how racism against "colored people" existed in some areas of the country. It was a painful and enlightening moment for the six-year-old.

The strict system of segregation laws in Atlanta included rules that stated African American people:

- Could not swim in public pools
- Could not go to any public park
- Could not attend the schools for white students
- Could not attend any of the theaters
- Could not use the same restroom facilities and water fountains as white people

Even with these barriers in society, his parents implored him to never let himself feel unworthy of respect.

King's parents discussed some of the insults that they themselves had confronted as a result of racism. The stories shocked the boy. Then he gained experience firsthand, when he visited a shoe store with his father and a clerk told them to sit in the back: As Black people, they would not be served in the front.

It was these humiliating experiences during early childhood that fueled Martin Luther King Jr. to his crusade for equality. In his autobiography, King admits that he began to hate white people. But his parents maintained the opposite—that as a Christian he should love "the white man," not hate him.

King was the third generation to become a Baptist minister at Ebenezer Baptist Church, the church where his father and, years earlier, his grandfather, preached. Moreover, he grew up in a family where love was at the center of all their relationships. He was able to perceive the universe as a friendly place because of his family life.

A committed Christian, King's mother filled all of her children with a sense of fierce self-respect. King admired his father for his Christian character, integrity, and commitment to moral principles, and for confronting injustice. His father always stood up for himself and spoke his mind.

As well as playing a central role in King's childhood development at home, religion determined the direction of his adult life. King attended universities and seminaries across the country in the 1950s, after graduating early from high school at the age of fifteen. He moved back to Atlanta in 1960 and became a co-pastor with his father at Ebenezer Baptist.

In his youth, one subject King had a problem with was oration. While training to become a minister at Crozer Theological Seminary in Upland, Pennsylvania, he received a C in public speaking. He must have worked hard at this skill; he delivered his famous "I Have a Dream" speech with memorable power and influence at the age of thirty-four. Martin Luther King Jr. is now known as one of the great orators of the twentieth century.

Following my tour of the King dining room, Diane walks me into the adjacent kitchen—and I instantly fall in love.

The big, bright twelve-by-twelve-foot space just feels like home. Sunlight flows in from two tall windows bordered with white and blue cotton curtains.

Wooden wainscoting painted dark green rises to waist height and complements the mint-green walls. The linoleum floor, covered in a checkered pattern of light green, yellow, and beige flowers, is so cheerful it makes me want to dance.

I can see that a box of Wheaties holds a prominent spot on a small central table that is set with bowls and spoons for breakfast.

"Wheaties was the young King's favorite breakfast cereal," says my tour guide.

I comment, "With Martin Luther King Jr.'s never-ending courage and stamina, I should start eating the Breakfast of Champions."

A skillet, coffee pot, and double boiler sit atop the early black-and-white gas stove and oven.

A cook's apron hangs off the back of one of the simple wooden chairs, ready for service. The surroundings remind me of my own childhood kitchen table.

A wooden icebox sits against a wall to prevent spoilage of the King family's groceries. Steel ice tongs hang nearby to move

blocks of ice during deliveries. A standalone piece of furniture called a Hoosier cabinet catches my eye; it sits against the rear wall, the upper shelves filled with 1940s spices, coffee boxes, salt, flour, and sugar.

Diane tells me that it was King's grandmother who oversaw the kitchen, preparing many of the family meals. She was an important family figure, since the parents' work as a minister and choir musician often took them away from home.

She indicates that King loved a few of the famous specialty recipes of the South, which would have been at the center of many meals in Georgia households.

"A favorite meal in the King house that was held in the dining room was the Sunday supper of fried chicken, collard greens, black-eyed peas, and corn bread," says Diane. "It was the family discussions from these traditional Sunday suppers that would have a tremendous influence on the later life of Martin Luther King Jr."

If food and meaningful discussion were prominent parts of Martin Luther King Jr.'s life, I want to learn how to make traditional Southern dishes, in hopes of understanding what he was eating and feeling in his mind and body while he and his family were sitting at that dining room table. I don't think I can get the full experience of visiting the King house and the great city of Atlanta without it—and I cannot help but think there are some Southern dishes that might be fabulous for Franny's dinner.

So, for the final leg of this culinary adventure, I attend a Heart and Soul traditional Southern cooking class at The Cooking Schools, just steps away from the house where Dr. Martin Luther King Jr. grew up.

When the classroom doors open, I am the first of some twenty-odd Southern cooking devotees to walk in. The class is held in a restored warehouse, with rustic furniture and eclectic art. The front of the room is dominated by a long counter with gas burners, multiple ovens, and high-end appliances. Classroom seating is provided at a dozen dining tables that seat three to four students each. My fellow cooks are a wonderful mix of people, all ages and all backgrounds—which I find makes the best classes.

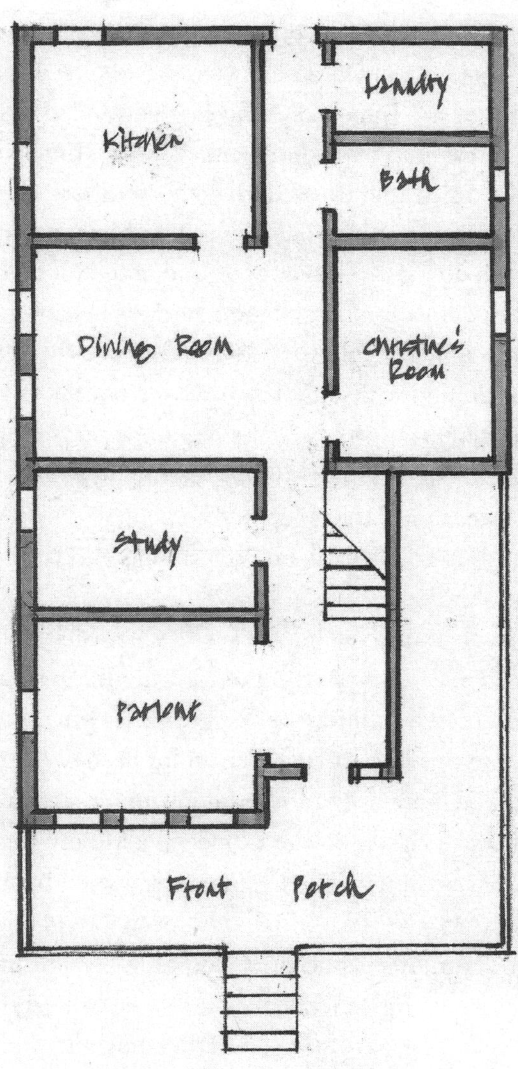

Martin Luther King Jr., childhood home

Our instructor, Rick Westbrook, is an energetic gentleman with horn-rimmed glasses and a baseball hat. Rick introduces himself as a long-time chef of Southern food in the Atlanta area; it gives me great confidence when he tells us that he knows this cuisine backwards and forwards. Rick says that his inspiration for cooking comes from happy memories of Sunday dinners at his grandmother's house in Cumming, Georgia, where she would prepare loads of fried chicken for his large extended family.

To kick off the class, Rick presents us with a bunch of collards, explaining that these dark leafy members of the cabbage family are a staple side dish in Southern cooking. The thick, coarse, paddle-like leaves were one of the most common plants traditionally grown in kitchen gardens because, more resilient than spinach or lettuce, they could last through the winter weather and withstand the heat of a Southern summer. Rick demonstrates how to use our sharp knives to split the large leaves down the middle and cut out the tough, woody stems. He places the leaves in a large soup pot along with chicken stock, mushrooms, butter, olive oil, and seasonings and turns on the burner. We're off!

When I booked the cooking class with Chef Rick, I told him I have a special interest in Martin Luther King Jr. As I stand in front of the cooking stove with him, he suggests that King, naturally, grew up eating this fare and was known for his hearty appetite.

In adulthood, King was a frequent customer at Atlanta restaurants that served Southern food. In addition to providing warmth and nourishment, the restaurants, owned by African Americans, were a backdrop for Atlanta's civil rights movement. Paschal's Restaurant and the Busy Bee Café became centers of change where civil rights leaders could meet, talk, and strategize. In the 1950s and 1960s, other civil rights movement icons such as Andrew Young, John Lewis, and Jesse Jackson were also frequent diners.

Of course, Southern cuisine wasn't the primary influence in the formation of the civil rights movement, but I do wonder whether, maybe on a subconscious level, there was a connection between King's memories of the tastes, aromas, and feelings during family talks around his childhood dining room table and his political actions.

Chef Rick announces that the next dish we will make is candied sweet potato. Franny loves sweet potato; I'm going to pay special attention. The origin of this dish comes from yams, which are an important part of West African food traditions and were used to feed enslaved prisoners on ships during the transatlantic slave trade. In their new environment, where their homeland ingredients weren't available, the enslaved Africans found a substitute for yams: the North American sweet potato.

Rick instructs the class to chop the sweet potatoes into large chunks. Away I go—*chop, chop, chop*—and I place my sweet potato chunks into a large pot. Chef Westbrook tops them off with honey, butter, cinnamon, water, salt, pepper, and what seems like a dump truck load of brown sugar. The pot comes to a boil and then Rick adds a large dollop of his secret ingredient, agave syrup. I can hardly wait to get at this.

Over the next hour, we chop and slice at our tables as our cooking instructor shares some knowledge of the history of Southern cooking. He tells us that the dishes we are preparing are what is sometimes known as "soul food" and that they originate from a cuisine traditionally prepared and eaten by enslaved people in the Southern United States. During the days of oppression, when Black people endured slavery, only slave owners had access to the best cuts of meat, like roasts and hams.

The less desirable meats (pig ears, feet, and intestines) and leftover vegetables went to the enslaved people. Nevertheless, they used their creativity to turn plain food into delicious dishes, cooking that has become part of Black Southern culture and has been enjoyed through the generations.

In the early twentieth century, more than six million Black people left the South due to poor economic conditions and intense racism in a massive relocation now called the Great Migration. Having to deal with the traumatic circumstances of encountering further racism as they sought new housing and employment, they brought their Southern culinary traditions with them as a reminder of comfort and a sense of community in different, unfamiliar surroundings.

As Rick presents us with a lively show of cooking and storytelling, we make a béchamel sauce of butter and flour, which is added to elbow macaroni and four types of cheese for a baked mac and cheese. And then, before I know it, I am folding together a batter of wet and dry ingredients that is poured into a cast-iron skillet and popped into the oven for corn bread. Time flies when the cooking is fun.

For the main dish, Rick has us prepare classic Southern fried chicken. He has already been marinating chicken thighs and breasts for an hour in buttermilk along with salt and pepper. His personal addition to the traditional marinade is pickle juice.

Chef Westbrook gives me the job of dredging the chicken pieces in a flour/breadcrumb mixture, dipping it in an egg wash, and then dredging it again until it is completely double-coated.

Then, on to the dramatic frying process. With metal tongs, I carefully dip the heavily dredged chicken pieces into two inches of hot peanut oil (peanut oil has a high smoke point, making it a good choice for frying foods), and the frying process begins. The peanut oil pops, sizzles, and smokes, the aroma of frying chicken fills the room, and the anticipation for good eating builds. To feed this large class, we have to fry a whole mess of chicken. I become mesmerized by the spectacle of the breaded chicken pieces floating in a hot, bubbling pool of oil.

Finally, once all the dishes are complete, they are laid out on a long table. Everyone grabs a plate and digs in.

My first taste is of the mac and cheese, which packs a rich, satisfying creaminess and combines the gooey four cheeses with the al dente pasta. This dish is impressive, but I know there is much more to come.

The hot corn bread is light, crunchy, and exquisitely soaked in brown butter from the bottom of the sizzling skillet. Next into my mouth are the collard greens braised in chicken broth. Their earthy, savory flavor is the perfect light vegetable accompaniment to the heavier mac and cheese.

A real surprise is the candied sweet potato. I've always loved its soft, creamy texture and natural sweet taste, but tonight, the humble sweet potato has been pumped up into culinary glory with the brown sugar, honey, cinnamon, and agave. The bright orange tuber presents as a vegetable—but with its candied syrup, it could easily be a decadent dessert. That clinches it—this dish will definitely be on the menu for Franny's birthday dinner.

But now I am ready for the main course—the Southern fried chicken. My stomach rumbling with anticipation, I look down at the fried chicken thigh with a golden-brown coating full of crunchy ripples and speckled with spices. I picture young Martin Luther King Jr. getting ready to dive into a piece of fried chicken in his childhood dining room. I pick up the warm golden-colored thigh in my fingers, bring it up to my mouth, and bite down.

It is a stunner. The first sensation is a resounding *crunch* from the breadcrumb-and-flour-coated skin. Then the magnificently spiced taste engulfs my tongue. My mouth is in ecstasy as the

juicy, flavorful dark chicken meat falls away from the bone. As I chew, the tender meat blends with the crispy breading into a jumble of amazing flavors. I look down to see wisps of steam wafting from the thigh, and I breathe it all in.

It is really about the skin. As I chew and allow the flavors to unravel in my mouth, I realize the crust—its tasty fat, its umami essence—is a perfect enhancement to the meat's mild flavor. Like two dance partners in sync with each other, making each other better than if they were alone.

But wait. There is something else going on here. There is a hint of tang, an ingredient I can't put my finger on, that is making this dish even more pleasurable. At first, I think it is the buttermilk—but no. Then I figure it out. It's Rick's secret marinade ingredient: pickle juice. The pickle juice is not prominent, but it adds a touch of extra brightness to the chicken.

Of course, I eat with my hands. I need plenty of napkins. I gnaw on the thigh bone and pick it clean. I can hardly wait to make this dish at home.

As we joyfully dine, Chef Rick brings up the future of this cuisine in Atlanta.

"Tonight we're making traditional Southern dishes, but a number of contemporary African American chefs are rethinking soul food," says Rick. "Rather than staying static, the cuisine is going in different directions."

Some Atlanta chefs who are expanding their repertoire are swapping in lighter alternatives for classic ingredients, frying fish and meats in olive oil rather than lard (pork fat), for instance, or making their collard greens with smoked turkey instead of the traditional smoked pork.

Another huge focus is giving dishes a fusion spin, including Southern fried tofu, using collard greens in ramen, and vegan mac and cheese made with cheese from soy, nuts, and vegetable oils. In some ways, this feels like a return to the origins of Southern food, when most of the time meat was not available—fried chicken was only for special occasions.

The goal of some Atlanta chefs is to improve the reputation of Southern food, "elevating" dishes via presentation (think small plates) or creating more refined renditions. On this trip, I've had the honor of meeting Chef Sonya Jones, who is famous for her signature sweet potato cheesecake at the Sweet Auburn Bread Company. Chef Sonya tells me that when she attended culinary school, the teachers considered Southern cooking to be substandard fare.

"They spent a lot of time promoting Italian food and making polenta," she says. "I thought, that's great—but what about grits?" They're the same thing, Sonya says, and it's true: Despite slight differences in the type of corn used, both polenta and grits are a dish made of ground corn.

Determined to elevate Southern cuisine with a high-end dessert, Sonya created a cheesecake combining two Southern staples—sweet potato in the cream cheese custard, with a pound cake crust. Mission accomplished. Tasting Sonya's sweet potato cheesecake is a heavenly experience, and the dish is surely now a Southern classic.

Back at the cooking school, I sit alongside my classmates in the dining area and we enjoy the sumptuous Southern dishes that we have made together. After chopping, dredging, baking, and frying together, we have bonded. There is much merriment and laughter. When the evening comes to a close, there are hugs and selfies, and we exchange addresses.

I wonder to myself: What causes this fellowship? It would have been the same warmth and good feeling in the King family dining room, I'm sure. The same as the trust and solidarity of the civil rights leaders eating at the Busy Bee Café. What is it about fried chicken?

The food is basic, unpretentious, and filling. But maybe it is the honesty and history embedded within it that allows it to emit a spiritual effect. Traditional Southern cuisine is more than just a meal. It has the power to bring people together, a reminder of what a group of people can all have in common.

The tastes of the evening make me recall my recent visit to the childhood dining room of Martin Luther King Jr. I try to picture the King family gathered around the table for Sunday supper, eating the same Southern foods and discussing the pressing issues of the day, with King's grandmother bringing more steaming dishes in from the kitchen. Standing in that space, I was overwhelmed with the feeling of family love and support radiating around me.

I have seen grander and more elaborate dining rooms, but after visiting Sweet Auburn, I think the King dining room might be the most important one in America.

It changed humankind.

Martin Luther King, Jr. National Historical Park

450 Auburn Avenue NE, Atlanta, Georgia, United States

nps.gov/malu/contacts.htm | (404) 331-5190 ext. 5046

Dear Franny,

I had an emotional day in Atlanta at Martin Luther King Jr.'s childhood house.

I feel sure that his loving family, dinner conversation, prayers, and Southern dishes would have all contributed to giving him confidence and opening his mind to fighting for equality. A number of things jumped out at me that would have made his Sunday dinners a special meal in his great dining room.

I learned in the King house that you don't have to have a ton of money to make a beautiful and hospitable dining room. The King dining table is modest—but it is also approachable and refined, all within a room where people could share wonderful Southern dishes, converse with ease, be listened to, and create happy memories.

And, like the Kings, we can lean into simple elegance with a few choice pieces to rejuvenate the dining room, design-wise: a gravy boat, a water pitcher, and cloth napkins chosen with thought and care.

With our friends turning to vegetarian, vegan, and gluten-free food, I want to tweak a few traditional recipes for your dinner. Like Dr. King, we want to bring everyone to the table.

Martin Luther King Jr. was a remarkable person. His dream was that people of all races and creeds could join hands at the same table. In the spirit of Dr. King, I want to commit to a hospitable dining room. I want to welcome new friends to our table. I know you do too.

XOXO

J.

8

FRIDA KAHLO'S CASA AZUL DINING ROOM, 1939

Mexico City, Mexico

COME WITH ME TO A dining room in Mexico City strewn with multicolored banners and patio doors that open onto a garden of cacti, yuccas, and marigolds, all the while being serenaded by the romantic harmonies of a live mariachi band.

Imagine sitting down to a Mexican feast starting with a soup of cubed red snapper, Mexican oregano, onions, tomatoes, and serrano chiles. Next, a grilled zucchini salad with avocado and crumbled añejo cheese in a lively vinaigrette sprinkled with cilantro. And then, the sensational main course: *mole de pato* (duck stewed in a sauce of chocolate and chiles) alongside a dish of *pico de gallo con xoconostle* (a piquant fresh salsa of diced tomatoes, onions, and tart, underripe cactus fruit).

One might expect this to be a menu from a magnificent, high-end restaurant in modern-day Mexico City. But it is a sample of the food that would have appeared on the dining room table of the renowned artist Frida Kahlo.

Frida Kahlo—her name evokes so many colorful and passionate images. She was one of Mexico's greatest artists, best known for her brilliantly colorful self-portraits (always depicting herself with a steady gaze). Her expressive hairstyles and clothing, and heavy, connected eyebrows, also marked her identity.

It was the color in Kahlo's paintings that first caused to me to fall in love with her art. I was mesmerized by her still lifes and self-portraits, drenched in bold reds, greens, yellows, blues—crying out her pain, her sorrows, and her love. Her art has always moved me.

Kahlo is one of the best-known female artists of the twentieth century, a fascinating personality noted for her ideas about love, sex, death, the body, gender, Mexico, class, and race. A consistent theme in Kahlo's artwork is her physical and emotional pain. She spent a large amount of time in the house convalescing.

Frida Kahlo lived with her husband, Diego Rivera, in a house called the Casa Azul on the outskirts of Mexico City from 1936 to 1954. The building was Kahlo's birthplace, the home where she grew up and where she later died in a room on the upper floor. Today, the house is open as Museo Frida Kahlo, a museum dedicated to her life and work, displaying her art, clothing, jewelry—and also her cooking utensils and dining room furniture.

While most people are familiar with Kahlo's artwork, few know that Kahlo was just as passionate about food as she was about painting. As a lover of Mexican cuisine, I became aware of how Kahlo cooked and entertained from the book *Frida's Fiestas: Recipes and Reminiscences of Life with Frida Kahlo* by Guadalupe Rivera and Marie-Pierre Colle. In it, the authors recount Mexican feasts like the one I described as the kind that Kahlo served to guests in her dining room.

From my own experience, I have noticed that for people who like to eat, food also brings joy into their life. And when I consider the importance that food and the dining room played in Kahlo's life, I have to find out more. That only adds to my longstanding wish to visit her house in Mexico City.

If Frida Kahlo found joy in eating, there had to be more to her life than misery. And I would love to express Kahlo's passion and artistry in my dinner celebration for Franny.

As I venture out on the streets of Mexico City's historical downtown, my head spins from the whirl of chaotic traffic, crowded sidewalks, colorful streamers, musicians, and street vendors selling Mexican ceramics, tacos, woven blankets, and bizarre wrestler's masks. Founded in the early fourteenth century by the Aztecs, Mexico City is one of the oldest capital cities in the Americas—historical buildings, ruins, monumental parks, and museums are everywhere. I do love to explore, but while I bite into an empanada I bought from a street vendor, I remind myself of my main purpose for being here: to find the house of Frida Kahlo. To achieve my goal, I board a bus that will take me to the smaller community of Coyoacán, on the outskirts of Mexico City.

After an hour-long bus ride that travels past historical monuments, open-air markets, and bustling neighborhoods, the bus enters a comfortable, rustic-looking enclave of tree-lined streets and single-story houses. I do not see any signs, but I can only assume I am entering Coyoacán. The bus stops with a loud squeak and a jerk, and the driver calls out a list of Spanish names. When I hear "Frida Kahlo," I am out of my seat in a flash.

As I jump off the bus, I am met by a young woman with long dark hair and large brown eyes. She immediately gives me a big hug and exclaims, "Señor Ota! Welcome to Mexico!"

I had been told in advance that the people of Mexico are very warm and friendly; this heartfelt greeting only puts an exclamation mark on this statement. After the embrace, she introduces herself as Estefania Morlett, my Museo Frida Kahlo tour guide.

After I tell Estefania how glad I am to meet her, she explains that Frida Kahlo's house is a block away. As we walk under the Coyoacán palms and past colorful houses that have been built right up to the street line, Estefania tells me about herself.

"I love to share my knowledge of Frida Kahlo, her house, and art with people who visit Mexico from around the world," she says. "I have carried out research with the curators here at the Casa Azul, and we go beyond some of the inaccuracies about her life. It is a deep passion for me."

I am glad to hear this. I tell Estefania that in my own research, I found, at times, that so much about Frida Kahlo focuses on her unconventional romances, bisexual orientation, and sensational lifestyle that I fear there might be instances when stories about the artist can become distorted.

Estefania goes on to say that, earlier in her life, she had studied art history here in Mexico City and in Milan, Italy, and then earned an honorary doctorate from Universidad Iberoamericana, Mexico City. It sounds like Estefania is the perfect person to tour me through Frida Kahlo's Casa Azul.

Estefania points out the house just ahead of us, at the corner of Londres and Allende Streets. But there is no need for this heads-up: in the distance, beyond the single-story houses that are scrunched together along the street, I spot a house with vibrant cobalt-blue walls popping out of the streetscape. In front of it is a long lineup of people waiting to enter the famous house.

This two-story corner building looks more likely to be found in an idyllic village than in a city of millions. I hurry ahead to stand at the front door and take in the simple lines of this brilliant blue house rising straight up from the sidewalk. Casa Azul translates to "Blue House," appropriately so named by the famous artist. The house is a work of art in itself.

As we wait in line to enter, Estefania begins to recount some details of Kahlo's life to me: "Frida Kahlo was born in the house we are standing in front of in 1907, a house that was built by her father. But at age eighteen, Kahlo was tragically injured in a horrific bus accident that was to change her life. It led to a continuous series of surgeries and recoveries. She spent long periods of time bedridden in casts, and underwent over thirty operations trying to fix her broken bones. She led a lifetime of pain."

It was then, Estefania explains, that Kahlo began to paint as a way to pass the time. She found a way to use her condition as the inspiration for many of her masterful paintings. Kahlo transformed her physical pain into works of art.

"But she also suffered psychological pain caused by her conflicting relationship with her husband, Diego Rivera," says Estefania.

Rivera was a famous painter whose bold large-scale murals helped establish mural painting as a respected medium in Mexican history and culture.

Kahlo first met Rivera in 1922 when he was painting a mural at the Bolívar Auditorium of the National Preparatory School she attended. They met again five years later when Kahlo took various pieces of her artwork to get a critique from the well-known artist. Rivera was impressed by Kahlo's art and immediately taken with her bravery. He soon began to be a regular visitor to the Kahlo residence. They were married in 1929, when she was twenty-two and he was forty-two.

"They were married twice, divorced once, and separated countless times," Estefania says. "Kahlo and Rivera each had numerous affairs."

At the time of their first separation, in 1939, Kahlo painted one of her most tragic works, *The Two Fridas*, an emotional pairing of two portraits of herself. One Frida is dressed in European clothing torn open to expose a broken heart; the other Frida is in Mexican clothing. The two Fridas hold hands and are connected by an artery running between their hearts.

Frida Kahlo created some of the most compelling images of the twentieth century. She produced about two hundred sensual, haunting paintings, primarily still lifes and portraits of herself, family, and friends that combined elements of surrealism, fantasy, and folklore—all figurative. Unlike many of her contemporaries, she did not experiment with abstract art. Although she received occasional requests for commissions, Kahlo sold relatively few paintings during her lifetime. Today, her paintings sell for exorbitant prices. In 2025, a Frida Kahlo self-portrait sold for nearly $5 million.

During her life, Kahlo challenged social norms and broke taboos by addressing themes such as the female body, gender, cross-dressing, identity, and trauma in ways that continue to inspire today's artists. On top of it all, she has energized the imaginations of countless artists around the world. After she passed away in 1954 at the age of forty-seven, her reputation grew into the frenzy that art experts now call "Fridamania." The lineup winding around the outside of the house gives an idea of the masses who love her.

"She would be so proud of her legacy today," says Estefania. "Today, Frida is a rock star."

As true fans, Estefania and I talk nonstop about Kahlo, completely forgetting about the lineup we're in. But after twenty minutes of standing in the warm Mexican sun, still engaged in Frida stories, we enter through the house gates.

Thankfully, the first space Estefania takes me to is the cool, lush courtyard garden. As we stroll in, I feel like I am entering a magical oasis. Birds sing from the trees, visitors glide through the grounds, and I can smell the blossoming flowers everywhere we walk. We find a garden table and chairs to sit and admire the floral beauty around us.

"While we all love the paintings of Frida Kahlo, an important aspect of her life that is sometimes lost is that she and her husband, Diego Rivera, were Mexican nationalists," says Estefania. "In the nineteenth and early twentieth centuries, the rich and elite of Mexico turned their eyes to Europe, and France specifically, for their art, architecture, and culture. The prevailing sentiment was that France provided the standard for high culture, and Mexicans ignored their own culture, which they felt was not worthy of recognition."

I am initially taken aback to hear this. But when I reflect on it, I remember that it was almost an international belief of the time that France set the bar for culture around the world. I am glad that Frida and Diego decided enough was enough.

"As proud Mexicans," Estefania continues, "Frida and Diego promoted Mexican art, architecture, fashion, food, and jewelry. They wanted Mexicans to rediscover their Indigenous and native history and love everything about Mexico, even though it was unheard of at the time."

We get up to stroll the courtyard, a fulsome Mexican botanical garden. Estefania points to flowers that Frida planted from all over the country, including yuccas, bougainvilleas, cacti, jasmine, agave, and banana and orange trees. As she bends down to smell the scent of a bloom, Estefania tells me that Frida loved botany.

"She broke with traditional garden designs of the time, which were modeled on European flora and statues. She grew Mexican flowers and incorporated pre-Columbian idols across the walls of the courtyard that Diego loved collecting as part of his Mexican heritage."

Estefania leads me over to the house to get a closer look at its striking blue walls.

"You would not know it today, but the house was originally built in a white French colonial style with decoration of classical friezes and pilasters," my tour guide says. "When Frida and Diego moved in, they removed all of the European architectural references and flattened the walls to make it appear more like a modest, rural Mexican house. Then in 1932, they painted it a beautiful Anil Azul blue"—an indigo-colored dye that comes from a shrub on the Oaxacan coast—"the color deriving from a Mayan belief that this shade of blue removes evil spirits from the house. She made it her own heavenly space. The window frames were painted red to support Diego's belief in communism."

Estefania knows that I am eager to see the dining room, so we make our way into the house.

The ground floor includes the living room, kitchen, dining room, and bedrooms. One of the paintings on the walls is *Viva la Vida*, a still life of watermelons sliced open, revealing vivid red, green, and white, the national colors of Mexico. Kahlo painted it just days before her death, and some have interpreted the fruit as embodying her open heart. Estefania tells me that in Kahlo's last days, she had lost her leg and was in enormous pain and misery. While Kahlo's cause of death is believed to be pulmonary embolism, Estefania insists that the famous artist took her own life. "We in Mexico know the truth," she says.

On the second floor we visit Kahlo's sunlit studio, which features her original furniture and art supplies, including an assortment of brushes, paint-covered palettes, a mirror, and pigments in bottles, waiting to be mixed for use. I am especially moved to see a wheelchair in front of her easel. Kahlo underwent multiple operations to treat the injuries from her bus accident, and she used a wheelchair as part of her recuperation.

Evidence of recovery from her surgeries is also visible in her bedroom, next to the studio where she spent much of her adult life. On the underside of the bed canopy, a mirror was hung so that, even while lying in the bed, she could still paint self-portraits.

Finally, Estefania takes me downstairs, and I sense that we are finally approaching the dining room, my main focus for the visit.

I step through a blue-painted door frame into an astounding fourteen-by-twenty-foot sunlit room. The first thing that I notice about the dining room is its astonishingly vibrant color scheme: Its bright blue and white walls make me feel like I am standing inside a Frida Kahlo painting. The brilliant yellow floor that appears in much of the ground floor continues through the dining room. Estefania tells me that Frida mixed a brilliant yellow pigment into the Mexican *hormigón* concrete floor to achieve the brilliant hue.

Kahlo's dining room has been made into a unique art piece. The color of the walls brings me joy; the yellow floor radiates a warm, heavenly glow. It is immediately my favorite dining room of all time. With its surprising explosion of color that lifts my spirits to the blue Mexican sky, it is the most elaborately decorated room in the house, filled with red flowers, paintings, masks on the walls, hand-painted ceramic animal figures, pots, jugs, fruits, and multicolored bowls.

In the center of the room, a long table painted bright yellow is covered in a white linen tablecloth, upon which sit dishes in vibrant colors and patterns. I try to imagine the tabletop covered in fresh fruits, vegetables, and flowers bought during Frida's numerous forays into the Coyoacán market.

Arranged around the table are simple wooden chairs with an insert of rush weaving. While the chairs appear to match one another—the legs are painted the same yellow as the table, with accent stripes across the wood joinery—a closer look reveals that the striped pattern on each chair is unique.

I look up into open ceiling joists and spy a large skylight bringing overhead sunlight to further brighten the colors of the dining room and add airiness to the space.

The white walls have a three-foot band of cobalt blue painted around the lower section, defining the room's perimeter. Above this level, the walls are decorated with still life paintings of fruits and vegetables, with ceramic bowls and wood spoons hanging off the walls. Another wall holds a fireplace made of Mexican lava rock; flowers and ceramics adorn the mantel. All around me, there are handmade ceramic pots, cupboards painted with fanciful swirls, and animal dolls hanging in the corners.

But my favorite feature of Kahlo's dining room is the wood shelves, painted bright yellow, that display the artist's collection of colored glassware, earthenware pots, plates, and Indigenous artifacts. They are indicative of her pride in and promotion of Mexican artistic and cultural heritage.

"Frida was deeply influenced by Indigenous Mexican culture, and you can see it here in her use of bright colors and all the artifacts throughout the dining room," says Estefania. "In the early twentieth century, Mexican folk art was discriminated against and looked down on. Nevertheless, Kahlo collected it. To her, the pieces defined the essential characteristics of Mexicanness."

Standing in the middle of the dining room, I fall in love with

Kahlo's exuberant collection of Mexican folk art—decorated ceramic animals, jugs, embroidered textiles, children's toys, earthenware piggy banks, papier-mâché Judas figures, and devotional paintings, all lining the walls.

So much about Kahlo is in her dining room. You can feel her presence in the walls.

The bright colors of the walls and floor and the eclectic collection of handmade artifacts emit a lively ambience and visual joy—they reflect her interests, passions, and personality. So much about Kahlo is in her dining room. You can feel her presence in the walls.

And people loved coming to this dining room. On any given night, Frida and Diego might be serving dinner to communists, capitalists, artists, poets, musicians, or intellectuals of her day. Her list of friends included Nelson Rockefeller, Orson Welles, Gary Cooper, André Breton, Marc Chagall, Georgia O'Keeffe, Isamu Noguchi, Pablo Picasso, Joan Miró, and exiled Russian revolutionary Leon Trotsky, with whom Kahlo had an affair. The upper echelons of society all had an invitation to dine with them. Guests were served chiles in walnut sauce, spicy shrimp cake, or stuffed corn tortillas, while the mariachi—the traditional village musicians—played throughout the night.

"Whenever people of prominence came to Mexico, it was a very important part of their visit to see Frida and Diego," says Estefania. "Frida looked at food as a means of being more Mexican. She wanted everything in her house to be Mexican."

Being at the center of Mexico City's circle of artists, intellectuals, and leftists, the famous artist couple entertained here; it was where they would come together with their many famous guests to eat, drink, and engage in long conversations. The dining room was the heart of their intense social and cultural life. Frida and Diego earned a reputation for their raucous dinner parties. They wanted everyone to experience the best of Mexico.

According to the book *Frida's Fiestas*, Kahlo especially loved celebrating her birthday, which was on July 6. To set the festive atmosphere for her birthday party, the dining room would be decorated with colorful paper streamers and Kahlo would hire mariachi. In celebration of her Mexican heritage, Kahlo asked her female friends to dress like women from Tehuana (a region known for being matriarchal, making the clothing a symbol of female strength). The guests were advised to come "ready to eat every kind of food and to let their hair down and to sing their hearts out."

The schedule for Kahlo's July 6 birthday party would have been:

Early afternoon: Guests start arriving loaded with presents—perfume, dolls, necklaces. Those invited would be relatives and friends, as well as many of Mexico's artistic elite, along with members of the communist party, to which both Kahlo and Rivera belonged. They would be greeted at the door of the Casa Azul and handed their choice of a glass of tequila, a mug of beer, or a jug of almond-cured pulque (a Mexican alcoholic beverage made from fermented agave sap; agave is a plant with spiky leaves that grows in arid regions).

Mid-afternoon: The mariachi make their appearance, shattering the calm of the Coyoacán district. They sing and play their trumpets and guitars among paper lanterns, streamers, and colorful papier-mâché doves. Frida sings loudly with the mariachi, while guests stroll around the house and garden.

Late afternoon: Guests begin helping themselves to the endless pitchers, platters, plates, and bowls that fill the dining table. There is more pulque, tequila, and other refreshments. The tables are decorated with colorful fruits and flowers laid out on green, yellow, and pink tablecloths. The buffet is an explosion of color:

Shrimp broth, made from dried shrimp with potatoes, carrots, parsley, and guajillo chile puree, and served with lime quarters
Country-style *chiles en frío*, stuffed with chopped meat and bathed in a sweet-and-sour sauce of tomatoes and sliced onions
Romeritos (a Mexican green vegetable that is naturally salty and tastes like spinach) with shrimp tortitas (Mexican pancakes) and sour prickly pears
Refried beans smothered in cheese and garnished with totopos (corn tortilla chips that have been fried or baked)
Manchamantel, a Mexican stew of chicken, pork, vegetables, and fruits braised in a chile-spiked sauce
In addition, there might be serving bowls of beans, avocados, radishes, panela cheese, steaming bowls of white and red rice, traditional Mexican cabbage in green sauce, and cheese-filled peppers.

Early evening: Desserts are placed in the middle of the table: a sweet potato-pineapple pudding with pine nuts, mamey mousse, pine nut flan, meringues, nougats, and taffies.
Nightfall until dawn: Tequila is liberally consumed while the mariachi band plays into the night. Guests sing and dance. Only Kahlo's laughter is loud enough to rise above their celebrating. Kahlo entertains guests with jokes, told in her characteristically rowdy voice. They party until dawn.

Whenever I hear the strumming guitars and emotive voices of a mariachi band, a magical wave of love and longing comes over me. The roots of the mariachi go back hundreds of years; it is a uniquely Mexican sound with suave harmonies from singers and stringed instruments, written to open up emotions.

"For many years, Mexican society kept young people of the opposite sex separated. The music was a way of communication from a young man to a woman that he was courting," says Estefania. "The music was a message of love delivered by the mariachi on his behalf. It is no wonder that Frida and Diego loved mariachi. The sound was a huge part of their dinner celebrations and a point of pride of their Mexican cultural heritage. No doubt the music caused their guests to fall further in love with Kahlo, Rivera, and Mexico."

To add even more color and energy to the party atmosphere, Kahlo used the power of clothing to seduce, distract, captivate, and entertain. She loved jewelry, makeup, and perfume to set the stage, emphasizing her thick eyebrows that met in the middle and leaving her upper lip unplucked as part of her personal style. She used semiprecious stones, custom jewelry, pre-Hispanic ornaments, and combined frills, lace, silks, and glittering fabric to accent her artistic wardrobe. Frida wore her thick hair in braids that she intertwined with colorful ribbons and yarn, then piled onto her head and adorned with fresh flowers to make her fashion statements.

Like she asked of her friends attending her party, Kahlo also proudly wore the Tehuana dress. The basis is the huipil, a loose-fitting blouse traditional in Mexico, composed of cotton with elaborate embroidery on necklines, sleeve openings, and hem. For her lower garments she wore long, full skirts in bright, colorful patterns decorated with embroidery, ruffles, and frill or lace hems.

"Her clothing was her cultural statement and her visual identity," says Estefania. "She did not copy the American Hollywood look in women's or movie magazines. She had her own style—strong, flamboyant, colorful, and traditionally Mexican. It was her trademark."

Talking about her birthday dinner with Estefania, I am besotted with Frida Kahlo and her approach to hospitality and generosity. I would have loved to be one of the guests at such a birthday dinner—but I might have disappointed her. I don't think I would make it through the night. While at one time in my life, I might have been able to keep drinking tequila with her (barely), that time has vanished into the mist.

Kahlo underwent several surgeries toward the end of her life, in the late 1940s and early 1950s, often with prolonged hospital stays. She frequently turned to alcohol and drugs for relief. Nonetheless, she continued to paint and draw.

But even as her physical illnesses grew worse, the painter still found pleasure in eating and drinking with company. She physically could no longer access the dining room, so she moved the dinners to her bedroom, where she consumed enchiladas with mole (pronounced MOH-lay; more on that to come) and drank tequila.

"But her life was also filled with joy," says Estefania, her face brightening.

In the face of constant struggles with her health and her marriage, Kahlo took pleasure in the everyday joys of life. She smoked cigars and told off-color jokes. She played the guitar and sang Mexican folk songs to her friends and dinner guests. And of course, she took great pleasure in eating and drinking.

Kahlo's ill health caused her to attend her first solo exhibition in Mexico in 1953 lying on a bed. In her last year, her life was full of physical pain. Rivera was absent from her for days. And yet she threw another big party for her birthday, with a hundred guests, turkey with mole, chiles, and tamales, and atole (a comforting warm drink). Irrepressible and exuberant, she loved entertaining as much as art. Frida Kahlo knew how to celebrate any occasion with her guests, whom she indulged lavishly.

I want to do the same.

As the climax to my Frida Kahlo dining adventure, I decide to attend a cooking class in Mexico City that promises to make Kahlo-inspired birthday dinner recipes. The class is in a three-

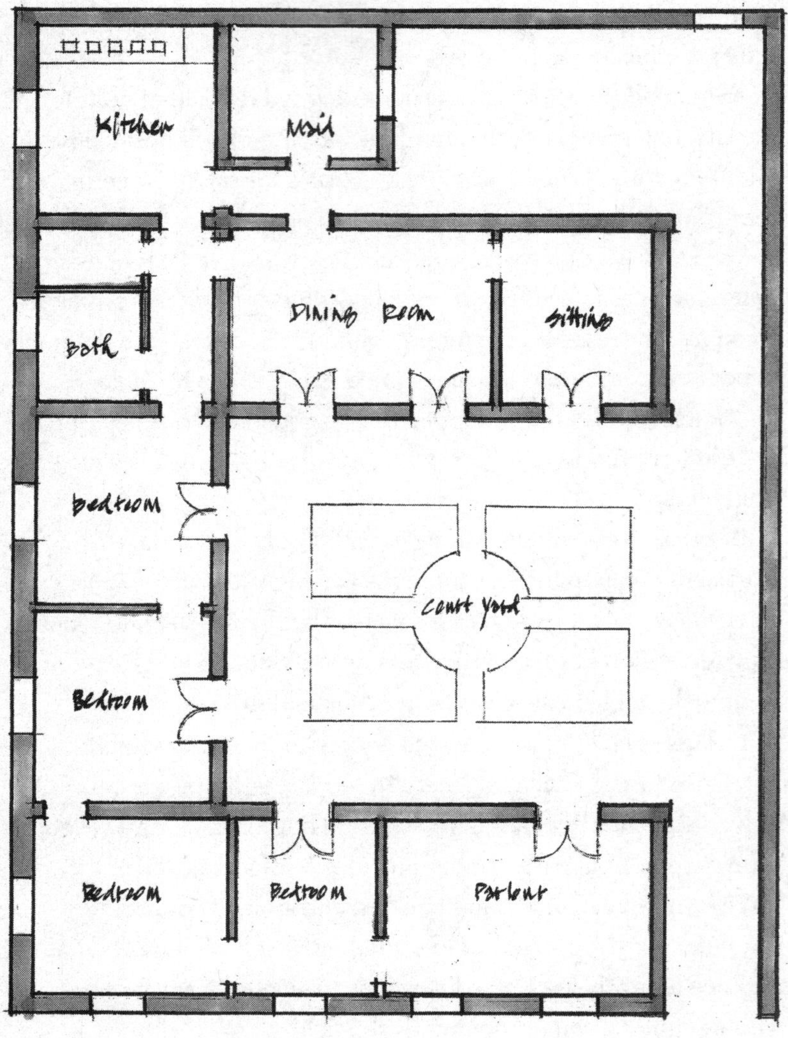

Casa Azul

story walk-up just steps away from the historical city center. In my excitement, I arrive twenty minutes early, which gives me a chance to explore the high-octane downtown neighborhood with its historical building facades, cobblestone streets, and street food stands.

At 9 a.m. I knock on one of these historical, heavy wooden doors, and as it opens, I am greeted by two handsome gentlemen wearing aprons: my cooking instructors for the day. They introduce themselves as I enter their interior courtyard. The first is a fair-haired man named Tim Dubitsky, a former New Yorker now living in Mexico City, and the other is Javier Martinez, born in Mexico City. Both work professionally as chefs, and Javier is also an architect; we laugh about what a wonderful combination it is to be passionate about historical buildings and food. Today, they offer cooking classes in Mexico City as well as culinary excursions to Mexican farming communities.

Tim and Javier escort me along a historical corridor painted white and then up a skylit flight of cast-iron stairs. When the doors open to their apartment, I step into a gorgeous double-story loft of colorful Mexican paper hangings, woven carpets, clay ceramics, blue dishware, and strings of lights, enhanced by mariachi music that wafts out the open windows.

I immediately take a place at the massive kitchen table and am thrilled when Chef Tim hands me a knife and a round wooden butcher block and asks me to start chopping vegetables—tomatillos, garlic, onions, chiles—for a salsa verde to spread over roast potatoes. The class has begun!

Tim is a lively chef with many years of experience cooking in restaurants in New York and Mexico City. Currently residing in Mexico City's Centro Histórico, he is living his dream of operating a cooking school and is also enrolled in the master's extension program at Harvard's culinary psychology program. As I chop, Tim gives me a crash course in the traditional past of the cuisine we're about to make.

"The history of Mexican food can be traced back over two thousand years, with its roots in the Mexican Mayan and Aztec cultures," he begins.

Tim goes on to tell me that the Mayan people's diet included corn, beans, and other local fruits and vegetables. Aztecs introduced chocolate, honey, and salt as food sources. Tomatoes, potatoes, and chiles were first domesticated in the Americas by Indigenous Peoples, but spread around the world after Europeans began to explore and conquer the New World. The Spanish introduced chicken, pork, and beef. Additionally, garlic, onion, wine, and rice made their way into cooked dishes. Traces of all these early Mesoamerican cuisines are found in Mexican dishes today.

"In the marriage of Frida and Diego, food always played an important role," says Tim. "They used traditional ingredients in their cooking as an expression of their love of Mexico and their connection to the Indigenous culture of the country."

Tim reveals that in solidarity with the poor, at their wedding feast, Diego decreed that the food was to be eaten by hand with tortillas rather than knife and fork. Dinner was a social activity and a political statement at the same time.

Tim hands me a comal, a heavy Mexican cast-iron skillet, and we pop the chopped onions, tomatillos, and peppers into it to roast over the gas flame. The intention is to get a nice char on the vegetables to give the salsa a smoky flavor.

Just as I finish, Chef Javier announces that this morning's salad will be a cactus salad. Since I am the sous-chef, my job will be to slice the cacti into thin strips. Javier tells me that he was trained as an architect and has been making Mexican dishes that he learned from his family to share with the cooking school. His passion comes from his strong interest in Indigenous foodways, Mexican history, and building rural communities.

Javier tells me that Kahlo loved Mexican food: tequila with salt and lime, sangrita, tacos, black mole, chile peppers, and black beans. Good cooking would be an important part of her life; however, while she oversaw the cooking in the house, she generally left the actual preparation of such dishes to her cook, Eulalia. Instead, Kahlo devoted herself to the organization of the family mealtimes, menu planning, ordering the food, and table decoration.

Kahlo would have special Mexican delicacies sent to Rivera's art mural sites for lunch and for dinner, sometimes delivering them herself. She would bring a blue pewter dinner pail divided into compartments, each holding a different dish and topped with warm tortillas and bread, complete with cut fruit and flowers artistically arranged. She knew that the way to keep Diego happy was through his stomach. He eventually grew to over three hundred pounds.

Over the next three hours, Tim, Javier, and I chop and slice. The two of them talk nonstop about their views on Frida, Diego, Mexican art, architecture, Mexican festivals, ingredients, peppers. The air is filled with the aroma of peppers roasting and onions sizzling; all the while the room hums with Mexican vocal and guitar music. I feel like I'm at a Mexican fiesta.

I tell my chefs that I appreciate the way they have set the table in a Frida-inspired style with bowls of fruit, vases of freshly picked flowers, bunches of herbs, assorted Mexican ceramics, and a carved stone egg holder in the shape of a bird.

"For Kahlo, setting the table was an art project," says Chef Tim.

It served as a way for Kahlo to experiment with color and form. Lavish flower arrangements, often with blooms freshly picked from the garden, color-coordinated crockery, and compositions with fruits and vegetables all combined with a lace tablecloth, simple plates, handblown blue glasses, and heirloom cutlery. In 1937, Frida celebrated Leon Trotsky's arrival in Mexico with a fiesta, decorating the dining room table in the Casa Azul with flowers spelling out "Viva Trotsky."

The kitchen is now in high gear. Tim directs me to use a mortar and pestle to grind the roasted tomatillos, onions, jalapeños, garlic, sea salt, cilantro, and Mexican oregano for the salsa verde. Javier slices corn off the cob. Later we roast the corn, add cream to the bowl, and top the salsa off with cheeses. This will be delicious.

A pot on the stove boils away to soften the peppers that will then be fried as the main course. Tim beats egg whites that will become the light batter for the fried peppers. I chop sections of plantain on an elevated wooden butcher block.

While we are all busy prepping Frida Kahlo recipes, we gush over the artist's kitchen.

It is no surprise that two people who run a Kahlo-inspired cooking class are intimately familiar with the Casa Azul. Like her dining room, Kahlo's kitchen featured bold blues and a sunny yellow across its tiled walls, painted floors, and spacious central table, with rustic touches like wooden spoons hung on the walls and traditional pottery on the counters. Frida and her cook spent much of their time at the kitchen table, where there were several vegetable-shaped clay tureens and painted terra cotta plates and pots. Everything was handmade and embellished with images of animals or traditional Mexican designs.

"My favorite feature in the kitchen is the white ceramic tile backsplash with the blue and yellow tiles embedded in the counter," says Tim. "It is such a bright and happy space."

Javier is excited about the wood stove. "Even though gas ovens were already well established by that time, Frida preferred using a wood fire to make simple Mexican dishes using traditional earthenware pots and copper vats."

But we all agree that the biggest statement in this kitchen is love and passion, shown through tiny ceramic pots. Kahlo attached these colored pots to the walls to form words and images: One wall spells out "Frida + Diego," another depicts two doves tying a lovers' knot.

"Often we see the kitchen as a utilitarian space," I say. "But Frida made it a room that bursts with romance and love."

As we wind down our Kahlo kitchen talk, Javier steps up to the stove to stir a large round ceramic pot. He is the mole chef, and the time has come to pay special attention to his dish. Mole is used as a sauce for many dishes, including pulled pork, chicken, to top enchiladas, or as we'll be enjoying today, with roasted plantains.

Javier tells me that mole is complex in taste, that it gets its distinctive earthy flavor from combining Mexican dried chiles, seeds, nuts, dried fruit, onion, garlic, spices, and dark Mexican chocolate. In the minds of many, chocolate is the ingredient that has come to define mole, but there isn't just one kind of mole—the word derives from the Aztec *molli*, which just means "sauce," and so there are hundreds of different kinds, with some leaning sweet, salty, spicy, hot, or cold—and the chocolate should never dominate, even if it tends to get the main billing over the fruit and various spices that also go into the sauce.

Tim chimes in that mole can take hours and even days to prepare (Javier started his mole before I arrived), with as many as thirty different ingredients added in different ways. The exact concoction depends on the cook: chiles, tomatoes, dried fruits, sugar, spices, bread, nuts, or seeds might be in the mix. The ingredients are ground together into a powder or a paste that creates a layering of flavors. Once the paste is formed, it's mixed with water or broth, and then simmered until thick. When it's complete, the mole should be a balance of flavors. Nothing should stick out.

I go over to the stove to investigate; the mole has been simmering for hours in a large clay pot. The thick brown sauce is gently warming as Javier stirs it with one of his handmade wooden spoons. I mention that the clay pot is a thing of beauty. Javier agrees and tells me that it has other attributes besides being good-looking. Food almost never burns in the thick walls of the pot, the handles on the rim make it easy to move around, and its low price makes it accessible to all Mexicans.

Javier's mole today is made with cocoa beans from the state of Tobasco in Mexico. He invites me to taste one, and as I do, I detect a rich, thick, slightly bittersweet chocolate flavor with the texture of a roasted almond.

"Each family has their own recipes for mole that are handed down through the generations," says Javier. "And each region of Mexico has their own versions of mole. Mexicans are very social people, and food is at the center of their lives. Each region is very proud of their mole, and during town festivals, the people get excited about sharing their mole with others."

After a morning of chopping, slicing, stirring, and boiling, I'm ready to eat. And finally, our dinner is ready.

Beautiful blue plates are waiting on the big wooden table. I take my place with great anticipation.

First in my mouth is the *sopa de frijol negro*, a velvety black bean soup with garlic and herbs, topped with panela cheese, dried oregano, and crispy tortillas. The soup is thick and has a full flavor, the black beans made complex with a paste of cumin, onion, epazote, tomato, garlic, and Mexican oregano. I tell Tim and Javier that this is a great way to start the meal.

We move on to the *ensalada de nopal*, a grilled cactus salad with diced tomatoes, green onions, cilantro, sliced radishes,

Mexican oregano, crumbled añejo cheese, and a vinaigrette. The cactus has a slight crunch on the outside and, as I bite into it, a soft inner flesh. The vinaigrette adds a touch of acidity that is offset by a lovely pink radish marinated in honey.

The main course is *chiles rellenos*, lightly battered pasilla peppers stuffed with Oaxacan and Manchego cheese and fresh herbs. Tim removes a corn tortilla from his lava rock tortilla warmer and lays the pepper on it, along with leafy greens and fresh crema. I wrap the pepper in the tortilla and take a big bite. The stuffed pepper is divine, with a light tempura-type crispy batter on the outside. The inside has a perfect chew of the roasted pepper, and then the creaminess of the mild cheese oozing from the center finishes off the bite.

Accompanying the chiles rellenos is an enticing side dish of *esquites*, fire-roasted corn kernels sautéed in butter with onions, chile pequín, and epazote, served with *queso rayado*, crema, and chile dust. A touch of juice from a lime section brightens the charred corn.

But the dessert is the finale: *plátanos en mole negro Oaxaqueño*, a classic mole with twenty-eight ingredients served with slices of roasted plantain. It's a wonderful blend of chocolate and spices, sweet and bitter; nothing stands out. The mole is a perfectly balanced accompaniment to the charred plantain slices.

Black Bean Soup

Nopal Cacti Salad

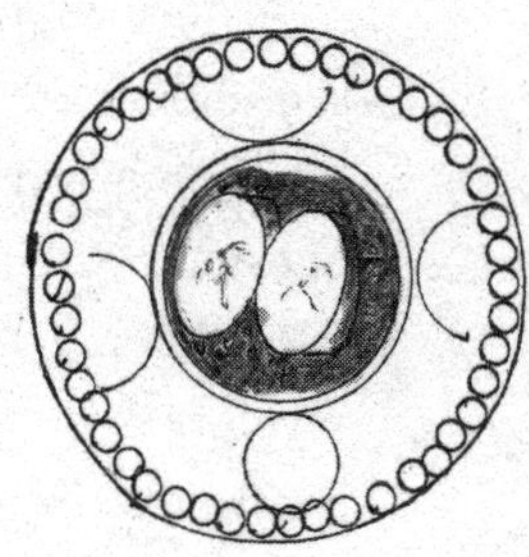

Plantains & Mole

During the meal, there is much oohing and aahing as I taste each new delicacy. I try to picture Frida and Diego sitting around the table, enjoying the Mexican repast with us, a mariachi band serenading us in the background.

The Frida Kahlo–inspired dinner is amazing. And then I realize it is also entirely meat-free. The tastes are so sensational and complex, I did not miss the meat at all.

As I spoon the last traces of mole from my dish, I ask Javier what Kahlo means to him. A smile comes to his face.

"She was one of the most important women in Mexico," he says. "There are so many things to admire about Frida Kahlo. She was a great artist, she was a fashion icon, her affairs outside of her marriage; she was bisexual at a time when it was not acceptable, which was super controversial. But the thing I admire most about Frida was that she was building a new Mexican culture. It was based on historical traditions combined with contemporary culture. And then she introduced it to the world. Frida developed a new way to understand Mexico."

Javier goes on to say that one of the ways that she did this was to hold magnificent dinner parties in her home.

"She invited people from around the world to her dining room, where they could eat, drink, and fall in love with Mexico. She showed them the best of Mexico so that they could take it back to their own countries. Look at what we are eating today on our table."

As Javier speaks, I look across the table at the variety of sensational Mexican dishes that we are indulging in. I can see that it's a combination of historical food traditions and contemporary ingredients. This meal is traditional, but modern.

"Frida Kahlo and Diego Rivera led a Mexican cultural revolution—not with guns, but with Mexican moles, mariachi bands, tequila, color, furnishings, and discussion—all in her sunny yellow and blue dining room," says Javier. "Everybody wanted to have dinner with Frida. Her house was the Studio 54 of Mexico—world leaders, artists, movie stars all wanted to party, drink, eat, and be seen with her and Diego. She used food to make people love her country."

Before I came to Casa Azul, I thought Frida lived a sad and painful life. So much is made of the dramatic parts of her life—the macabre art, the debilitating injury from the bus accident, the turbulent marriage, the sensational love affairs, and the heavy drinking and drug use.

But what I found was much more. As Kahlo's work became more popular, Mexicans developed a new, deeply rooted sense of what it meant to be Mexican. The food, music, bright colors, and traditional customs became a nationalist renaissance, the emergence of a once-forgotten cultural identity.

To me, the ambience of all dining rooms is created with the food, art, furniture, plates, and glasses that reflect the host's interests, passions, and beliefs. The room tells guests who they are.

In this dining room, there is no question who she is. Frida Kahlo is Mexico.

Museo Frida Kahlo

Londres 247, Del Carmen, Coyoacán, Mexico City, Mexico

museofridakahlo.org.mx/?lang=en

Dear Franny,

To visit Frida Kahlo's dining room and to then cook some of her favorite dishes was an exhilarating and moving experience. Here are some thoughts that could be incorporated into your birthday dinner.

Kahlo's dining room walls are a lively collection of ceramic animals, piggy banks, religious objects, papier-mâché people, paper hangings, and banners. We don't have to only hang paintings—we could display artifacts, pottery, and souvenirs from past travels. Frida's influence is that we can break with convention.

The big statement is color. I asked Estefania why Kahlo chose bright yellow for her dining room floors; she said, "It made her happy." That reminds me of Claude Monet's ebullient yellow dining room and the gold wallpaper walls at Highclere Castle. We have to think hard about incorporating yellow in our remodeled dining room.

Kahlo's food was authentic to her values and her culture. She did not care about the latest food fads. She wanted to communicate who she was through her dinners—through the food, music, clothing, and surroundings. She wanted everyone to love Mexico.

The lesson that I learned from Frida Kahlo's dining room is the importance of loving without inhibition, for everyone to see. More and more, I realize we're not here forever. And when I look around, I find that good times can be fleeting. In the past, there have been times when I have been guilty of hesitating, playing it safe. With her failing health and pain, Kahlo seemed to understand her mortality—she passed at forty-seven years old. She savored every bite, every painting, every second of singing with the mariachi band.

And don't we all wish we could live like Kahlo? A life of passionate love, being in the moment, expressing our delights and pains without inhibition—living every second to the fullest?

Standing in the splendor of her yellow, white, and blue dining room, I could hear Frida asking me, "Why not, John?"

Why not?

XOXO

J.

P.S. I hope you like mariachi. I'm thinking of having a band at your birthday dinner.

9

FRANK SINATRA'S TWIN PALMS PATIO, 1950

Palm Springs, California

BEFORE THERE WAS MADONNA, before there were the Beatles, even before there was Elvis . . .

There was Frank Sinatra. Sinatra was the first musical teenage heartthrob in the 1940s, before there was even such a thing.

Charismatic, melodious, inspirational, the American singer was one of the most popular and influential musical artists of the twentieth century. He is one of the best-selling music artists of all time, having sold more than 150 million records worldwide. He was awarded eleven Grammy Awards. Even after he was past his prime, he attracted large audiences. My parents went to see Sinatra at the Canadian National Exhibition in Toronto in 1972. While his best singing years had passed, my parents were still entranced. "It was his presence," my mom enthused. "He still had it."

Not only could he sing, but Sinatra also forged a highly successful career as a film actor. After winning an Academy Award for *From Here to Eternity*, he starred in *The Man with the Golden Arm* and *The Manchurian Candidate*. He appeared in musicals such as *On the Town*, *Guys and Dolls*, and *High Society*, and he won a Golden Globe for *Pal Joey*.

But Sinatra might be best known as the leader of the Rat Pack: a hard-drinking, fun-loving, all-night-carousing group of entertainers who made films and hung out together in Las Vegas casinos and included Dean Martin, Sammy Davis Jr., Joey Bishop, and Peter Lawford.

With his wildly successful singing and acting talents that audiences could enjoy on stage, television, radio, and film, combined with his own personal charisma, Frank Sinatra was a blockbuster American entertainment package. He is a legend.

But as a fan of historical architecture and eating, I admire Sinatra most for building his modernist house at a time when most stars still wanted classical Renaissance. He could have played it safe and gone with convention, but of course, he did it his way. Sinatra's house in Palm Springs defines the most significant style of all the mid-century modern houses, a style called Desert Modernism.

In my opinion, his glamour and presence stoked a revolutionary change in entertaining—the backyard barbecue. Millions of North Americans moved the dining room from inside the house out to the patio and the pool. His profile and aura led to the institution of the pool party, a completely different approach to dinner, food, and drink that changed lifestyles across North America.

By the 1960s, it even reached the modest little Ota House in Toronto. We were barbecuing in our backyard, and my parents were serving whiskey sours as their guests dipped Polynesian bo bo balls in sweet-and-sour sauce and popped them into their mouths.

To truly understand the mid-century modern dining phenomenon—not to mention Sinatra—I decide I have to visit Palm Springs. I would love to imbue some of the informal glamour of Sinatra's patio dining into Franny's birthday dinner.

I always think you really get to know somebody when you visit them at their house. So I am off to the California desert to find out more about the famous house and the man many consider to be one of the greatest singers of the twentieth century.

As I drive the main street of Palm Springs, Frank Sinatra romantically croons "The Way You Look Tonight" on the car stereo. With the bright sunlight, the desert backdrop of palm trees, and most of all, the swoopy, modern architecture around me, I am falling in love with the town.

It is February and I have arrived in time to participate in the city's modernism week, a festival of tours, seminars, and parties that attracts admirers of architecture from around the world. Palm Springs is recognized as the world capital of mid-century modern houses. In reaction to the overdecoration of mid-nineteenth-century buildings, modernism—a style that was developed in a number of countries after World War I—is based on simple design with clean lines and minimal ornamentation. The movement led to today's buildings of concrete, steel, and glass that use a modular system of construction. Mid-century modern was a continuation of the modern design movement.

The new architectural form was aerodynamic (inspired by the contemporary obsession with jets, rockets, and outer space), eye-catching, and unconventional. The future was now. Rooflines slanted skyward, walls of glass and indoor/outdoor design emphasized continuity and wide-open space. These space-age homes, built from 1945 to the 1970s, also featured simplicity and an integration with nature, encouraging residents to explore the world in new ways.

But what differentiated modern houses in Palm Springs from those in the rest of the world was an enormous injection of fun, pleasure, and hedonism. At the end of World War II, Americans began to indulge. After years of rationing and restraint, there was a widespread readiness to celebrate and enjoy the good life.

In the 1950s and 1960s, Hollywood stars built vacation houses in Palm Springs because their studio contracts prohibited them from being more than 120 miles away from Los Angeles. Actors and entertainers such as Dinah Shore, Lucille Ball, Desi Arnaz, Dean Martin, Bob Hope, Bing Crosby, Jack Benny, Liberace, and Zsa Zsa Gabor built spectacular, sprawling homes, but were always on call to the studios and had to report back within two hours for filming if necessary. The result: LA celebrities commissioned sleek modern homes within the two-hour restriction in Palm Springs. The sole purpose of this city was to wallow in pleasure.

One of the first to lead the way was Frank Sinatra. Sinatra and his friends, and their imitators, cultivated a glamorous lifestyle in Palm Springs. One of poolside barbecues, fish fries, brunches, buffets, designer fashion shows, themed Western and luau costume parties, moonlight hayrides, and most important, celebrity entertainers.

To find the Sinatra house, I drive the palm-lined streets past blocks and blocks of 1950s and 1960s houses, replete with angled butterfly roofs, geometric screened walls, and shiny mosaic tiles. I am in the famous Movie Colony neighborhood near downtown. I almost expect to see Frank and the Rat Pack strutting the sidewalk.

I find 1145 East Vía Colusa and pull into its circular driveway. In front of me is a striking geometric silhouette set against the stark beauty of the Palm Springs desertscape. I have made it to the Sinatra house.

I bounce out of the car, taking in the spectacular surrounding landscape. Framed by the shallow foothills of Mount San Jacinto State Park, Sinatra's house became known as Twin Palms, named for the two signature palm trees perched together on the property. Today I am sharing the house with dozens of other Sinatra fans who have come to Palm Springs for modernism week. There is a joyful atmosphere; we all are agog at being at a house that defines the mid-century modern period.

I approach the house. Twin Palms is a single story, with two wings on each side of a central entranceway. But that is where its conventional house design ends. My modernism week guidebook reads: "Built in 1947 and designed by architect E. Stewart Williams, the Twin Palms residence is one of the finest examples of modernist architecture in Palm Springs . . . The Sinatra residence remains remarkably intact and has been only slightly modified over the years."

To me, the house is an elegant gem in the desert. Standing in front of the building, I admire the minimalist composition. Horizontal lines from its deep overhangs, thin steel columns, and clerestory windows (windows positioned high on a wall to allow light into a space while maintaining privacy) give it a light, airy appearance.

Below the sleek, angled roof are broad windows and clean lines of natural stone and wood accents. A sculptural chimney of Arizona flagstone pairs perfectly with the angular steel construction.

I love how the natural materials and low profile help to nestle it into the surrounding desert, enhancing the views around it. A more solid, traditional house of classical columns would draw focus solely to itself and detract from the setting of desert hills, palm trees, and azure skies.

With all of its contemporary aura of celebrating a positive and energized postwar future, Twin Palms was a symbol of Sinatra's enormous success—especially for a man from Hoboken, New Jersey.

Francis Albert Sinatra was born on December 12, 1915, in an upstairs tenement, the only child of Italian immigrant parents. It was a modest background: His parents ran a bar, and young Frank would earn pocket money by singing on top of the player piano and on street corners.

Sinatra developed an interest in music from a young age; he was greatly influenced by the intimate, easy-listening vocal style of Bing Crosby. He began his musical career in the mid-1930s swing era with bandleaders Harry James and Tommy Dorsey.

By May 1941, Sinatra's career was blossoming, and he polled as the top male singer in *Billboard* and *DownBeat* magazines. He was known as a crooner, meaning a male singer who performed in a smooth style and emphasized romantic lyrics. Crooning, with its suggestion of intimacy, was thought to be wildly attractive to women, especially to enthusiastic teenage girls known as bobby-soxers (the term came from the popular frilly ankle-length socks that they wore, called bobby socks). One step further: Fans who fainted away at the sound or sight of Sinatra were called swooners.

His appeal to teenage girls revealed a whole new audience for popular music, which had been recorded mainly for adults up to that time. Fans mobbed him wherever he went, sometimes leading to open riots. They would wait outside the theaters for a peek of him, and chant "Frankie! Frankie!" inside the auditorium while he was singing.

As the winner of a radio station's 1946 "Why I Like Frank Sinatra" essay contest explained, "He is one of the greatest things that ever happened to Teen Age America. We were kids that never got much attention, but he made us feel like we were worth something."

With all these women chasing after him, it might be a challenge to be the wife of Frank Sinatra. That honor fell to Nancy Barbato, whom he met in Long Branch, New Jersey. They married in 1939 and she became the mother of his three children (Nancy, Frank Jr., and Christina). She remained a source of stability and home-cooked meals for Sinatra for decades—even after they divorced.

The year 1947 was a dream for Frank Sinatra: The most popular singer in the world had just had the most prolific recording year in his career, and on top of it all, he'd expanded into acting in movies. It was in that year that he and his family moved from New Jersey to California.

Like many of his contemporaries, Sinatra wanted a vacation home, away from the commotion of Hollywood, not to mention the gossip and cameras. He scouted out Palm Springs to build a getaway home for his family. He became enamored with the dry climate and gorgeous mountain landscape that the city in the desert presented.

In May 1947, Sinatra walked into the Palm Springs office of architect E. Stewart Williams and asked him to build a house by that December, just six months away, so that he could throw a lavish Christmas party. He had recently signed a film contract with Metro-Goldwyn-Mayer, and had made his first million dollars. This house was a way for Sinatra to show off his newly found wealth and prestige.

Originally, the singer wanted a Georgian-style revival mansion perched in the desert—columns, pediment, stone balustrades, the works. But Williams had a different vision. This was his first residential project and he knew this location needed to be used for something special; still, he provided Sinatra with a design for the requested Georgian-style house, as well as a mid-century design that he believed would advance contemporary architecture. To his great relief, Sinatra chose the second design.

Work on the 4,500-square-foot house began immediately, racing against the clock to try to fulfill Sinatra's wishes. While they didn't meet the Christmas party deadline, the Twin Palms estate was ready in time for Sinatra to throw a star-studded New Year's party (more on that later). It quickly became known as a glamorous and cutting-edge home.

As I step through the front doors just off the circular roundabout, I know immediately that I am in the house of a movie star. The abundant sunlight and elegant use of wood, stone, and glass create an atmosphere of luxury and vitality suitable to a rising singing star.

I walk through the light-filled front vestibule and enter an open-concept space designed with sculptural, streamlined, continuous lines. Looking around, I find that the tranquil design of the four-bedroom, seven-bathroom interior of Twin Palms has a gently calming effect on me.

The floor plan of the house is designed with a central core—where I am standing—of the dining area, kitchen, primary bedroom, and living area. To my left, beyond the publicly accessible spaces, is a corridor that leads to the children's bedroom wing. In front of me, through glass doors, I glimpse the patio and pool.

I enjoy how the space is open and airy throughout. The long, angled clerestory windows perched high on the walls allow sunlight to enter the house from multiple directions, making the rooms feel larger.

As I move into the open-concept living area, I am immediately cocooned in comfort and warmth. The living room ceiling was built stretching upward to allow Sinatra a spectacular view of the mountains and the sky. Sinatra could revel in the peace and quiet of his desert bungalow while he lounged on his wraparound sofa.

Music was Sinatra's life, so built-in cabinets in the living room had a state-of-the-art music system for Sinatra to listen to and record in when the mood struck him. He could make a recording himself, inscribing it onto vinyl to produce an actual record right then and there.

I enjoy the memorabilia and personal photos, highlighting Sinatra's career, that appear on the living room walls. Spread throughout the estate are colorful paintings, pottery, and textiles, reflecting his love of art. Sinatra was also a passionate collector, owning works by Pablo Picasso and Joan Miró. He even painted some works himself.

The house was completely air-conditioned, something almost unheard of in the 1940s. The impressive structure cost $150,000 to build at the time, the equivalent of about $1.7 million today.

Straightforward, with no unnecessary flourishes, the white kitchen captures the functional aesthetic of the time. A ten-by-twelve-foot carefree space, it boasts a mix of upper and lower cabinets and easily maintained vinyl flooring. The streamlined cooking area gleams with a stainless-steel counter and wall-hung refrigerator. I picture Nancy cooking Frank's favorite dishes, such as spaghetti and meatballs, clam linguini, roasted peppers, scrambled-egg sandwiches, and steak, which he liked pounded flat.

Looking around the kitchen, I know that the dining area, the focus of my visit, is not far away. As I leave the utilitarian cooking space, I look back and observe that the kitchen is separated from the rest of the house by a pass-through counter so that meals could be served directly from the kitchen and carried to the outdoors.

Floating through the house's open spaces, I enter the dining area. It is immediately evident to me that the airy, spacious dining area has the most prominent position in the house. Its central place in the floor plan is a reflection of the importance that Nancy Sr. placed on dinner for her family. Lit by a white over-the-table sunburst chandelier, the minimalist wood dining table seats eight on steel-framed chairs.

An eye-catching feature in the dining area is a sculptural wall of rough-finished stone that mirrors the presence of the distant San Jacinto mountain range. Laid in a horizontal ashlar style, the beige-and-taupe-colored masonry resembles a natural rock outcropping and brings the rugged beauty of the desert into the heart of the house.

I admire how the blurring of boundaries is most evident in the dining area, where the table looks out to the pool and the patio. But it's more than just a means to a pretty view. When you open the sliding glass doors, the interior dining area flows out to the patio and then to the pool, becoming one large space for parties. There is no such thing as inside and outside; it all becomes one. Even the stone floor is built with no threshold, to minimize separation.

The warm weather of Palm Springs allowed outdoor living to become part of the interior of the house. Overlooking the pool, floor-to-ceiling glass windows and doors along the rear wall were used to visually extend the indoor space. I love how the gentle ripples of the swimming pool reflect on the wood plank ceiling surface.

There is no such thing as inside and outside; it all becomes one.

But the big wows in this house are the pool and the patio. Stepping through the glass doors, it is clear that everything is built around the pool. Walking the patio, I can see that the now-famous piano-shaped pool was a result of a design to bring two wings of the home into a cohesive unit. Williams wanted a sinuous curve to play against the building's linearity.

Astonishingly, shadows from the trellis next to the pool form patterns of light and dark that resemble piano keys. Even the shadows have been designed to complement Sinatra's music.

Swimming pools became the trademark of Palm Springs in the postwar period. The combination of fine weather, beautiful people, and great times transformed the resort town from a run-of-the-mill vacation spot to the city with the most swimming pools per capita in the US. Having such a great number of pools remodeled the way Palm Springs projected itself to the outside world. Postcards featured lavishly decorated pool decks, and hotels marketed the quality of their aquatic facilities over the comfort of their rooms. Everything was about the pool.

Even today, Palm Springs is first and foremost a resort town, filled with boutique and chain hotels that still boast some of the finest pools and patios on the West Coast.

At Twin Palms, the expansive patio offers plenty of space for glamorous lounging and outdoor entertainment. Lounge deck chairs line the edge of the pool on the concrete patio floor. A tall hedge and curving shrubs provide a garden backdrop that gave the Sinatra family some privacy.

The turquoise blue of Sinatra's pool beckons me to jump in. But, being on my best behavior, I decline. I don't think Sinatra would approve. He would want me to first change in the pool house at the far end of the patio; it offers additional accommodation and comes equipped with a kitchenette and "his and hers" cabana showers.

During Sinatra's residency at Twin Palms, parties were a priority. Partying and Sinatra were synonymous. And the 1948 New Year's party that opened his new home was a bold statement about his show business success.

Sinatra's star-studded dinner party set the trend for glamour and popularized poolside dining. His Twin Palms did more than blur the lines between inside and outside; its true legacy is that, with its backyard barbecue, it moved the kitchen and dining room to the fresh air during the summer months. Barbecue pool parties changed the way we cook, eat, drink, and entertain outdoors to the present day.

While patio life spread far beyond California, it was all inspired by Palm Springs. The warm weather, glamour, and celebrities set the bar, and Frank Sinatra at Twin Palms was the epicenter. The dress code was casual and there was always partying, dancing, swimming, cocktails, lounging in the sun, movie stars, and long, light-hearted, boozy evenings.

Beautiful women, bathing suits, a buffet of fashionable food, raucous laughter, music, and a bar stocked with plenty of alcohol would be requisites for Sinatra get-togethers. (Later, when Sinatra opened his shows with the Rat Pack in Vegas, he would wheel out a bar cart of booze as he came onstage and start drinking—the audience loved it.)

Famous for his party antics, Sinatra would demonstrate how to tear away a tablecloth without upsetting any of the dishes on top of it, or maybe make a run to a hot dog stand wearing a tuxedo, then come back for a game of darts and a sauna with showgirls in tow. Socializing with Bing Crosby, Jack Benny, Danny Kaye, and Dean Martin, he was always the center of attention. Everyone wanted to please Frank. He would drink and carouse until the

wee hours of the morning, and if anyone went home early, they would earn a dirty look. It is said that Sinatra knew how to throw a party because he *was* the party.

There is no record of the menu for Sinatra's 1948 New Year's patio dinner, but he surely would have wanted to impress the Palm Springs crowd with the latest food fads.

Finger foods and finger sandwiches were a big cocktail party fad in postwar America. Anything that was colorful and cheerful that you could eat with one hand while balancing your cocktail glass in the other was fair game.

So Sinatra's New Year's menu might have included these finger foods—some classics that are still with us, others forgotten in time. Which do you recognize?

Mushrooms stuffed with bacon, cream cheese, Parmesan, and Worcestershire sauce
Meatballs, either Swedish, sweet-and-sour, or porcupine (a Depression-era mix of beef and rice cooked in tomato sauce)
Bacon-wrapped cocktail sausages, shrimp, or scallops skewered with a toothpick
Shrimp, beef, or fruit kabobs
Deviled eggs
French onion dip, alongside chips and pretzels
Peanut butter and pimento cheese–stuffed celery
Savory cream cheese and minced olives with Ritz crackers
Pigs in blankets
Pinwheel roll-up sandwiches made with colored cream cheese and a gherkin pickle center
Ribbon finger sandwiches with layers of deviled ham and egg salad
Polynesian bo bo balls (deep-fried, battered pork balls with sweet-and-sour dipping sauce)

While finger food is perfectly suited for outdoor dining, the real revolution was the ascent of the barbecue. With the rise of the middle class in the twentieth century, the conventional gender roles adopted by North Americans had men toiling at the office or factory during the day while women stayed at home, brought up children, and cooked in the kitchen. Those roles stayed fairly constant right through to the 1970s, when, with the advent of the women's movement, more women entered the workforce. However, an exception to cooking roles occurred after World War II, with the popularity of the barbecue.

In the late 1940s and 1950s, many North Americans celebrated their newfound leisure time and greater prosperity through casual outdoor dinners. After the frugality of wartime living, postwar home cooks invested in grills and other accessories for their suburban backyards. This was especially the rage in California, where outdoor living was a natural complement to the swimming pools, patios, and sunshine. North Americans were looking for a fun, frivolous change from formal indoor dining. Casual in food, cooking, dress, furnishings, and manners, barbecuing was the perfect answer. It also led to many men taking on a new role in the household: Boss of the Barbecue.

Barbecuing equals manliness, and in the mid-century period, manliness counted. So, over a roaring flame—or more realistically, the glow of charcoal—husbands took to their backyards, clad in aprons and mitts, to char hunks of meat while knocking back a bottle of cold beer. Men reveled in cooking for their families or party guests, a role that had previously and unquestionably belonged to women. On any weekend evening or national holiday, the man of the house became the great provider and the center of attention.

Flaming up the barbecue also fit perfectly with the manly image of cowboys eating round the fire during the cattle drive, like in the Western dramas that saturated televisions and movie theaters. Think *Gunsmoke*, *The Rifleman*, and *Have Gun—Will Travel*, in which men were portrayed as tough, strong, silent cowboys and women were stereotypically weak, fragile, and needy.

Certainly, women did the planning, marketing, preparation, and hosting. But the actual barbecuing—that was a man's job. Even today, as conscious as we are of questioning gender roles, I've noticed it is still often men who do the grilling. And as culinary author Sylvia Lovegren says, "If women are smart, they'll keep it that way."

But back to Palm Springs. Whatever the ego-boosted man thought, it was the meat that was the real star of the barbecue. It was another example of the greater prosperity many families enjoyed after World War II. Plentiful jobs, a burgeoning economy, and a spirit of optimism fueled an obsession with barbecuing and drove North Americans to buy massive amounts of meat—the most expensive meat of the time being sirloin steak. Like serving turtle soup in the Gilded Age, it was a form of boasting to friends about your wealth and achievements when you could afford to serve sirloin steak to everyone at the barbecue.

I think that if Sinatra truly wanted to impress his friends with his first million dollars earned, he would have served them steak from the poolside barbecue. Steak was manly, and in 1948, Sinatra was the epitome of manliness (at least the mid-century definition of manliness). He was rich, he smoked, he gambled, he had close connections with organized crime—and women loved him. He had relationships with the most beautiful stars in Hollywood, including Ava Gardner, Lauren Bacall, Juliet Prowse, and Angie Dickinson. Written accounts of Sinatra portray him as a complicated man. He was moody, temperamental, tempestuous, a perfectionist, but he also had a soft side to him and could be generous to friends. When his friend Sammy Davis Jr. suffered the loss of his left eye in a car accident, Sinatra came through with both financial and emotional support.

Also, Sinatra liked to drink—did I mention that?

Sinatra, a Jack Daniel's devotee (legend has it that he was even buried with a bottle of Jack Daniel's by his side), would hoist a flag with the whiskey company's name at Twin Palms as a signal to his neighbors and nearby friends: It was party time at Frank's house.

Popular mixed drinks of the time included champagne cocktails, Manhattans, old-fashioneds, highballs, gin punches, and of course, martinis. But Sinatra had his own drink that would have been the headliner for his New Year's house celebration, called the Sinatra 3-2-1. He kept it simple:

3 ice cubes in a rocks glass
2 "fingers" of Jack
1 "finger" of water

A "finger" of whiskey or water is a bartending term that's fallen out of use, referring to holding a finger horizontally around the bottom of the glass and pouring to the top of your finger. To be more precise, one finger is approximately three-quarters of an inch of the liquid in a standard old-fashioned glass, or about one ounce, thus making Frank's "two-finger" serving of whiskey roughly two ounces.

"That's the nectar of the gods, baby," he once said.

Being by Sinatra's pool and thinking about his alcohol-filled, star-studded New Year's party makes me feel a little envious that I missed it. I love a good party.

As I step down the walkway on my way out of Twin Palms, I look up and try to imagine the iconic black Jack Daniel's flag snapping in the wind above the trees.

For some reason, my throat is dry.

I'm feeling unusually thirsty. And I would love a barbecued steak.

A few weeks later, back in Toronto, I find myself really missing the Sinatra vibe of Twin Palms and the glamorous outdoor magic of Palm Springs. I regret that, since it is a pristine museum piece, I was not allowed to cook on the patio of Frank Sinatra's house. I still have barbecued sirloin steak on my mind.

To address my emptiness, I invite myself to the home of Carol Moore-Ede and Jim Keffer, to grill them a sirloin steak dinner along with some mid-century modern finger foods that I have been experimenting with. I have been to their gorgeous house in the Cabbagetown neighborhood of Toronto; it has a magnificent curvy aquamarine swimming pool reminiscent of the Sinatra pool, an expansive patio, and a well-used barbecue.

Carol is a friend and a renowned architectural historian who has written widely on modern architecture. I am sure she will sympathize with my feelings of mid-century modern deprivation.

Her husband, Jim, is a professor emeritus at the University of Toronto and, as I am about to find out, a big fan of Sinatra and the resident master barbecue expert. He is perfectly suited to this Sinatra barbecue endeavor of mine.

When I arrive at their spacious backyard, the pool water is shimmering and the patio stones are gleaming in the sun. A rugged wooden table serves as the bar, surrounded by matching wooden lounge chairs that overlook the pool. Around the perimeter of the patio is a mixture of flowering lilies, shrubs, and summer cone flowers that add color and vibrancy to the landscape. I take note of a monster-sized barbecue that will provide the cooking heat for our steaks.

To set the atmosphere, I wear my loud red-and-yellow swim trunks, sunglasses, and a short-brimmed straw hat similar to one I had seen Sinatra wear in a photo and I turn on Sinatra tunes.

Bustling around my temporary kitchen on the patio, I tell Jim about my research on Sinatra and his house in Palm Springs.

"He had a great voice," says Jim, without hesitation. I smile. Whenever I bring up Sinatra with people of a certain vintage,

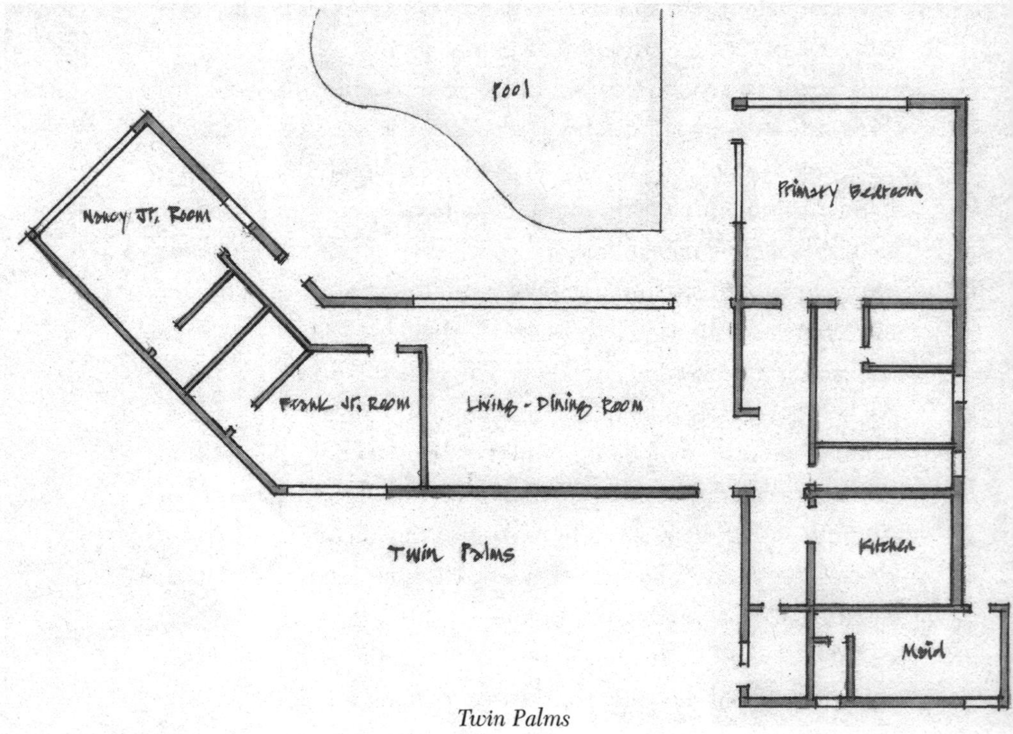

Twin Palms

without exception, this is their first comment. Then come smiles and countless stories and superlatives about his artistry, talent, and power of connection.

"He left Bing Crosby in his dust," Jim says. "He could do this thing called a tremolo—he could quiver his voice. That made the young women crazy in love with him. And of course, he had those blue eyes."

With such positive vibes coming from my hosts, I enthusiastically get going on my Sinatra New Year's–inspired menu, which is as follows:

Stuffed mushrooms
Bo bo balls
Gazpacho
Potato salad
Coleslaw
Garlic bread
And, of course, a thick, marbled sirloin steak

As we sit by the pool in the sun, Carol, forever the architectural historian, reflects on the new industrial ideas that came from the postwar period.

"The birth of mid-century modern was after the war, and new materials such as steel and plywood set a new style," says Carol. "With the new technology developed for the war, manufacturers developed products for a civilian future. Aluminum pipe and plastic webbing were used to make folding chairs, sheet aluminum covered the sides of swimming pools, and wrought iron was molded into patio furniture. Aluminum frames were used for a new idea: giant sliding glass doors, which encouraged people to go outside and be healthy."

Carol also tells me about the discovery and production of the charcoal briquettes that are used for barbecues. A man named

Edward G. Kingsford, who was Henry Ford's brother-in-law, was disturbed by the wastage of wood that Ford created during the car-making process. Kingsford suggested that they build a factory that would compress the wasted wood into charcoal briquettes. With briquettes offering the advantages of consistent heat and longer burn time than the existing fuel of wood (dried oak, hickory, or maple) or lump charcoal, a new product was added to a barbecuer's cooking methods.

During our spirited discussion, I lay out all the condiments and salads on the patio dining table, and spread briquettes in the barbecue to put Kingsford's genius to good use. Jim is in charge of the barbecuing, since he is more familiar with his own grill. I am his assistant (and Carol admits she doesn't know how to use the barbecue).

After the steak has been grilling on the red-hot briquettes for about ten minutes, the aroma of fat, smoke, and meat cooking makes us delirious with anticipation. I pierce forkfuls of steak and sit them on our plates.

Finally, after all these weeks, I bite into a perfect medium-rare morsel of sirloin. As my teeth come down on a lovely caramelized crust that gives a faint crunch, juices ooze from the sides. I can taste the perfect char. My teeth continue to bite through the tender flesh, which releases more juices and a sensational beefy flavor. The texture is like velvet in my mouth. Inside, the medium-rare steak is an effortless chew. In fact, I don't even think about the chew—it is all about the intense beefy flavor and juices.

We all groan in pleasure. We eat with our hands, popping each thick slice of steak into our mouths like candy. It is too much trouble and a waste of time to use knives and forks.

I only wish Sinatra were here to share the steak goodness with us. We're doing a splendid job of paying homage to his beloved Twin Palms, I think. Although he maintained residences in Los

Angeles and New York, they were temporary stations. Palm Springs was his haven, his home. A place where he could get away from it all. And with Carol and Jim's splendid pool and patio along with Jim's and my—if I may say so—superb grilling, we're certainly leaning in to the essence of abundance that would have animated his postwar-era parties. It was a time to take chances and indulge, two of Sinatra's Palm Springs pursuits thanks to E. Stewart Williams's architectural push and Sinatra's patio—especially with everything I imagine that they entailed: barbecuing as a display of leisure, a steak-centered menu, and flowing cocktails.

People used to have more fun in those days, I muse. They let loose. They drank more. They ate more. They partied harder.

Carol laughs and tells me, "Everyone used to get into the pool. If you didn't, they'd throw you in—that's what they did!"

She stares at me—like a dare.

With that, I spontaneously whip off my shirt, sunglasses, and hat and do an exuberant running belly flop into the pool. There is an enormous splash. Water spills onto the deck chairs, towels, and my hosts. The turquoise water is exhilarating, refreshing. Suddenly, I feel like I'm in Palm Springs all over again!

Can somebody please pass me a bo bo ball?

Twin Palms Frank Sinatra Estate

1145 East Vía Colusa, Palm Springs, California, United States

sinatrahouse.com

Dear Franny,

As a person who enjoys modern architecture, I loved Frank Sinatra's pool, patio, and dream house in Palm Springs. If we lived in it, I would feel compelled to maintain Sinatra's reputation for sensational pool parties. It might be fun to try! But it might also be hard on my liver. Here is some inspiration that I picked up at Twin Palms for your birthday dinner.

Food, drinks, music—Sinatra set the bar as an unparalleled host.

The Palm Springs pool party crowd had it right—barbecued skewers, crudités, and finger food for informal dinners by the pool. Charred steak is superb, and we can grill up veg-friendly goods as well—the stuffed mushrooms I made for Carol and Jim were very tasty.

We can give our patio party a dress code and then decorate for the theme. This was big in mid-century modern land: They threw Hawaiian Night or Roman Toga parties. The past century didn't have the most culturally sensitive takes—we can do better!

Nothing says indulgence like some good potables: fizzes, and nonalcoholic drinks too, since people seem to be drinking less liquor these days. Not everyone is drinking like it's 1947.

Put on some Sinatra music and the next thing you know, we're dancing! We can foxtrot. How romantic, under our string lights and near our inflatable wading pool. Wait . . . I can almost hear Frank and daughter Nancy singing:

And then I go and spoil it all by saying something stupid like, I love you . . .

I love you . . .

I love you . . .

XOXO

J.

10

JACQUELINE KENNEDY'S STATE DINING ROOM AT THE WHITE HOUSE, 1962

Washington, DC

I ADORE A WELL-SET dining room table. Wine and water glasses glistening, dinner plates with gold edging shimmering in the candlelight, silverware set precisely—all of this on an expressive tablecloth that pulls everything together. It doesn't have to be elaborate or expensive-looking. I really like if the setting reflects something unique about the host's personality or history: a mother's silverware that nobody else wanted, a hand-me-down platter, or a set of salt and pepper shakers from a flea market with a funny story to them.

Brainstorming ideas for how I might set the table for Franny's birthday dinner, I remember an impressive display of First Ladies' glassware that I once saw on a tour of the State Dining Room of the White House in Washington, DC. Although the practice has been discontinued, each First Lady was once allowed to commission their own glassware for White House dinners. To me, almost all of the glassware looked similar—traditional, heavy, cut crystal glasses with geometric etching. But one stunning exception to the rule stood out from all the others—elegant, minimal, paper-thin wineglasses, water glasses, and champagne glasses with a complete absence of adornment or etching.

It was the glassware of First Lady Jacqueline Kennedy.

Try to imagine what the other First Ladies might have whispered to each other if they'd seen Mrs. Kennedy's modern wineglasses.

Try to imagine that a young First Lady moved into the White House with a desire to change not only the glassware, but also the design of the dining room, the chef, the food, the seating arrangements, and the entire concept of a state dinner. To the extent that it affected home entertaining across the entire country.

And imagine for a second, if you will, that you have been invited to the most famous White House state dinner of the 1960s.

Just imagine . . .

Some people compare their houses to humans; houses do have histories, experiences, and, some of us believe, souls. They are the places people have so much emotional attachment to, where they can come home and be themselves. Throughout human history, the house has always provided comfort and shelter—from the earliest humans who lived in caves to the president of the United States. It doesn't matter who they are; to sleep, eat, and re-energize, human beings crave the comfort of home.

The White House has held more than three hundred presidential state dinners over the years. Ronald Reagan takes the prize for hosting the most: fifty-nine during his presidency. But one of the most impressive state dinner parties ever seen was the Malraux Dinner, a 1962 event at which President John F. Kennedy and his wife, Jacqueline Kennedy, welcomed France's minister of cultural affairs, André Malraux.

The Kennedys have been compared to King Arthur's famed Round Table in the mythical castle, Camelot, where kings and knights would congregate. Arthur's legendary kingdom was based on courage, romance, loyalty, and lofty principles. It was a place of idyllic happiness.

In the early 1960s, America had its own version of Camelot. A prominent component of this idealistic administration was dining and entertaining that also brought men and women of its time together to experience culture, art, and mutual understanding.

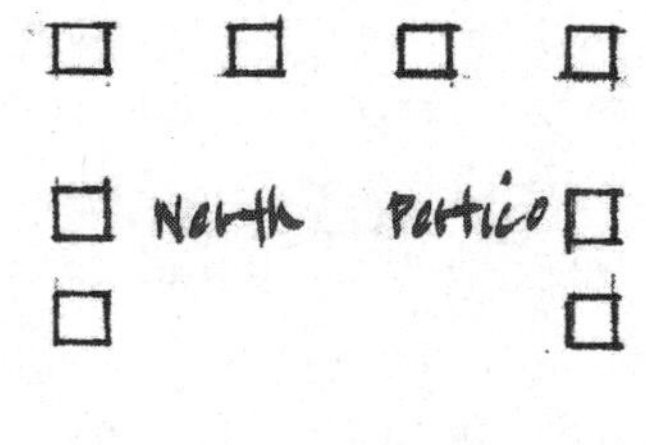

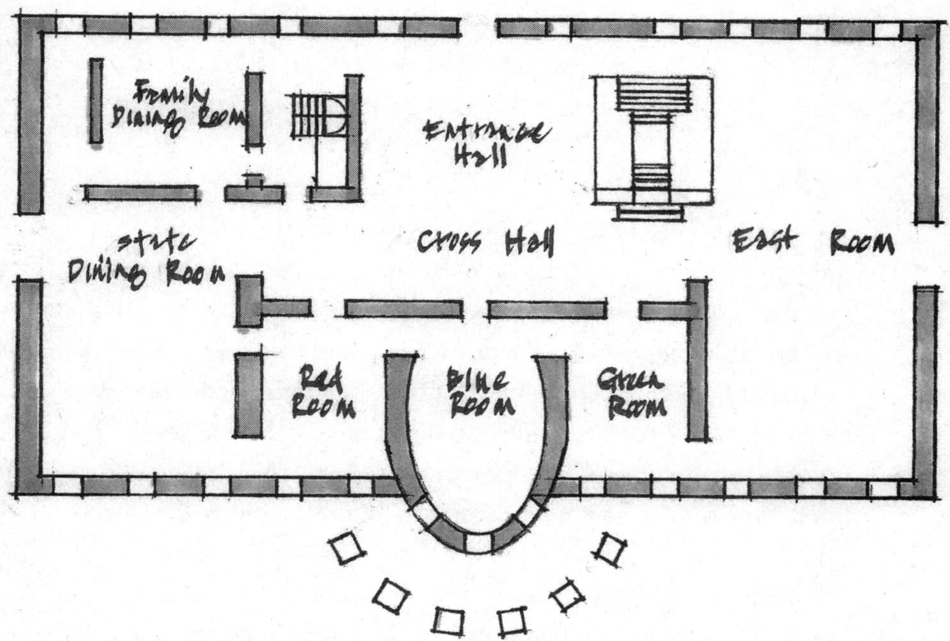

The White House, State floor

Instead of King Arthur, this Round Table was led by a First Lady of the United States, Jacqueline Kennedy.

On January 20, 1961, many people watched nervously as John F. Kennedy, of Massachusetts, was sworn in as the thirty-fifth president of the United States. At first, they were not sure he was up to the job. Most presidents were on the other side of sixty; at forty-three, he was the youngest man ever elected to the position. But he proved them wrong. Progressive, handsome, and princely, President Kennedy was given to heroic words and gestures.

The public also had doubts about Mrs. Kennedy, his artistic wife, who at twelve years younger, was the nation's third-youngest First Lady. In 1961, Mrs. Kennedy would become a style trendsetter (soon enough, women around the world wore the stylish pillbox hat she popularized), but her influence went beyond fashion. She would make meaningful contributions during her husband's presidency.

The 1950s was a decade when people followed strict conventions in home entertaining. The United States stuck close to past traditions.

Suddenly, Mrs. Kennedy burst onto the scene.

Her aim was to make the White House into a stage for promoting American culture, to make it, as she said, "a showcase for great American art and artists." She considered all aspects of culture, including the visual, culinary, and performing arts.

Up until this time, the White House was considered temporary lodging for the president and not thought of as a place to spend funds for an architectural restoration project. But Mrs. Kennedy hired interior designers, fundraised to support the budget, and oversaw the restoration of all of the White House's public rooms. She paid special attention to the State Dining Room, where she repainted the paneling bone white, regilded the chandelier and sconces, and added a new white marble mantel. Mrs. Kennedy also campaigned to bring back furniture that former presidents had taken away from the house.

Once Mrs. Kennedy achieved her vision, she hosted the first-ever televised tour of the White House on a 1962 CBS broadcast seen by 56 million viewers in the United States. Mrs. Kennedy won an Emmy Award for her tour; she was the only First Lady to win an Emmy.

Mrs. Kennedy introduced architecture, food, fashion, art, and culture into American life in a way that has not been matched since. Later on, Mrs. Kennedy made more big changes in the dining room—I'll speak to that soon.

A fashionable State Dining Room was not always a high priority for the First Family. The White House was designed by James Hoban from South Carolina after he won an architectural competition in 1792, and it was built partially by enslaved people and workers. George Washington, who was on the selection panel, liked the image of a handsome, modest Irish country house. It took eight years to finish construction; President John Adams and his wife, Abigail, moved in even before it was finished in 1800. President Washington oversaw the construction, but he left the presidency in 1797.

The mansion was built with a gray sandstone facade, and in 1797 it was painted with a light whitewash to prevent the porous walls from freezing. So it always had a whitish look. The story that the building was later painted white to hide burn marks from the invading British is a myth. The official name for many years was the President's Mansion, but people, including presidents, always referred to it casually as the White House. In 1901, Theodore Roosevelt made it official, naming the building the White House after its nickname.

At first, there was no State Dining Room at all for the president of the United States. The southwest corner that it now occupies was an area of smaller meeting spaces. At the time, there wasn't much use for a large dining room, since there were few events. It was only when America's legendary hostess, First Lady Dolley Madison, came to live in the White House in 1809 that she turned the meeting rooms into the official State Dining Room. Mrs. Madison had a great interest in entertaining guests.

The most significant dining room renovation was undertaken by President Theodore Roosevelt in 1902. Along with changes to other rooms, Roosevelt gave the State Dining Room an Old English baronial appearance, with tapestries on the walls, cooking racks over the fireplace, dark English oak paneling, and oak flooring. A noted animal hunter, President Roosevelt mounted a large moose head above the fireplace and placed other game trophies on the natural oak panels—bison, caribou, Alaskan sheep, and a Kodiak bear.

After Roosevelt left, one of the first things First Lady Ellen Axson Wilson did upon occupying the house in 1913 was to remove the game trophies from the State Dining Room.

When I toured the State Dining Room, I was surprised at the modest size of the space as the entertainment site for the most affluent country in the world. Although President Roosevelt had expanded it in 1902 by relocating a stairway, I found the forty-eight-by-thirty-six-foot room to be small. However, that reflects the political philosophy of Washington, Jefferson, and the other Founding Fathers, who, when it was being constructed in the late eighteenth century, wanted the house to be built for a common man, not a king. Today the room seats 140, and it serves as the center of White House hospitality.

I admired the State Dining Room's aura of extreme elegance. At the center, an elaborate gold chandelier of multiple curving arms hangs over a long wooden table. Atop the table is a monumental centerpiece of gilded bronze and mirrors that was acquired in 1817. The influence of Theodore Roosevelt's imposing personality endures in the surrounding walls, built with wood paneling and pilasters in the classical Georgian style, painted bone white. The room is accented by gold drapes around tall windows and lit by gold sconces, another Roosevelt addition.

A striking feature is the image of a contemplative Abraham Lincoln that hangs over the fireplace. It is the only painting in the State Dining Room.

But to me, the most significant feature of the dining room is the inscription on the mantel, from a letter that President Adams wrote to his wife, Abigail, in 1800: "I pray Heaven to bestow the best of Blessings on this House and all that shall hereafter inhabit it. May none but honest and wise Men ever rule under this roof."

A state dinner honoring a visiting head of government is one of the grandest and most glamorous of White House affairs. Of course, it is also a chance to put the dining room on display.

The first official state dinner was hosted by Ulysses S. Grant on December 22, 1874, for David Kalākaua, the last king of Hawaii. Grant's dinner was a multicourse meal that began with fruits, flowers, sweetmeats, bread, and soup for the first course. This was followed by a croquette of meat and then a third course of meat and potatoes. Additional dishes included partridge legs, as well as a rice pudding dessert. Wine was abundant. During the dinner, the king had Hawaiian food testers who stood behind him and sampled the more than twenty dishes before he ate them. Indigestion probably wasn't the main threat on his mind.

Another impressive state dinner was given by President Theodore Roosevelt for the powerful prince of Prussia. The men-only dinner was held at one sprawling U-shaped table overflowing with flowers, fine china, and crystal. The impressive culinary display offered a gourmet presentation of ten courses that included oysters on the half shell, consommé, roast duck, beef fillet, capon, asparagus with sauce mousseline, champagne, and ice cream with melted cherries.

President Dwight D. Eisenhower was an accomplished cook in his own right; his recipe for green turtle soup was served to the prime minister of Canada and the president of Mexico in 1955. (I wonder if President Eisenhower was using a recipe from *The White House Cook Book* that I saw in Edith Wharton's kitchen.) But overall, he preferred simple food. His basic state dinner menus had more to do with the customs and food preferences of the 1950s.

When the president, with First Lady Mamie Eisenhower, hosted King Paul and Queen Frederika of Greece in 1955, the menu displayed mid-century sophistication and the Eisenhowers' personal charm. Among some of the many dishes served were shrimp cocktail, saltine crackers, white fish in cheese sauce, Boston brown bread sandwiches, crown roast of lamb stuffed with Spanish rice, toasted Triscuits, and caramel cream mold.

And then along came Mrs. Kennedy.

She wanted to transform state dinners, making them less reserved and formal. While Eisenhower's food was conventional, Mrs. Kennedy inaugurated a whole new way of entertaining. Instead of the usual five to six courses of classic American fare for dinner, Mrs. Kennedy streamlined meals down to four courses from a French menu. She wanted to leave enough time for post-dinner entertainment and conversation.

Mrs. Kennedy wanted the state dinners to be high-toned but relaxed, distinguished, and fun. During the Kennedy presidency, she oversaw fifteen state dinners.

No other White House dinner epitomized the entertaining style of Mrs. Kennedy more than one evening honoring French Minister of Culture André Malraux in the State Dining Room on May 11, 1962. As a novelist, art historian, Spanish Civil War fighter pilot, World War II resistance leader, and cultural supporter,

Malraux had garnered enormous admiration from President and Mrs. Kennedy for his diverse talents and accomplishments. They were both greatly attracted to Malraux's commitment to culture, humanity, and social justice.

In addition, Mrs. Kennedy had a special interest in French culture. She had earned a bachelor of arts degree in French literature from George Washington University in 1951, which included studies and French courses in Paris at the University of Grenoble and the Sorbonne.

The origins of this famous dinner began nearly a year before the night at the White House, during the Kennedys' official presidential visit to Paris.

Tragically, days before the Kennedy visit, Malraux had lost his two sons in a car accident. However, Malraux continued to escort Mrs. Kennedy to Paris museums while President Kennedy was working. Deeply moved by this act of friendship, the Kennedys decided to host the state dinner for Malraux as way of expressing their thanks.

During their tours of art museums, Mrs. Kennedy and Malraux developed a personal bond. And according to a *Vanity Fair* article by Margaret Leslie Davis, there were also some light-hearted moments.

Malraux inquired, "What did you do before you married Jack Kennedy?"

Mrs. Kennedy replied, "*J'étais pucelle.*" (I was a little virgin).

And during the visit, France fell in love with her. Mrs. Kennedy's language skills, extensive knowledge of culture and history, and fine sense of fashion were highly respected by the French people.

The Paris trip was a success for Mrs. Kennedy; the center of attention shifted from President Kennedy to her. The French media frequently published photographs of Jacqueline Kennedy in the foreground, walking ahead of the president in her pillbox hat and fashionable wardrobe. While his meetings with the French government were not entirely productive, Mrs. Kennedy, fluent in French and social charms, so captivated the country that at the conclusion of the visit, *Time* magazine noted, "There was also that fellow who came with her."

At their final dinner in Paris, Mrs. Kennedy told Malraux about her dream of bringing Leonardo da Vinci's *Mona Lisa* to the United States.

I can only guess that Malraux did a double-take when she asked for the *Mona Lisa*. This was a big request. But with her own brand of dinner table diplomacy, Mrs. Kennedy made her pitch to bring one of art history's greatest masterpieces and the most famous painting in the Louvre to America.

Upon the Kennedys' return to the US, official invitations were extended for Malraux to visit Washington; after several refusals, he agreed to meet the president and First Lady in May 1962.

Once the dates for the visit had been formalized, Mrs. Kennedy jumped into action. The First Lady spent five weeks meticulously preparing for the minister's arrival. Observers were amazed at the energy and high level of detail she put into this event.

Mrs. Kennedy's handwritten notes for the dinner have been preserved and are occasionally exhibited at the Kennedy Library and Museum in Boston. On yellow legal paper, she scribbled detailed notes regarding entertainment, guest lists, seating plans, menus, table settings, and flower arrangements. You can see the intensity of her thought process through her handwriting, corrections, and revisions. The president also had input into the evening, as evidenced by his handwritten comments on the papers.

The seating charts were penned in calligraphy. Mrs. Kennedy carefully brought together each table grouping to include a variety of people; she wanted to encourage conversation and unique perspectives. Her notes reveal that she even specified the type of candy to be left in the public rooms for guests following dinner.

In addition, Mrs. Kennedy put her interior design skills to work to enhance the atmosphere of the dining room for the Malraux Dinner. She brightened the uninspiring green State Dining Room by repainting it in shades of white: clean, modern, indicative of a new wave of entertaining.

She refined the lighting, replacing the bright light of the chandeliers with bulbs that emitted a mellow glow and candlelight at each dinner table. (Perhaps she knew of Edith Wharton's preference for candlelight from her book *The Decoration of Houses*.) The president and First Lady were to be seated at separate tables, and each of the other tables was hosted by a high-ranking guest.

Mrs. Kennedy replaced the existing old velvet chairs with lighter, gold, bamboo-inspired chairs she had seen in France.

The number one interior design change Mrs. Kennedy made was to remove the cumbersome horseshoe table and replace it with round tables that seated eight or ten people, to encourage conversation between guests.

The guest lists for prestigious White House state dinners were traditionally tailored to military leaders and political figures. To create a more festive atmosphere, Mrs. Kennedy expanded the guest list to include writers, actors, university professors, and cultural personalities. Her goal was to introduce Malraux to the most fascinating people in American society, including significant members of the arts scene.

Mrs. Kennedy's goal was to introduce Malraux to the most fascinating people in American society, including significant members of the arts scene.

The Kennedys invited so many guests that the dinner had to be held in two rooms. Plans were made for President Kennedy to host twelve tables in the State Dining Room while Mrs. Kennedy would host five tables in the smaller Blue Room. Traditionally, husbands and wives sat together at dinner, but Mrs. Kennedy decided that husbands and wives were to be seated at different tables, so that guests were able to meet and converse with a variety of people. She juggled the names at each table in the seating chart to create a mix of personalities.

As the date for Malraux's arrival drew near, Mrs. Kennedy set up a special tour for him of the National Museum of Art in Washington for the morning of Friday, May 11, 1962. Photographs from that day show a smiling Mrs. Kennedy leading Minister Malraux and his wife around the museum.

While they were admiring the artwork, Mrs. Kennedy again mentioned her idea of bringing examples of great French art to the United States.

"You should lend us some of your artworks," she said to him. "I would love to see the *Mona Lisa* again and show her to the Americans."

There is a newspaper photograph of Minister Malraux looking pensive with his hand on his chin as they tour the National Museum. I can only imagine that he is thinking, *Oh no. Mrs. Kennedy has asked for the* Mona Lisa *again. We consider this painting a cultural treasure, and there would be outrage if any harm came to it. What am I supposed to say?*

In the weeks leading up to the dinner, Mrs. Kennedy spent considerable time on selecting her dress. This was not an occasion where she was going to pull an old dress out of her closet. It was apparent that she had her own approach to international diplomacy: She wanted to make this dinner an extra-special occasion for Malraux—right down to her gown.

Imagine you are an up-and-coming visual artist in 1962 and you have heard that your paintings have come to the attention of First Lady Jacqueline Kennedy. One day your doorbell rings, and when you answer, a delivery person hands you a large envelope stamped Special Delivery. It is an official-looking envelope with an image of the White House in the top left corner. When you open the envelope, out slides a beautifully embossed invitation, an RSVP card, and a stamped return envelope. The invitation reads: "The President and Mrs. Kennedy request the pleasure of your company at dinner on May 11, 1962."

You have been invited to the most famous state dinner of the 1960s: the Malraux Dinner.

What will you say? What will you do? At this once-in-a-lifetime event, you will want to remember every detail to share with your friends and family.

It's finally May 11, 1962, and in the early evening, you arrive by private limousine at the North Portico entrance of the White House. Dressed in formal attire, you are escorted to the East Room; a White House aide announces your name as you enter the room.

You might feel nervous—that is natural. The East Room is packed. The atmosphere is electric, with guests chatting and drinking, excited about the upcoming evening. Around you, the fireplaces are lit and there are multiple bouquets of lilies of the valley, baby's breath, red and white tulips, blue irises, daisies, lavender, and lilies. Mrs. Kennedy has given the public rooms the look of a family home. She has also arranged for an open bar; much champagne will be served all evening.

The most astounding aspect of this event is the people in the room. Look around and there are Pulitzer Prize–winning writers Archibald MacLeish and Thornton Wilder and future Nobel Prize winners Saul Bellow and Tennessee Williams. Dramatist Paddy Chayefsky is here, as is filmmaker Elia Kazan, playwright S.N. Behrman, and choreographer George Balanchine. You will recognize Leonard Bernstein, Julie Harris, and Arthur Miller. Artists Mark Rothko and Franz Kline are also in the room. As a visual artist yourself, you're hoping for an introduction.

Suddenly, a hush comes over the crowded room. A White House aide announces, "The President and Mrs. Kennedy."

Trumpets blare. The Marine Corps Band strikes up "Hail to the Chief."

President and Mrs. Kennedy step out, close the door of their second-floor residence, and descend the Grand Staircase.

Like their guests, the Kennedys are dressed in formal attire: he in a finely tailored tuxedo and black tie, with a small pink rose in his left lapel.

But everyone's eyes are on Mrs. Kennedy, ravishing in a daring strapless silk gown designed in an eye-catching shade of pink by Guy Douvier for Christian Dior. The design is fitted with a series of bows at the back, which flares down into a slight train. She has accessorized her gown with pink heels, diamond earrings, elbow-length white gloves, and a tiara-like jeweled ornament in her upswept hair. She is instantly the center of attention.

At the bottom of the stairs, the couple pose with André Malraux and his wife, Marie-Madeleine. Madame Malraux is wearing a white floor-length gown with pearls adorning the neckline. She wears a small diamond-and-pearl pin in the shape of a bow in her dark brown hair. Minister Malraux is also wearing a simple black tuxedo.

A member of the color guard leads President Kennedy, Mrs. Kennedy, and the Malraux couple away from the steps, and they form a receiving line to greet you and other dinner guests. Everybody is smiling and shaking hands. It seems incredible, doesn't it, that you would get this face time with the president and First Lady?

Once the guests are assembled in the State Dining Room, President Kennedy rises and clinks his glass with a spoon. He raises his glass in a toast to honor the distinguished French visitor.

"I suppose all of us wish to participate in all the experiences of life, but he," President Kennedy says of the distinguished Malraux, "has left us all behind."

President Kennedy is sitting next to Madame Malraux. He is also chatting with a gentleman at his table who turns out to be Charles Lindbergh, the first person to fly solo nonstop across the Atlantic Ocean in 1927. Also seated at the president's table are artist Andrew Wyeth, author Irwin Shaw, actress Geraldine Page, and fashion designer Nicole Alphand.

Review the elegant calligraphy of the dinner table plan and you can see that you are to be seated in the Blue Room.

Take your seat at a small table of ten, set with your name card. (Remember to keep this card and the menu as mementos. After dinner, you can ask your tablemates to sign it; this is a unique tradition at Mrs. Kennedy's dinners.) As guests join you at the table, you can see in the distance that Mrs. Kennedy is seated in the center of the Blue Room, accompanied by André Malraux.

Although she is smiling at all the guests, she is mostly talking to Malraux, who is sitting to her right. They are both enjoying each other's company, maybe talking about the art tour that she led at the National Gallery earlier in the day. The jeweled ornament in Mrs. Kennedy's hair glitters in the candlelight.

Tonight, the table is set with colorful and majestic china that President and Mrs. Abraham Lincoln purchased in 1861. The white dinner plates are designed with an American eagle, wings spread, gripping a shield with the American red, white, and blue colors. The eagle holds a bundle of sharp arrows in its right-side talons and an olive branch in its left, while gazing to the olive branch side that symbolizes peace. The country's motto, *E pluribus unum*, floats on a ribbon underneath the eagle. The design is encircled by a royal-purple border dotted with gold, with a gold cable design around the edge of the plate. This is a favorite set of dishes of Mrs. Kennedy, which she also uses for smaller, private dinner parties.

Folded white napkins are placed on President Lincoln's plates and gilt-edged place cards are laid on top of the napkins. At each setting is an urn of cigarettes, a salt dish with a tiny spoon, an ashtray with White House matches, and an individual nut dish.

The cutlery is minimal and is not silver but vermeil (silver covered in gold), and two of the knives have gleaming opalescent pearl handles. Four long-stemmed tulip-shaped glasses are set beside each plate. One is for water, two for wine, and the fourth for champagne to toast.

Everyone notices that Mrs. Kennedy has unfolded her napkin and placed it across her lap. Dinner is about to be served.

The quality of food at state dinners was an enormous priority for Mrs. Kennedy. Not long after her husband's inauguration, Mrs. Kennedy hired a French chef, René Verdon, to lead the kitchen. The menus soon changed from featuring saltines and beef stew to more sophisticated fare, like sole Véronique and chocolate almond tuiles.

The Kennedys had met Verdon when he was working as an assistant chef at the Carlyle Hotel in New York, where they had a penthouse apartment. He made a natural choice when Mrs. Kennedy was looking for someone to take on her preferred French cuisine, and she enticed him to leave the Carlyle, first on a temporary basis to cook for special events, then later permanently when she established him as the first-ever executive chef.

Chef Verdon's cuisine was widely covered by the popular media during his time at the White House, bringing attention to the refined tastes of President and Mrs. Kennedy. He was known, for example, to pick fresh herbs for dinner from the garden he planted on the roof. Verdon's appointment also highlighted Mrs. Kennedy as a Francophile—her menus at these dinners were even written in French.

While Verdon's influence was felt throughout the country—coinciding with the publication of Julia Child's book *Mastering the Art of French Cooking* and her popular public television program *The French Chef*—some media sources criticized Mrs. Kennedy's French dinner culture for not being patriotic. She responded by contacting the press to clarify that American wines, not foreign ones, were served at certain White House meals, and that dishes were now being called by their English names. The president even began to take domestic sparkling wine abroad on state visits to introduce American wines to the world.

Tonight for Malraux, though, the menu sitting on the table is written in French. It might strike you as very impressive and international.

It consists of:

Consommé Madrilène Iranien (consommé soup—a traditional way to start a French meal)

Homard en Bellevue (aka lobster en Bellevue—a stunning salad of chilled, meaty lobster tails surrounded by vegetables, creamy from its dressing and sweet with a hint of the sea)

Bar Farci Polignac (sea bass stuffed with spinach—it seems so elegant)
Pommes Parisienne (potatoes Parisienne)
Asperges de Floride (Florida asparagus)
Corton Charlemagne 1959 (a dry white wine, this will be amazing with the opening course and the sea bass)
La Galantine de Faisan au Porto (pheasant aspic salad)
Château Gruaud-Larose 1955 (a prestigious full-bodied Bordeaux red wine to pair with the pheasant)
Le Croquembouche aux Noisettes (cream puffs garnished with nuts—a fabulous treat)
Dom Pérignon 1952

This is definitely a special menu to impress the honored guests.

The centerpiece of the evening is Chef Verdon's bar farci Polignac. There are expressions of delight and amazement as the sea bass is set before everyone at the table. It is a work of art in itself, each individual whole fish filled with a spinach stuffing and baked to perfection.

But it's not all about the visual. Biting into it, you will find that the first sensation of the sea bass is the slightly crispy skin, then the firm yet flaky texture, revealing delicately sweet flesh with a touch of fattiness. This is a fish that is light but substantial. The interior spinach stuffing, with fragrant hints of garlic and buttered mushrooms, adds a perfect balance of vegetables to enhance the flavor of the bass.

The climax of the dish, though, is the sauce. This is where Chef Verdon stands out as a culinary genius. The wine, broth, and sour cream cooked together make a tasty experience—but it is the leek that adds the depth of flavor. If an onion had a brother with a gentler, more mellow temperament, it would be a leek. Leeks are a favorite ingredient in French cooking, prominent in Verdon's kitchen. Related to onions, they are more subtle, sweeter, not as harsh.

You will find the creamy leek sauce brings all the flavors of the mushroom, spinach, and bass together to form a Mozart string quartet in your mouth.

The final indulgence to dinner is the French croquembouches. I am sure that Mrs. Kennedy hopes that you enjoy the crunch of the baked exterior pastry and hard spun sugar. However, it is the thick, sweet custard oozing from the center that is the star of the show. Allow the US Air Force Strolling Strings to serenade you as you and your fellow guests sip champagne.

After dinner, you are escorted into the East Room, where Mrs. Kennedy has chosen the entertainment for the evening as carefully as the food: a virtuoso performance of violinist Isaac Stern, cellist Leonard Rose, and pianist Eugene Istomin playing the Schubert Trio in B Flat Major, Opus 99, in four movements.

After the performance, everyone dances. Even though women are wearing formal long gowns and men are in tuxedoes, the guests will break into the new dance sensation, the Twist. Keep an eye on Vice President Lyndon Johnson—he is especially fond of this move.

Another new practice introduced by Mrs. Kennedy is the mixing of men and women guests at coffee after these state dinners. Formerly, the men went with the president to the Green Room for coffee and cigars, and the women went with the First Lady to the Red Room for coffee. At Mrs. Kennedy's events, you should feel free to enter whichever room you choose.

As the elegant state dinner winds down, you can see that Malraux is delighted to have been honored in such a magnificent manner. He is leaning over to Mrs. Kennedy and whispering to her. Whatever he is saying causes her to break into a radiant smile.

You might wonder if he has just whispered that he would look into sending Mrs. Kennedy France's cultural treasure—the *Mona Lisa*—as a loan to her and President Kennedy. After being treated with such magnificent hospitality—food, drink, company, entertainment, and dining room surroundings—how can Malraux refuse?

And indeed, in December 1962, Mrs. Kennedy's dream came true. The *Mona Lisa* reached American shores, stopping first at the National Gallery in Washington, then at the Metropolitan Museum of Art in New York. The loan had to overcome strong resistance. The painting is considered a national treasure in France, but André Malraux prevailed for Mrs. Kennedy.

During its stay at the National Gallery, the *Mona Lisa* was seen by more than 500,000 people, many of whom waited in line for hours just to catch a short glimpse before being told to move along. Security was insured by two rifle-bearing marines stationed on either side. The painting subsequently traveled to New York for a nearly month-long residency, where the Met welcomed over one million visitors to see the painting. Thanks to her dining room diplomacy, Jacqueline Kennedy had brought the best of the visual arts to the American people and, in doing so, created a history-making blockbuster show.

So much has been made of Mrs. Kennedy's glamorous image. It is true that she brought culture, fashion, and the *Mona Lisa* to America, but she did more than that.

The Malraux Dinner gathered the most accomplished men and women of the American cultural scene. It not only emphasized the Kennedys' support for the arts, but also demonstrated Mrs. Kennedy's social and entertaining skills, which added prestige to her husband's presidency.

With her public image, cultural inquisitiveness, and linguistic capabilities (she was fluent in English, French, Spanish, and Italian), Mrs. Kennedy helped gain allies for the Kennedy administration. When relationships between the president and world leaders became tense, it was the First Lady who seemed to be able to ease the waters.

French President Charles de Gaulle was impressed by her command of his language, saying that she "knew more French history than most French women." In India, where relations with the US were strained, Mrs. Kennedy earned praise when she paid a visit to the grave of Mohandas Gandhi, laying a wreath on his memorial. And after Mrs. Kennedy asked Soviet Premier Nikita Khrushchev about the Russian dog who was sent to space, Khrushchev sent the Kennedys a puppy—one of the offspring of the space dog.

Jacqueline Kennedy continued to dedicate her time to the promotion of the American arts and the preservation of the country's history. She hosted lunches and dinners in the State Dining Room that brought together elite figures from politics and the arts. She restored the White House from being an overlooked dwelling for a passing series of presidents to a respected and iconic symbol of leadership for the country.

Mrs. Kennedy redefined the role of First Lady to make it a dynamic and contributory role to the presidency that continues to this day.

She was a welcome breath of fresh air.

The White House
1600 Pennsylvania Avenue NW, Washington, DC, United States
whitehouse.gov

The John F. Kennedy Presidential Library and Museum
Columbia Point, Boston, Massachusetts, United States
jfklibrary.org

Dear Franny,

Jackie Kennedy designed a dinner for French Minister of Culture André Malraux, and went all out. I want to do the same. Here are some ideas I learned from Mrs. Kennedy:

Whether it's a small dinner for four or a large dinner for a hundred, Mrs. Kennedy showed that it's important to plan. Menu, seating arrangements, clothing, right down to the candies in the bowls. It was all in the interests of relaxed hospitality and making her guests feel welcome.

I like her seating plan. She thought ahead to place certain people with particular points of view next to each other to inspire conversations. I also like separating couples from sitting together. They have enough time to be together on the drive home.

We don't have a famous French chef to cook for your dinner, but it's a nice touch to make a feature dish in honor of a special guest, a main or a dessert to make that person feel special. I could even make something new and name it after you. How about Sweet Potato Franny or Steak Frances (derived from the famous Steak Diane) or Hot Fudge Franny Sundae (my fave)!

Whether it's a world-class chamber orchestra or a game of charades, it's an idea to have some form of entertainment for after dinner. In the 1960s guests would play the party game Twister—you know, where players placed their hands and feet on colored dots on a mat, trying to stay standing and outlast their opponents. The laughter and accidental rubbing of bodies up against each other kept the evening lively.

It's always nice to dress up for dinner. It shows your commitment to making a totally elegant evening for the guests. It doesn't have to be a pink gown and tiara—but something different to brighten up the evening. (Wait a minute. That tiara is not a bad idea . . .)

The Malraux Dinner was uniquely Mrs. Kennedy. She changed food, dining, and entertainment attitudes in North America to the present day. My takeaway from Mrs. Kennedy's example for your birthday dinner is that just because things were done in a certain way in the past doesn't mean we can't change things up.

I know you love croquembouche, but I won't be making that for dessert. Even Chef Verdon advises this is an all-day project for a trained French chef.

You probably remember that I tried once, and I almost set the kitchen on fire.

XOXO

J.

11

THE NORBRATEN AND LICHTI DINING ROOM, 2024

Toronto, Ontario

FRANNY IS EXCITED, I can tell.

She had her hair done at the stylist today, a pedicure yesterday, and she has donned some fancy slacks. She looks sensational. I'm excited too.

We have been invited out to dinner.

Even though dinner has become a more casual event in the twenty-first century compared to, say, the Edwardian Downton Abbey period, I am dressed up as well. We want to communicate to our hosts that we appreciate their efforts to entertain us and that we are grateful for their generosity. Being invited for dinner to a person's dining room is still a big deal for us! We want to look our best for them.

Franny and I are about to visit some good friends who live in our favorite contemporary house in the city. It is a place we love to visit. Our friends transformed a once-unloved dining room into a glorious, unique space of color and light. Located in Leslieville, a proud neighborhood of working people and artists in Toronto, the house perfectly fits the entertaining lifestyle of the owners, who generously share luncheons, dinners, and parties with friends and family.

It is summertime and we haven't seen our friends in a while. To celebrate the return of the sun and the easy lifestyle of the season, I have an idea to cook some unique dishes for them to enjoy in their dining area.

Over the years, I have seen many current-day house renovations (open spaces, futuristic appliances, bidets in all the bathrooms), and while I notice that so much effort goes into the redesign of the kitchen and bathroom, the dining room is sometimes left behind. This should be no surprise, but my feeling is that if we truly value hospitality and sharing good times with others, the dining room should be at the top of the list. It is the room of celebration, memories, and coming together.

Today, I am searching for inspiration for Franny's birthday dinner in a contemporary setting. I have explored great historical dinners and learned all about their customs, but I want to see if my vision can come true in modern surroundings: creative food and animated discussion in a dining room that expresses warmth, hospitality, and rejuvenation. To see how it can be done in this day and age, we are off to dine with our friends.

Enjoying the warmth of the late-afternoon sun on our faces, Franny and I walk, toting bags of groceries, past colorful wood-frame cottages and front porches that create a happy-looking streetscape. Admiring the lush front gardens of alliums, daisies, and cone flowers, I see our friends' abode ahead of me.

Arriving at the house's front, we remark at how it has been carefully designed to fit in with the architectural scale of the late-nineteenth- and early-twentieth-century surrounding structures of basic brick walls, modest wooden front porches, and bay windows. Yet it has a contemporary vibe. The exterior facade has been composed with dormers with clean lines that pop out of the slanting roofs. The walls are clad with shingles painted an edgy flat black. The house sits on the street like a cool, handsome dude sporting an all-black ensemble of shirt, pants, and elegant tuxedo jacket sans tie.

"It's the best-dressed house on the street," says Franny.

Juggling our grocery bags, we dash up the front concrete stairs and press a luminous white doorbell. I am eager to get inside and start cooking. I have dreamed up a special Saskatchewan-themed menu, in honor of the home province of one of our hosts, that I think will pump up this summer celebration dinner.

In a few seconds, the door opens and out pop two handsome gentlemen who greet us with enthusiastic hugs and huge smiles: our friends, Garth Norbraten and Greg Lichti.

Hug number one comes from Garth, a prominent architect in Toronto and the son of a prairie carpenter. I know that he is responsible for the design and was hands-on during the entire renovation. He is the one who originally hails from Saskatchewan, the province situated on the Great Plains of Canada. I love sitting down with Garth to chat about life in central Canada, as well as our common passion for modern architecture.

Hug number two comes from his partner, Greg, who is originally from Listowel, Ontario. He is associate vice president of development for the Princess Margaret Foundation, which supports the premier cancer hospital in the city—but, with an enormous smile on his face, Greg tells us that he has just happily retired from his office! So now there are two reasons for this celebration dinner.

"What the heck are those?" asks Greg in astonishment, pointing to the bags full of food, bowls, spatulas, and spoons we have deposited in the vestibule. "Are you expecting to feed an army?"

"It's a 'celebration of summer' dinner," I announce. "I'll be cooking traditional Saskatchewan dishes in tribute to Garth's home province. But now that we know Greg is retiring, we can also celebrate his new stage in life. It's going to be Saska-licious!"

My humor is on the corny side, but it works: There is enormous laughter and more hugs. It's going to be a great evening.

I have already given the couple a heads-up that the main course for tonight's dinner will be Saskatchewan bison burgers. As adventurous eaters who have enjoyed unconventional foods from around the world, including crickets in Mexico, they have already told me they are looking forward to tasting the prairie bison.

I go ahead into the house and get a glimpse of an expansive interior full of modulated light, lively color, and the silhouettes of multiple art pieces.

As our friends escort us through the vestibule, Franny and I admire the setting. We have been here before, but the immense beauty of the space makes it feel like we are seeing it for the first time. We continue on, and Garth explains that when they first bought the property, it was a "sad little house" from 1906. With sweat and commitment, they proceeded to strip back the deteriorating layers of its floors, walls, and roof, leaving a blank canvas to build their dreams upon. And today, we find ourselves in a spacious, contemporary, and light-filled blended dining room, kitchen, and living room.

Measuring approximately thirty by forty feet, the space that was once a small kitchen shed has been transformed into a main floor of long, colorful walls, high-tech spotlights, and a gleaming natural wood floor. It is a perfect example of a twenty-first-century great room, the kind of room that originates from a bygone era, where dining, entertaining, cooking, and partying can take place all in one space. What I find especially invigorating about the great room surroundings is that all of these activities, together, create a synergy through their combined actions that is sometimes lost if each activity is hidden away in a separate space.

We walk farther into the great room and get a peek through the floor-to-ceiling windows, with a view into a lush garden, that stretches across the entire back of the house. This view reminds me of the seamless connection between interior and exterior at the Frank Sinatra house.

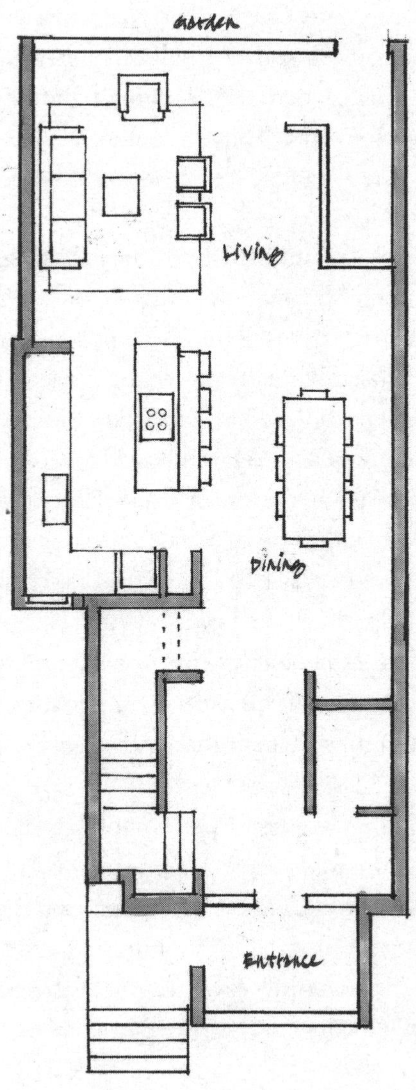

Norbraten-Lichti house

"Even though I'm standing here in the house, I feel like I'm in the garden," exclaims Franny, who is the gardener in our house.

"We get great joy from our garden," says Greg.

"The dining area was designed to blend with the flowers and trees of the garden," adds Garth. "The colors are a combination of a Japanese Shinto garden and an English country garden. But, as you can see, the English garden is winning right now."

I tell Garth not to worry. "Claude Monet reveled in his overgrown garden at Giverny," I say. "It might be the most-loved garden in the world."

A stunning aspect of entering this room is how the owners have set a welcoming mood through the modulation of warm light and music. I feel as though I have entered a whole new world of art, hospitality, and visual delight. There is no overhead lighting; I can tell that Greg and Garth have purposely designed the space with soft lighting to set a mood of relaxation and serenity.

To enhance the Saskatchewanian atmosphere, they are playing folksinger Joni Mitchell, another Saskatchewan native. Hearing her soulful voice singing "Big Yellow Taxi," I allow my shoulder and back muscles to relax. I feel welcome and carefree.

Taking it all in, I immediately think of my guiding principle to slow down for dinner. In this great room, lighting and music create a soothing setting that is conducive to easy conversation and sharing of ideas.

I realize that another reason I feel completely at ease in this great room is that the walls are wrapped in a vivid chartreuse. The color brings to mind bright green shoots impatiently poking through the earth and snow in early spring.

"It's so fresh and hopeful," says Franny of the stimulating hue. "You've brought the color of the garden right into the dining area."

I make an immediate mental memo to myself: Include something chartreuse in our new dining room for Franny's birthday dinner.

"I like to have color on my walls. Most modernists are great admirers of the color white," says Garth, an architect through and through, "but I come from an environment where it's gray for much of the year."

Further color accents are provided by carpets and cushions in hits of turquoise, mint, and forest green, playing off the narrow-planked hardwood flooring. The space is given additional sparkle from bright spotlights on thin wires that stretch below the ceiling.

But for me, the big architectural statement in this house is that the dining area is the first room that guests step into. It is such a different floor plan from all the other dining rooms that I have seen on my travels around the world, in which they are a standalone room, sometimes not in view to house visitors.

Garth and Greg's arrangement to immediately enter the dining area is consistent with many new house designs across North America, where, with their open-concept plans, the dining room has become the showpiece of the ground floor. The standalone dining room—at least as we knew it during the twentieth century—is rarer to find now.

We are in the middle of a return to the dining room—or in some houses, to a larger dining area. Let me explain. The shift from separate dining rooms to open-concept kitchen-dining areas is a result of a desire for a more casual, relaxed lifestyle and toward flowing, flexible, multi-use spaces. The new "all-in-one room" also allows for more informal entertaining, with views to the outside and maximal natural light.

Whether a house is designed to be open concept or it has a dedicated room for dining, the place where we dine is no longer only for eating. It is being reborn as a multifunctional space: It is also a library or a workspace, and as many people have stopped going into a corporate office daily, it is also an at-home office. The dining room—whether in a bachelor apartment or a magnificent mansion—is now the center of the home where we come together to do everything.

And informality is now a priority. Unlike under the strict rules of etiquette at Highclere Castle, homeowners want their guests to feel relaxed when they arrive for dinner. To achieve that laid-back atmosphere, contemporary dining areas might be designed with certain considerations:

- A beverage station with glasses, a bar, snacks, and even a soda fountain makes for easy, help-yourself refreshments.
- The dining table might have a long bench along one side that allows restless children a place to sit and still easily slide away to move around.
- There is often a close connection to the backyard deck, with an emphasis on plush outdoor furniture, the barbecue, and outside eating.
- Instead of a formal parlor, the first thing that guests see as they step into the house is a dining table set with eclectic dinnerware and surrounded by comfortable chairs.
- The dining table might be incorporated into the kitchen island so that cooking, dining, and socializing all happen in one large room.

The architectural message of the twenty-first-century dining area says, "We are active, we are informal, and we like to eat."

Having the dining area as the first space that guests enter in the house makes a statement about the significance that eating and gathering with friends play in the couple's lives. I can also see that the dining area is the largest space on their ground level, hearkening back to historical examples, including the Japanese tatami room, Claude Monet's house, and Martin Luther King Jr.'s childhood home. For Garth and Greg, the entire ground floor is a symbol of hospitality. We have returned to a time when the importance of coming together to dine is reflected in the architectural floor plan.

"We love to eat and entertain," says Greg. "This space is where we love to spend time with friends. We wanted to make the dining area the center of the house."

"Talking about eating . . ." I say.

There is a pregnant pause. We all look at each other and we are thinking the same thing: dinner!

Of course, a prerequisite to eating is that I must cook.

And so I swoop around the kitchen island and haul my bags of ground meat, jars of condiments, and boxes of berries up onto the counter. Even though the island separates the dining area from the kitchen, everything indeed feels like one open space. A gas stove is built into the island, and four bar chairs line one side for quick meals free from the more formal etiquette of the dining table. Behind me is a single row of maple cabinets that houses the sink and oven.

"Where did you get this charming backsplash?" asks Franny, as she gazes longingly at a wall of half-inch chartreuse mosaic tiles over the sink—the same color as the surrounding walls. The tiles add a liveliness and fun energy to the great room.

When I echo Franny's compliment of the brightly colored backsplash, the couple just laugh.

"The truth is that we bought these tiles from an architect friend," says Greg. "He got them from a building supply store that was going out of business. Garth was able to get enough to create this beautiful pattern."

While I turn on the stove to fry the bison burgers, Greg and Garth set the table that sits in the middle of the dining area. I admire the rectangular natural wood table supported by brushed metal legs that echoes the clean lines of their modern interior. Many of their furnishings have a Scandinavian flavor, reflecting the couple's past visits to Finland, Sweden, and Denmark.

Around the table are blond wood chairs that match the dining table. But these are not just any old dining chairs. As mid-century modern enthusiasts, Garth and Greg seat their guests in classic comfort designed by Arne Jacobsen, a visionary twentieth-century Danish architect and furniture designer. Jacobsen is remembered for his contribution to modern buildings and his simple, well-designed chairs with curvy, pleasing shapes.

Molded out of a single piece of plywood, the chairs have an undulating design against the home's rectilinear lines. To me, they look like waves of the ocean meeting the beach.

"Dining tables and chairs are so much more than just pieces of furniture," says Greg as he runs his hands over the curvy back of a chair. "They bring people together and create memories."

Greg's statement makes me recall the round dining table of Edith Wharton, a place of honest food and honest conversation.

As Greg and Garth open the drawers of their china cabinet, I peek over at their impressive collection of table settings. Like me, these two foodies are also dinner plate connoisseurs. As they set each plate, saucer, bowl, and cup onto the table, they outline the dishes' origins: Saskatchewan, Finland, Sweden, Denmark, and Japan. A special set of these dinner dishes that Franny covets are white Rosenthal china with a platinum border designed by famed Bauhaus architect Walter Gropius.

My favorite pieces are delicate crystal bowls called Ultima Thule made by Iittala, a Finnish glassware maker. I run my hands over the glass surface and feel subtle etchings and small divots on one of the bowls. The crystal's relief, Garth tells us, was inspired by the melting ice in Finland.

"That's it!" I exclaim to my tablemates. I make an immediate connection between the striated surfaces of the bowl and patterns of frost I would touch on my childhood bedroom window in winter. In addition, the bottom of the bowl has an enchanting texture that reminds me of ice balls left on the ground below melting icicles.

Once set, the table is covered in a collection of china and ceramics that is certainly eclectic, but it all works.

Once set, the table is covered in a collection of china and ceramics that is certainly eclectic, but it all works. Each item is a conversation piece with its own story, an enjoyable display of Garth and Greg's passions and travels. Their table setting reflects the current ideal of informality in the dining room, and unlike in earlier periods, the meaning behind the pieces is more important than showing off their financial value. The more varied, the better.

My chopping, slicing, frying, and baking take a little longer than anticipated, but as I step back to look at my culinary creations, it all seems worth the extra time—well, maybe not to everybody in the room. I can almost hear Franny, Garth, and Greg's stomachs rumbling like a thunderstorm.

I have never tried bison before, but I know that this is a type of meat with a historically significant past.

Long before Europeans arrived in North America, an estimated thirty million bison roamed the continent's Great Plains. These majestic animals were a valuable resource for the Native people, not only for food but also for clothing and tools. Eventually, when settlers arrived and headed west, the bison almost became extinct through overhunting. Through careful resource management in the wild and animal husbandry on farms, the bison is back. It remains an iconic North American species, as well as a delicious meat for chefs and cooks. Bison hunting is legal in some provinces and states today, and is controlled by a limited number of government-issued hunting permits.

When I announce that my Saskatchewan bison burgers are ready, there are enthusiastic cheers from my hungry diners, who are patiently sitting around the table.

But first things first.

We toast Greg on his retirement. Toasts and dining room celebrations seem to go together. The tradition dates back to the Ancient Greeks of the sixth century BCE. The practice of toasting began as a tribute to their gods in hopes of a long and healthy life, continuing to the present as a spirited way to start a dinner.

I know that when I hold my special birthday dinner for Franny, I will commence the festivities with a toast. Giving a toast can be an intimidating proposition, so to be of some help, here are . . .

My Top 5 Tips on How to Give a Toast:

1. Start with thanks, expressing gratitude for being able to share the moment together.
2. Acknowledge the person and the occasion.
3. Recount a personal story.
4. Share a quote.
5. Raise your glass. Cheers!

We toast Greg with hopes that the days ahead will be ones of fulfillment, discovery, and joy. We applaud and whoop. Greg replies with sincere gratitude. Then he raises both hands and proclaims, “Enough of this. Let’s eat!”

Following Greg’s lead, I get to work. I lay out the buns and burgers on the kitchen island and everyone comes up, dinner plates in hand, to help themselves, buffet style.

Greg, Garth, and Franny place the bison patties on their buns along with condiments, including tomatoes, Dijon mustard, relish, and cheese, and then return to the table. I decline any condiments so that I can focus on the pure taste of the bison.

“Saskatchewan!” I proclaim, and then we all take a big bite at the same time.

There is a slight pause—and then there are eruptions of *mmms* and groans of pleasure.

Together, we enter the gates of burger heaven.

First, I inhale the familiar aroma of grilled meat, oils, and the baked goodness of the bun. This only intensifies my appetite and anticipation.

The first bite’s sensation is the softness of the flour-dusted brioche bun—soft, puffy, and with a subtle, sweet, eggy taste. The sesame seeds add a hint of chewy nuttiness to the bread. A thin layer of butter adds extra richness.

Next is the texture of the sandwich: an irresistible crunch from the caramelized crust on the outside of the burger that’s a wonderful combination of fat, salt, sugars, and meat.

And then I finally taste the perfectly cooked bison patty. Juicy, with a slightly sweet undertone, this bison patty has a similar flavor to any great beef burger but with a little more oomph. I am surprised at its mildness; it’s not gamy or bold-tasting, like a lamb burger.

The purity of the undressed burger, with its meaty flavors and textures, is a thing of beauty. Without condiments, this bison has a leaner taste than a beef burger.

Burgers are a favorite meal in our house. Biting into a deliciously juicy and perfectly grilled burger releases happy feelings that spread from my brain through my body. I am sure a culinary psychiatrist would tell me that besides satisfying my hunger, burgers bring back memories of family barbecues in the backyard and good times with friends at the local drive-in.

I chew slowly to savor every moment.

Another joyous feature of this dining area is the owners' ceramics collection, which further brightens the chartreuse walls. The plates, vases, and sculptures are displayed on natural wood shelves that wrap around the great room.

"I feel like I'm eating in a gallery," says Franny, while adding more smoked Gouda to her bison burger.

The dazzling pieces bring even more liveliness to the dining area. Shaped in organic curves, circles, and ridges, the ceramics play off the straight lines of the modern architecture. One in particular is a small sculpture of interlocking rectangles, with some of the surfaces faced in gold leaf. It was made by an artist from Garth's native Saskatchewan. I am attracted to the way the candlelight on the dining table catches and flickers off the gold leaf surfaces.

To further meld the spaces of the great room together, the exhibition of pottery spreads from the dining area into the living area and right into the kitchen, with rows of plates and vases placed above the sink and work surfaces.

When I praise the couple on the vastness and beauty of their ceramics collection, Garth only rolls his eyes and laughs.

"Thank you, but it's getting a little out of control," he laments. "I'm running out of storage space in the basement."

I think back to the dining room at Highclere Castle, where the walls act as a portrait gallery to outline the history of the estate and its owners. This great room's dining area is also a showroom of sorts, but Garth and Greg's display of sculpture, glassware, and ceramics is a highly pleasing and artistic way to express their interest in artists they admire. It reminds me of the exhibition of Mexican artifacts in the Frida Kahlo dining room.

I am so engrossed in the dinner table conversation that I don't notice something is missing. I suddenly realize that, in my concentration on making perfect Saskatchewan bison burgers, I have forgotten two bowls of salad in the refrigerator.

I stumble up from my Arne Jacobsen dining chair and fetch first my crispy green salad, a bountiful bowl that features sliced apples and walnuts with an apple cider vinaigrette.

Then I announce, "I bet a Saskatchewan potato salad would not go amiss." I present my second salad, a traditional potato salad based on my mother's recipe, made with diced potatoes, onions, celery, mayo, and hard-boiled eggs. It's essentially the classic potato salad that appeared at every church picnic and potluck throughout my childhood.

"But in honor of this occasion, I have added a Saskatchewan twist," I announce. "My culinary research has revealed that Saskatchewan is one of the few places that adds mustard to their potato salad. I hope you enjoy."

A little-known fact is that Saskatchewan is the world's largest exporter of mustard. The popular image of the province is that it is covered in wheat fields swaying in the wind—but it also grows a broadleaf, oil-seed mustard crop with yellow flowers for the international condiment market. If you have been squeezing mustard on your hot dog your whole life, chances are that that mustard originated in Saskatchewan fields. Tonight, I am using one that is grown and made in the town of Gravelbourg, a French-speaking, mustard-growing community in the province.

We dig into the prairie mustard potato salad, and we all agree it is a winner, creamy and flecked with savory herbs. The splash of

Saskatchewan mustard into the mayo infuses an extra burst of tang that gives the potato salad a mild sweet-and-sour flavor.

I look over at Franny to see what she thinks. "Very good, John," she says with a big grin. "This is amazing."

I grin back. I decide on the spot that this potato salad will be on her birthday dinner table.

Topped with a sprinkle of paprika and salt and pepper, this potato salad turns into a monster temptation at the dinner table. All my discipline vaporizes into the summer air. I cannot resist coming back for more. Again, the taste and satisfaction must stir something from a happy past. I indulge in this potato salad so much that, eventually, I quietly loosen my belt buckle a notch.

Not to worry. I can try to eat intelligently tomorrow.

And although Greg, Garth, and Franny tell me they are entirely satiated from the Saskatchewan bison burgers and potato salad, they still ask what is for dessert. When I tell them that I have prepared another Saskatchewan favorite—a Saskatoon berry crisp—they go crazy.

"Saskatoon pies and tarts are what my mother made every summer," says Garth, with an enormous grin.

A fruit that is not well-known outside of the prairies, Saskatoon berries grow wild in fields and roadsides, ripening in late June or early July. A common memory for many Saskatchewanians is taking buckets and bowls to pick the berries throughout their childhood and then enjoying them in sumptuous desserts.

While preparing the crisp, I noticed that the Saskatoon berries are similar to blueberries, but smaller and with a shinier, deep purple appearance. I am really looking forward to tasting these little purple jewels.

As I take the steaming crisp out of the oven, the ground floor eating space fills with the aroma of home baking. I set large portions of the dessert on each plate and garnish it with generous scoops of vanilla ice cream. While the crisp is homemade and rustic in appearance alongside the melting ice cream, it is perfect in its imperfection—the picture of prairie baking delight. We pick up our spoons and indulge with gusto.

There is immediate applause from the diners.

Biting into the confection, I'm met with the crisp, golden-brown crust. Crunchy with a perfect combination of brown sugar, rolled oats, and generously laced buttery richness, it crumbles in my mouth into pure deliciousness. Next, the sweet creaminess of the ice cream melds with the slightly salty crisp.

But the star of the show is the Saskatoon berries. They are a complete sweet, tangy surprise. The little berries literally burst with a juicy, nutty flavor and have a slight chewiness that gives a unique, unexpected texture. We agree that the Saskatoon berries are a great change of pace from the more conventional blueberry experience and probably have more flavor per molecule.

"I love Saskatoons and how they bring about a warm coziness," says Greg.

"They're deliciously different," adds Fran. "They're sweet but earthy, like drinking a cup of tea."

"They're cranberry meets blueberry meets almond," enthuses Garth. "And if you want to sound like you're from Saskatchewan, you don't call them Saskatoon berries. Everybody there knows that they're berries. We just call them Saskatoons."

One of the great pleasures of my life is to taste something completely new and sensational, like these Saskatoons. It gives me even greater pleasure if I can share that first-time culinary experience with my wife and great friends at the table. There's nothing like the first time.

Whatever we call the berries, the dinner is an evening of new tastes, lively conversation, and happy celebration—all in comfortable, informal, dreamy surroundings.

A criticism of some contemporary architecture is that it can appear lifeless and severe. But this combined kitchen, dining, and living area, with its chartreuse walls, lively ceramics, and pops of pastel tiles, is as delightful and refreshing as biting into an icy cold lime ice pop on a sweltering hot day.

Historically, the conventional layout of the house was to design a vestibule at the front door; after passing through this space, guests would be escorted into the parlor for conversation and then into a separate dining room for a formal dinner.

What is great about our contemporary period is that those traditional rules of the house can either be kept or changed. In this house renovation, guests are immediately brought into the dining area. Garth and Greg have taken matters into their own hands and turned the conventional floor plan on its head to put their priorities first: leisure, generosity, and sharing take precedence over tradition.

In this house, we eat first and converse later.

And what a conversation it will be.

Garth Norbraten, Architect
johnsonnorbraten.com/garth.php

Dear Franny,

I know you loved our celebration dinner in Garth and Greg's great room—I did too. Fun, relaxed, and leisurely, it sparked some ideas that we can incorporate into our dining room and birthday dinner.

Just like the yellow in Frida Kahlo's dining room, G and G have rejuvenated their dining area with color. Chartreuse green is unique to them, but maybe we can find a way to add some hits of the fun color into the dinner atmosphere—napkins? plates? placemats? I'm all in.

I loved the way G and G could slow down the evening with prairie music and by being surrounded by prairie ceramics. It all fit with the menu too.

It was really fun talking to our hosts about their different china dishes and ceramics that were on the table. The informal, eclectic look of the table just adds to a relaxed atmosphere between guests.

And the number one most important lesson: At Greg and Garth's dinner, not everything had to be perfect. The dishware can be mismatched, the food can be eccentric, and the music can be from 1969. The main thing is to get together and be with the people around the table.

Dinner is not about impressing people. It's about how much we love our guests.

I hope you liked the bison. I bought quite a bit. We'll be eating it for a long time!

XOXO

J.

12

CHEF MICHAEL STADTLÄNDER'S EIGENSINN FARM, 2024

Singhampton, Ontario

I HAVE TREMENDOUS RESPECT for farmers.

They are the ones who select and buy the seeds for their crops, plant those seeds, water and weed once they grow into plants, track the weather and tend to the crops accordingly, do the back-breaking harvesting, and finally haul the produce to market. They put up the money to buy livestock, then feed and care for the animals. It is an ongoing labour of love. We are so lucky to have them.

And while I have great admiration for the people who put food on our tables, I am a city person. I like the options that the city offers me. Films, theater, museums—there are more things to do and see than I have time for.

But I also like to eat.

More and more, Franny and I are growing concerned about the quality of our food. We want to know where our pungent garlic was grown, if the apples we're crunching into were sprayed with pesticides, what chemicals might have been added to our spicy mustard, and if the chickens we're grilling are free-range.

We'll enjoy our barbecue more knowing that the chickens were happy chickens during their lives.

So I was intrigued when I learned that one of Canada's premier chefs decided to explore a different course and bought a farm in a remote section of the countryside. Chef Michael Stadtländer, his wife, Nobuyo, and their school-age son, Hermann, left the star chef life at glamorous restaurants to host dinners where customers indulge in menus based around their own farm-grown vegetables, their own livestock, and wild plants, berries, and mushrooms foraged in their own forest.

While the farm-to-table concept is commonplace these days, in the 1990s, Stadtländer's idealistic philosophy about sustainability, baking his own bread, and practicing organic farming was ahead of its time.

One morning, while sleepily scrolling through social media in bed, I spotted an announcement to book seats at a luncheon by Chef Stadtländer at his family's Eigensinn Farm.

I was heartily impressed when I read that the chef's menu would be a magnificent meal using ingredients grown entirely on the farm. And the crowning glory: The "dining room" would be outdoors, in the open air, surrounded by the fields of vegetables and roaming hogs and chickens, and right inside the forest of sugar maple trees that provide their syrup. A dining room surrounded not by gilded frame portraits and elaborately carved furniture, but by the vegetation and livestock that I would be eating from.

When I called the number listed, it was answered by a cheerful woman who introduced herself as Nobuyo Stadtländer, the chef's wife.

"Ota-san!" she exclaimed, using the Japanese honorific. "You must come for lunch. We would love to see you!"

Her exuberant response—despite us never having met before—clinched it: Franny and I were going to the country for a very special luncheon. To give myself a more rustic, farm-appropriate look, I went looking for my best Ralph Lauren jean jacket.

I was totally excited. The city guy was going to have a gourmet farm experience.

While I hold farmers in high regard, I'm embarrassed to say that I, myself, rarely visit farms. Though I love to cook, I feel oddly detached from the source of food production. Like many city people, I tend to take our food for granted. Unfortunately, I often pay more consideration to the bargain price of my apples or the convenience of the store where I can buy them than to the people who grew them.

My farm-removed psyche really hit me when I was looking for ingredients to make Edith Wharton's mock turtle soup. The historical recipe called for a calf head, so I sought one out at the farmer's market in Toronto. When I saw it, I was repulsed. Face, eyes, ears—all intact. I had to turn away. But then I thought, *Why should I be shocked? This is where meat comes from.* It is an animal—not a generic, faceless slab of red meat sitting in the refrigerator case of the supermarket. Just like real Brussels sprouts come from a farmer's field, they don't grow at the grocery store wrapped in a cellophane bag.

But I want to change everything that I know and that I do. It is time for me to discover where food really comes from.

Franny and I are driving north on a sunny May morning, bopping along to her favorite Ariana Grande song. We are on our way to Eigensinn Farm, near a small Ontario village called Singhampton. Over the heartfelt wails from the radio, I share my research with Franny on the background of Nobuyo and Michael Stadtländer. I tell her that we're about to meet one of the great food gods—I know I'm prone to excitement, but this time I am not kidding.

"Michael Stadtländer's current life is completely different from the life of a downtown celebrity chef," I begin. "Stadtländer was one of the first, if not *the* first, chef to lead the farm-to-table movement in Canada—even before there was such a thing."

Franny knows that I am fascinated by people who are "firsts." Claude Monet was one of the first to paint landscapes in the open air. Frida Kahlo was one of the first to celebrate Mexican culture in a Eurocentric world. Martin Luther King Jr. was one of the first to perform nonviolent protest to achieve civil rights. It's not easy being first. One must be rock solid in one's convictions. One has to be willing to take financial risk. One has to have incredible courage.

A farmer, artist, and environmental and food activist, Michael Stadtländer is also recognized as one of Canada's best chefs. He is one of a small group of chefs that believe in reflecting the land on which they work in their food. My summation of Stadtländer is that he is a culinary visionary.

Franny mentions that she has heard his name before, but hasn't seen him on any of the food shows.

"From what I can surmise, it appears that he is a modest person," I say. "He has shied away from the celebrity status that comes with being in front of a camera, which is part of his appeal to me."

Though not a household name, Stadtländer has been lauded as the father of the farm-to-table movement in Canada. His honors include becoming a Member of the Order of Canada and receiving the Governor General's Award for Leadership in 2010, and the 2011 Restaurateur of the Year award by the Canadian Association of Food Service Professionals for his restaurant Haisai (now closed) in Singhampton.

Buying, operating, and cooking on a secluded farm fulfilled a long-desired yearning in Stadtländer that began in his childhood.

Born in 1957, Michael Stadtländer grew up working on his family's farm outside of Lübeck, West Germany, where he fished, foraged, and hunted as a boy. The oldest of four brothers, he learned about cooking and eating with local ingredients from his mother and grandmother.

He eventually made his way to Switzerland, where he met Canadian chef Jamie Kennedy and joined him in opening the acclaimed Scaramouche restaurant in Toronto in 1980. This was one of the first restaurants to introduce nouvelle cuisine, an approach to cooking characterized by lighter, more delicate dishes with increased emphasis on presentation. With that, a cooking sensation was discovered and Stadtländer proceeded to open (and close) his own eponymous restaurant in Toronto, Stadtländer's, followed by a stint at the elegant Sooke Harbour House on Vancouver Island. It was there that the idea of operating a farm and restaurant of his own that featured dishes from the farm's produce was hatched.

In July 1993, Michael and Nobuyo got wind that a farm next door to a friend's place, near Ontario's Georgian Bay, was going up for sale. It was a chance that the Stadtländers found irresistible. They bought the land, returned to Ontario, and named the hundred-acre plot Eigensinn Farm (named after the title of an essay by poet and novelist Hermann Hesse; the German term translates to "single-mindedness" or "obstinacy").

"Obstinacy," says Franny, looking out the car's side window with an enormous grin on her face. "That sounds like a perfect nickname for you: Mr. Eigensinn!"

I just keep driving and act like I haven't heard anything. Sometimes my main job is just to keep Franny amused.

Right from the start, the chef's thoughtful, imaginative dinners drew food fanatics from around the world. A typical menu, all from his farm or locally sourced, offered foie gras, pigeon, rack of venison, and his own farm vegetables and fruits.

In 2002, *Restaurant* magazine in the UK named Eigensinn Farm one of the top 10 restaurants in the world.

Since then, the Stadtländers' farmhouse and restaurant have experienced a number of transformations. One iteration had guests taking their meals in the fields of the farm, each course in a different field. But one aspect never changes: The lunches and dinners exemplify Stadtländer's farm-to-table philosophy. The chef and his kitchen staff prepare multicourse meals with ingredients from the farm that they grow or raise themselves or source from nearby farmers.

As we pass by herds of dairy cows grazing in grassy fields, I tell Franny that I also admire Stadtländer for his advocacy work. He has a reputation for being outspoken about protecting the environment and advocating for sustainable, organic agriculture in Canada.

Probably his best-known protest was in October 2011, when he put on Foodstock, a "culinary protest." Pay-what-you-can ticket sales raised money to fight a proposal to transform arable farmland into a limestone quarry near the town of Honeywood, Ontario. A hundred of the country's top chefs sold amazing food that they cooked on open fires all over the fields, beloved musicians sang and played together for the crowds, and food experts gave lectures on cooking local, organic farming, and foraging in the wild.

A culinary protest. What an outrageous idea. Magnificent food, music, and supporting a good environmental cause too? Quick, where do I sign up?

After a pleasant two-hour drive on country roads, the pop FM station fades away from our car radio, proof that we have escaped the city. I spy a small hand-painted sign that reads "Eigensinn Farm," with a red arrow directing me to turn into a narrow gravel driveway bordered with wildflowers and tangled trees. As I pull in, I get a glimpse of a large, majestic barn to the left, a homey-looking wood-sided farmhouse next to it.

A few vehicles are already parked in a clearing at the end of the drive, so I steer that way. But to my surprise, from between the cars, out pops a woman who waves me toward an open parking spot.

"Ota-san!" she chirps. "Welcome to Eigensinn Farm! So nice to meet you. Park over here."

This must be Nobuyo Stadtländer, the spouse of the chef. She is a smiling bundle of energy. Buoyant, with long dark hair under a sun hat, she shakes my hand with affection through the car window. I introduce her to Fran and then Nobuyo is off, finding a parking spot for the next driver who pulls into the farm.

I am glad to have made it to the farm safe and sound. I open the car door and plant my feet on the ground to take a relaxing stretch. Suddenly, I am almost run over by a herd of small brown piglets scurrying around at my feet. Adorable, compact cylinders with stubby legs, they brush by my legs, then turn around to inspect me, giving me a once-over. And then, together, they turn back around and run down the parking lot lane, wagging their behinds, tails flagging in the air.

It's the first time in my life that I've been welcomed by a drove of pigs.

As they toddle off, Nobuyo hurries back to me and points to a gravel road rising up a low hill through the trees.

"Ota-san, the dining area is up that road," she directs me. "It is about a ten-minute walk. I'll see you there a little later."

Walk? Nobody told me this luxurious meal would involve a journey on foot up a gravel road.

In the city, I don't like to walk. I drive. My wife, on the other hand, her whole life revolves around getting her ten thousand steps in every day.

But the two-hour drive has left me starving and parched, in need of nourishment and a drink. So, reluctantly, I set out along the gravel road up the hill. After all, food is a great motivator.

Along the way, chickens, ducks, geese, and even peacocks (they don't eat the peacocks) roam free, following us wherever we go. And here come those pigs again.

As we head up the rugged road to the dining area, I quickly realize that this is not going to be an easy stroll. It is definitely not a pristine, interlocking brick paver path that you might find in the suburbs. The winding trail ahead rises and falls with sections of loose stones and grasses.

Within minutes, my feet hurt. Now, I realize it is probably not a good idea to wear tight, patent leather Oxford dress loafers to a farm—along with my designer jean jacket—but I thought I might meet some famous people at this meal. I always want to make a good first impression. At least, that's what I do in the city.

But now I am sure that I have pig manure on my loafers.

Stumbling around over gravel and stones, I fret that if I trip and twist my ankle, I will not get to meet Chef Michael Stadtländer or have his fabulous farm-to-table eating experience. I look around me. I don't think an ambulance could make it up this uneven road. I ask Franny, "Do ambulances even come to farms?"

My lovely wife just ignores my whining and breezes forward. "Hurry up," she says, looking back over her shoulder.

As we continue the hike, my legs begin to gain momentum. I am inspired by the bucolic beauty of the rolling hills that continue into the horizon, sprawling fields of spring grasses blowing lazily in the breeze, and noble structures of gray weathered wood and stone that appear like soft, flowing watercolor paintings.

But the visual elements that really take my mind off my cranky feet are the eccentric folk art sculptures that dot the landscape. I read that Stadtländer is also an artist who designs lively installations on his farm. I pass by a statue of a pig that doubles as a grill, a massive Mother Earth oven that gives birth to bread between her legs, and a giant Bacchus figure that pours wine, made from cement and wine bottles. I can see that they are lively works of art, integrating Stadtländer's passions of art, cooking, and regenerative agriculture.

I am beginning to fall in love with this place—even if my feet are killing me.

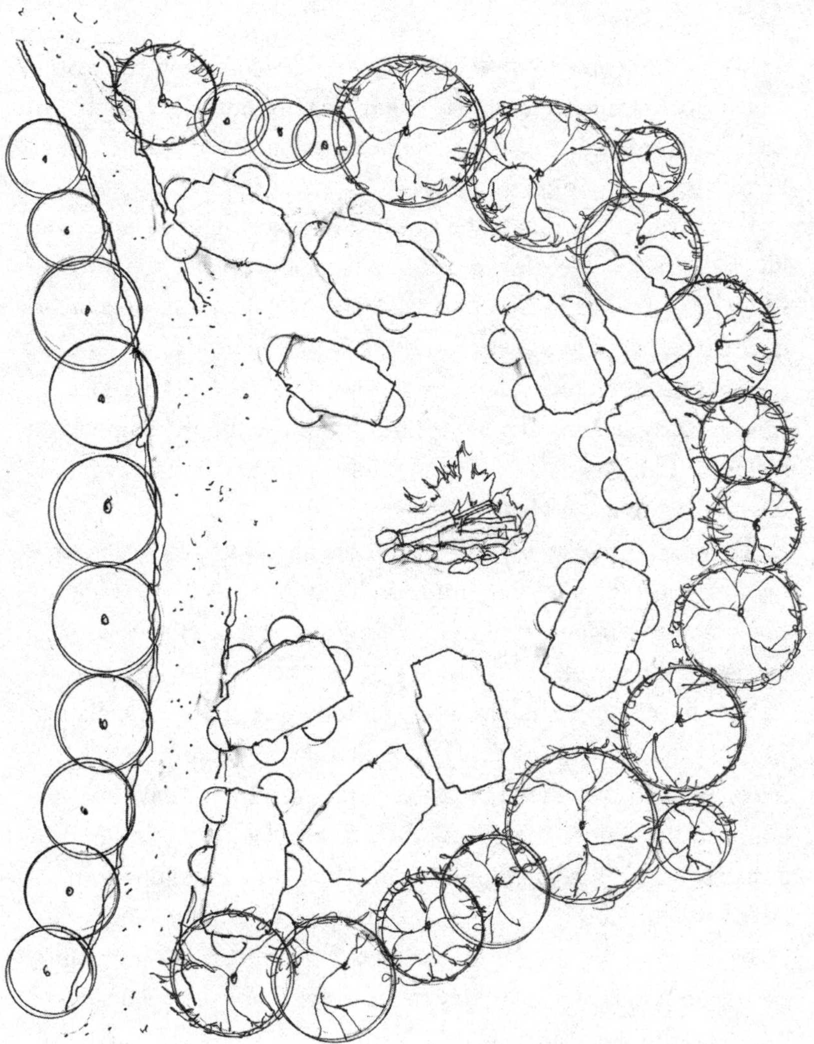

Eigensinn Farm dining room

After ten minutes of determined walking (for Fran, easy walking), we follow the dip in the road and enter a lush emerald-green forest with sunlight filtering through the tree leaves.

And before I even see it, I smell it: smoke.

The sensation of soot in the air sends me a signal that this meal involves open-fire cooking. I get the feeling that I should not expect nouvelle cuisine.

My patent leather loafers slide down a slight slope in the road, and at the bottom, a clearing in the trees pops out of nowhere. As though emerging from a dream, we have arrived at the Stadtländer forest dining room.

Looking over the dining scene, I take in a rounded clearing, about fifty feet in diameter, surrounded by tall-standing maple sugar trees, white pines, and endless wilderness. The forest floor is covered in an emerald carpet of ferns, leek, burdock, and fiddleheads.

The central feature is a roaring firepit that spits and crackles spectacularly. The focal point of the outdoor room, the flame roars as wisps of black smoke rise from the fire and find their way into my eyes, nostrils, and hair.

At first, the smoke is a bother. But the aroma and irritation to my eyes sets off something primal in my mind. It is like a wake-up call from the culinary gods to forget my standoffish city ways and engage in the forest.

Next to the fire are tables set up for food preparation and plating.

And then, around the central firepit area, set among the trees and wild growth of the forest, is the furniture. These are not precious, hand-carved mahogany pieces one might find in a traditional Edwardian dining room. These forest dining room tables are chiseled from unfinished, rugged slabs of ancient limestone from the shores of nearby Georgian Bay, and the dining chairs are rough-hewn, chunky tree stumps that have been sliced into shape with a chainsaw.

The entire design of the dining space is curvilinear—with uneven rocks and wood stumps, more randomly placed than planned. No electrical outlets are in sight. The kitchen helpers are even hauling tanks of water to the forest dining room with their own brute strength.

Architect Frank Lloyd Wright once wrote that *Nature* should always be spelled with a capital *N*, like *God* is always spelled with a capital *G*. He insisted that Nature was the best designer.

And here, unlike other dining rooms I have visited on my travels, Nature is certainly the designer, not a human being. Nature sets the message and the aesthetic.

At the central firepit stands Chef Michael Stadtländer. The first thing that strikes me is how impressive he appears. Towering above the kitchen staff, he seems to be at least six foot six. He has a shaved head and is dressed in a white, double-breasted chef's smock covered with a blue apron with white stipes. His athletic physique looks like he could be a starting tight end for an NFL team. Like the captain of a ship standing erect at the prow, he is preparing his mise en place, setting his workstation, checking ingredients, conferring with his cooking assistants, stoking the fire, and making sure all is ready.

Unlike other dining rooms I have visited on my travels, Nature is certainly the designer, not a human being.

I don't want to interrupt his cooking setup, but I cannot help but go up and introduce myself. He shakes my hand with a firm grip, gives me a big smile, and welcomes me to his farm. He is accessible and warm, humble and soft-spoken.

"We love to invite guests to our forest dining room," says the master chef. "Many of them have competitive and stressful jobs in the city. They tell us that being immersed in an atmosphere of nature is a peaceful, healing experience—especially in the spring, after enduring a long, hard winter."

We talk about how people around the world are engaging in an activity known as forest bathing: going somewhere in nature to slow down, smell the forest, feel the breeze, and let go of other thoughts. It's a therapeutic practice that can help reduce stress and improve mood.

"I am looking forward to all of this," I tell Chef Michael, "but the bonus is that I can soak in the relaxing attributes of the forest as well as enjoy your gourmet dishes."

Michael lets me know that he has titled the meal Leek Maple Waldhausen. He tells me that *Waldhausen* translates to "house in the woods"; it is made up of the German words *Wald*, meaning "forest," and *Haus*, or "house." This is the first hint I've had about the flavors to come; before we arrived at Eigensinn Farm, we weren't told anything about the menu, ingredients, or cooking approach. With the star ingredients coming out of the earth of his farm, there is a promise of some amazing food.

"Through food, you can actually taste the place where you are," Michael says, while looking across the forest landscape. "It's a beautiful thing if you can do that as a chef."

After a few minutes of pleasant conversation, I can detect that Chef Michael is preoccupied. He is very kind to chat with me, but my goodness—he is about to prepare a twelve-course meal for forty people over an open fire in the middle of the forest. When I excuse myself to let him get to work, he generously offers to chat with me again after the meal.

The afternoon is off to a great start. My sore feet are completely forgotten.

I turn to walk away, but before I do, I notice a sheet of paper hanging off a tree branch over the prep table. It is the menu for the day, in the chef's own handwriting:

Oyster on the half shell (from British Columbia, the only food item not locally sourced)
Pan-fried Effingham Inlet oyster with sautéed morels, wild leek, and maple syrup yuzu kosho butter
Cold-smoked Eigensinn Farm ham on sourdough bread with wild leek
Hot-smoked Lake Huron trout with wild leek and maple syrup yogurt, fennel, and bora nam radish
Soup from Jerusalem artichokes with green asparagus and wild leek
Head cheese roasted from suckling pig with fermented beets and wild leek
Stinging nettle dumpling with garden salad and wild leek and maple dressing
Ravioli of curried braised venison with sautéed saddleback mushroom and wild leek
Sorbet from sea buckthorn and wild apple cider and lemon balsamic
Wood oven–roasted Eigensinn suckling piglet, roasted blue potato gnocchi, wild leek, and Thunder Oak Gouda (I am especially looking forward to this, curious whether this meat from Stadtländer's sustainable farm will taste different from pork that I buy in my local supermarket)
Special forest cake
Chocolate wild ginger hazelnut maple-grappa truffle
Peanut butter miso wild cherry cookie

I look around and see that more guests are filtering into the forest dining area. They are couples or groups of friends, chatting, laughing, inspecting the fire, taking selfies with the famous chef, and uncorking bottles of wine that they have brought with them.

The Stadtländers' son, Hermann, is our maître d', guiding guests to their limestone tables. It is a festive atmosphere. I notice that no one else is wearing designer clothes or dress loafers.

I hear a sizzling from the fire and see that Michael has started cooking full-blast over the open fire. Beside him, Nobuyo is zipping around the cooking area, procuring ingredients, while kitchen staff collect wood to feed the fire.

Amidst the lively socializing, crackling central fire, and wispy embers floating above it, Franny and I find ourselves seats on wood stumps at a flat stone table—and none too soon. As soon as we are settled, friendly servers bring us silver knives, forks, and spoons wrapped in cloth napkins for the first course of the afternoon. Then we are off. Our star chef is working over the open fire, shaking his frying pan in that chef-style back-and-forth motion. With the pan's sizzling, fire flashing wildly from the open pit, and smoke rising above the dining area, I can hardly wait to taste what is coming out of his kitchen.

I don't have long to wait. After a welcome appetizer of oyster on the half shell that stimulates our taste buds for more, perched on top of a mound of green forest moss is a fat Effingham Inlet oyster pan-fried and accompanied by the luncheon's stars in their first appearance: maple and wild leek made into a decadent syrup. But wait, there's more. Crowning the oyster are four sautéed morels, like plump morsels of soft sponge. Soft to the bite, earthy, but not overpowering, the morels meld with the other ingredients so that I can taste the essence of the Eigensinn forest.

This creation sets the tone for all the following courses. Chef Stadtländer's mind has found curiously delicious ways to weave the maple and wild leek with other ingredients sourced from the farm.

Certain dishes shine a spotlight on each star ingredient. Arranged in a broad oyster shell, for instance, are cubes of head cheese with a mild pork meat taste and slight chew that is perfectly enhanced by fermented beets from the garden and sautéed wild leek. I mention to Franny that I could never imagine wild leeks adding so much spring freshness to the cuisine. "Can anything taste better than this?" I ask her.

As we spy wild leek plants growing around us, Franny observes that we are blessed to be attending this luncheon during wild leek season, a fleeting period between April and May. Wild leeks (also known as ramps) are considered one of nature's greatest gifts to foragers. They're really a type of wild onion with a unique garlicky flavor. Their popularity stems from this distinct pungent flavor, which cannot be found in commercial cultivation, and their rarity.

Historically, Indigenous Peoples and early pioneers would collect wild leeks in the forests after living through long, hungry winters. These leeks would have been the first vegetables they had eaten in months. Now, wild leeks are the darling of the gourmet world, with chefs sourcing them to inject a burst of springtime into their menus in pesto sauces, pickles, soups, pastas, and fish dishes.

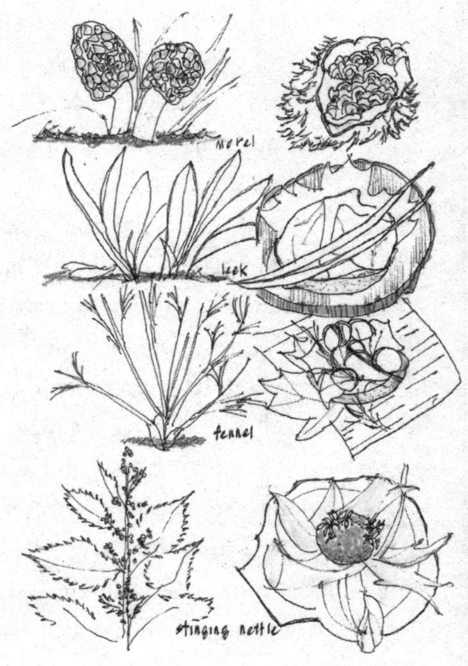

But for wild leeks, there's a downside to being popular. Overharvesting has become a threat to their future. The mantra of conservationists is: Just take the leaves, don't take the bulb. Wild leeks grow from both bulbs and seeds, and it takes about seven years for one wild leek seed to grow into a small shoot.

Springtime foragers often keep the locations of their favorite wild leek sites a secret. I decide that

I know nothing about the location of the Stadtländer wild leek patches. Nothing. I have not seen a thing. *Leeks? What are leeks?*

As for the menu's other feature ingredient, Franny and I welcome a delightful dark green dumpling made of stinging nettle, decorated with tiny nettle blossoms poking out the top of the ball. I place a morsel in my mouth; the nutritious herb has a peppery zing and tastes like wild spinach. Foraged from the Eigensinn meadows, the nettle is served on a bed of garden salad tossed with a dressing of wild leek and maple syrup, all arranged on a broad scallop shell. This is a dish where the sweetness of the maple syrup pulls all the forest flavors together.

I am a maple-holic. So at this meal, I am in my glory enjoying Eigensinn maple syrup. At home, I pour maple syrup over my salmon and my carrots, mix it into my yogurt and my coffee, and—ooh—there is nothing better than maple syrup pie.

In our modern age, many maple syrup processing plants are computerized, stainless-steel factories that resemble modern dairies. Industrial maple syrup manufacturing involves boiling maple sap in evaporators at high temperatures to concentrate the sugar to create a thick syrup. Bottling or canning is done on mechanized assembly lines.

In contrast, the Stadtländers take a simpler approach to making maple syrup. The harvest has also become a seasonal ritual.

"For us, it's what indicates the arrival of spring," Nobuyo explains, joining our table for a quick chat between meal errands. "Cooking down our maple syrup in the woods, usually over an open fire of pine wood—which gives it a nice smoky flavor—is part of our celebration."

And, despite how abundant maple syrup was on this afternoon's menu, Nobuyo tells me that they only tap about a dozen trees, even though they have a whole forest to draw from. To me, there seems to be something so right about only taking what you need from nature, without disturbing hundreds of trees.

"We use maple syrup like the Italians use olive oil," she says. "It's such a wonderful Canadian thing." Recalling all the maple dressings, maple yogurt, and maple butter I've just devoured, I heartily agree.

Nobuyo was born in Okinawa, Japan, and she tells me that she runs the operational side of the business. Having observed her keen expertise in greeting guests, catering to their every need, making sure the chef has everything he requires, and her overall appealing manner, I can see that Nobuyo is happily in charge at Eigensinn. And I know, from the way the husband and wife work together, that Michael is an appreciative fan of his wife. The farm's website even describes her as "the engine room behind the artist. Without Nobuyo, nothing happens."

In this dining room, conventional dishware is nowhere to be seen. My ham and sourdough delicacy, for instance, is presented on a rounded plank of natural cross-cut maple wood edged with bark from the forest—the same wood that was used to smoke the meat. There is even plateware that is made by Michael: Emerald jewels of ravioli topped with twirling fiddleheads are presented in a wavy, circular ceramic dish designed and handmade by the chef.

And to my delight, the climax of the meal has a special plate of its own: a handmade ceramic platter shaped like a piglet. The pork's crispy skin crunches like a potato chip, then there's an accent of creamy belly fat. This pork is indeed far superior in flavor, texture, and juiciness to anything we could purchase in the city.

As I savor the intense taste, I am mindful that this meat comes from animals on this farm. I have always loved eating meat, but I have become increasingly aware of animal rights and the ethics of the industrial processing of animals as food (I have a flashback to the calf head making mock turtle soup). My culinary conscience is eased by the knowledge that at Eigensinn, the animals are grass-fed, free-range in large fields, and raised in optimum conditions on diets consistent with their natural feeding patterns. This is yet another pro for the farm-to-table approach.

All around Eigensinn, industrial farming is changing the agricultural landscape. International corporations have bought up farms with the goal of ramping up intensive farming of animals and crops to maximize profits for their shareholders. For much of human history, agriculture relied on many small farms to produce a wide variety of foods. But today, small independent and family-run farms use less than 10 percent of all agricultural land.

Michael believes this movement toward big farming has led to a number of ominous effects on the land.

Chef Michael Stadtländer's Top 4 Reasons to Farm Organic:

Reason #1: To mitigate the wider use of pesticides to contain weeds, kill insects, and stave off fungi. "While these chemicals kill pests, they can also lead to adverse health effects for humans, including cancer. At Eigensinn, we do all the weeding of our fields by hand and on our knees with no chemicals."

Reason #2: Large-scale agriculture plays a major role in pollution. "These large industrial farms release manure, chemicals, antibiotics, and growth hormones into water sources—that poses risks to ecosystems and human health. We are risking our health for profits."

Reason #3: To counter exploitation and abuse of animals for mass production of food. "I am a supporter of high standards for animal welfare. We raise pigs, chickens, ducks, and rabbits. They have all been pasture-raised in the spring and summer, as well as with organic grain. In the winter, we have a large barn and open stalls with lots of space. Our Texas Red Wattle pigs have ten acres of field to roam; the ducks have their own pond.

We do everything we can to make the lives of our animals to be as super happy as possible while they are on our farm."

Reason #4: To support the family farm. All of Stadtländer's reasons for farming organically are in response to increased challenges that family farms have been facing: greater financial constraints, climate change, and competition from large corporate farms. Family farms are important because they play a critical role in providing jobs and income for local communities. They are often managed by multiple generations of a family, who can have a strong connection to the land and a commitment to sustainable farming practices.

Farming, let alone doing so responsibly, is not an easy job, nor is it cheap. What led Michael to this, when he could easily compromise his beliefs to be a star chef in the city?

"Our life on the farm inspires me to do the forest dining. I believe that the quality of the food you cook with should be under your total control," he later tells me. "Our greatest joy is growing the vegetables the way we like to see them: fully ripe, fully grown. Our pigs take fourteen months, not six, to grow. Our fowl are free-range; they take a half a year to maturity. All our grain is certified organic."

Michael and Noboyu grow more than one hundred kinds of vegetables and herbs on the farm, as well as raising pigs, chickens, geese, ducks, and rabbits—all organically. Ninety percent of the food on our plate today, I'm told, was grown at Eigensinn Farm or from selected farms that are also organic.

Michael emphasizes the importance of building relationships with local farmers and producers to inspire menus. "It's not that you just get this beautiful product from local farms," he says with conviction, "but you are keeping these small family farms in business." The small farms help the economy and add choice for consumers. His viewpoint is that, like Franny and me, more people want to know about the food they're eating: where it comes from, how it was grown, and if it has been affected by chemicals.

His farm restaurant customers seem to agree with him. As was the case for today's culinary feast, the Stadtländers sell out their meals; guests make reservations months in advance and pay a few hundred dollars each. My recommendation: It's worth it.

Taking a breather from the stream of Leek Maple Waldhausen courses, I realize that my appetite has become voracious and I am tasting each morsel of food with unprecedented delight. I wonder to myself, *Is it the fresh air? Is it the bewitching natural surroundings?* I surmise it is both these factors—but then it hits me. As I entered this magnificent forest dining room, I left any concerns back in the city. Tucked away in this wooded paradise, I am able to focus on the people around me, my hosts, my wife, and taste the delectable food without distraction.

"The cuisine is sensational!" I tell Nobuyo during one of her tableside visits. "I love that the same morels and leeks that we're eating are growing all around us!" I point to the forest. "It's almost like Michael can walk outside of the dining area to the forest floor, bend down, and pick more wild leeks out of the ground if he wishes."

Nobuyo reacts with an appreciative laugh and shares with me that at Eigensinn Farm, it is the seasons that dictate what is available.

"In our forest we find wild leeks, morels, saddleback mushrooms, dandelions, Queen Anne's lace, milkweed, burdock, daisies, chokecherries, spruce, pine, and hawthorn shoots, slippery jack, trout lilies, watercress, angel wings, cedar, wild blackberries, strawberries, and much more," she says. "For us, foraging is a science." And she is proud to tell me that they don't use GMOs (genetically modified organisms) at Eigensinn to increase yields. Everything they need is around them.

"One of the nicest things for us is to combine the gardens and the fish from Lake Huron, making our own maple syrup, and foraging in spring for dandelion, watercress, and collecting spruce shoot honey from our own bees."

She tells us that they have four beehives that produce enough honey for their seasonal kitchen needs. Beyond that, and perhaps even more important, she adds, "They pollinate." This allows plants to produce seeds in a natural way, making for sustainable crop yields. "Our lands are rich and green and full of wildflowers."

The sign that the meal has come to a close is Michael removing his blue apron and setting down his tongs. It's like a conductor putting down his baton at the end of a symphony.

I cannot eat another thing. (Did I say that already?)

Amazingly, Chef Michael has cooked, sautéed, and grilled the entire meal standing up, working over the flaming open fire, all the while remaining as cool as a cucumber, smiling, moving easily between fire and prep table, advising his kitchen staff, and appearing to enjoy the entire event.

The chef's performance makes me realize that the forest dining room is the ultimate open-air, open-concept dining room/kitchen. While for hundreds of years the kitchen was purposely hidden and isolated from the dining room, today the combined dining room and kitchen are integral to the dining experience. Smelling the aromas, seeing the flames leaping up from the grill, watching the cuts of meat being chopped, grilling the vegetables, hearing the tinkling of kitchen implements, and watching the actions of the chef are now features of the dining area. The messiness of dirty dishes, pots, and pans is less of a concern; diners want to be part of the action and see how their food is made.

Finally, Michael leaves the fire and makes the rounds of all the dining tables, chatting with guests, shaking hands, and posing for more selfies. We are all thrilled to spend a few minutes with him. When he comes over to our table, I give him a big hug (comically,

I only come up to his navel) and tell him that this was one of the best meals of my life.

As the chef continues to circulate and guests mingle between tables, I consider the fact that this meal was a lunch, not a dinner. While both involve a meal, I've gleaned that there seems to be a key difference in tone: Lunch, being in the middle of the day, can feel more relaxed, whereas gathering for dinner in the evening is generally considered a more formal occasion. Perhaps since many people work during the day, there isn't the same luxury of unlimited time for long, formal discussions associated with lunch—lunch comes with a shorter subconscious time limit. It seems to me that every detail goes this way: the table settings, conversations, dress codes. All of this makes me wonder if Franny's birthday celebration should be a lunch, not a dinner. I will have to ask her.

Unfortunately, the central fire quietly turns to gray ash and we collectively sense that the afternoon is coming to an end. It's time to go, but it's not easy to leave this magical place. Michael makes it easier for his guests by offering special cookies as a parting gift: a peanut butter miso wild cherry cookie, with a hole at the top so that they can be artfully offered to guests hanging on a twig from the forest. Peanut butter is my favorite kind of cookie, but I have never had one made with miso and wild cherries. I take a bite . . . crispy at the edges, chewy on the inside, a decadent melding of flavors: sweet, salty, umami, nutty—the astonishing cookie tastes divine.

There are hugs and handshakes all around the dining room, and commitments to attend the next forest dining event. We thank Chef Michael, Nobuyo, Hermann, and all the helpers for their incredible hospitality.

Michael puts his arm around me, and we look across the scene of his forest dining room full of people in the pleasure of each other's company who have just enjoyed a great meal.

"Exquisite dining rooms are the churches of our time," he tells me. "And the great chefs are like the priests."

We started off strangers with our fellow diners, but, isolated in the middle of this woodland and sitting on informal furniture, there has been an egalitarian effect, bringing everyone to the same level. Reflecting upon the afternoon's relaxed socializing, I realize that the forest dining room has taught me a major attribute of informal outdoor dining: It is more amenable to guests moving around to different chairs, and even neighboring tables, to introduce themselves and have spontaneous conversations. I find that when eating indoors at a formal dining table, there is an unwritten protocol to stay in your seat for the whole evening. The unfortunate outcome of this is that you miss talking directly to some guests at the other end of the table. At Franny's dinner, I will remember to remind guests that they are welcome to move around (maybe best during and after the dessert course) and they should not feel obligated to stay in one seat for the entire meal.

Reluctantly, Fran and I begin our hike back to the car. All dining rooms, I reflect, send a message from the hosts.

At Highclere Castle, the portraits of royalty and elaborate woodwork were intended to convey the owner's wealth and power. The jubilation of the color yellow in Claude Monet's dining room reflected his interest in uplifting the emotions of art audiences. The lively ceramics in Greg and Garth's contemporary dining room communicate their love of travel and Saskatchewan artists.

For the Stadtländers, the forest dining room surroundings exude the family's strong ties to the land and how inventive food is part of what makes Chef Michael an appealing chef. Their surrounding sugar maples, open fire, and natural ingredients are the stanchions of his belief in local farming and fine food.

I confess: For this culinary event, I was expecting something more manicured. But now that I've been here, I know that having a meal in the forest dining room has been one of the top 10 experiences of my life. By coaxing me to walk into the woods, the Stadtländers invited me to slow down, leave the city behind, and return to the land. Basic, unpretentious, the forest was the perfect setting.

Hospitality? Big checkmark. The Stadtländers made every person feel special. With all their expertise and top-notch ingredients, they could easily be food snobs, but they are not. They engage in easy conversation, make people feel welcome, introduce themselves, and chat with guests before and after the meal. These are habits that I must remember for Franny's dinner in my own dining room.

Compared to the walk in, the trip back out along the road is much more enjoyable. I don't even feel my feet or worry about my loafers. After this magnificent culinary party, Franny and I are completely rejuvenated.

When we make it back to our car, the little brown pigs have returned. They are so small, I have to be careful not to step on them. Together, they turn to me as if to say goodbye. And then, still as a choregraphed group, they turn around and trundle off down the path back into the farm, moving like the Keystone Cops in a slapstick film.

What a send-off.

Eigensinn Farm

449357 10th Concession, Singhampton, Ontario, Canada

stadtlanderseigensinnfarm.com/ | (519) 922-3128

Dear Franny,

I am so glad that we could visit Chef Michael and Nobuyo Stadtländer's farm together. Here are some thoughts that we can adopt for our home dining room:

Dishes don't have to be dishes. They can be whimsical! At Eigensinn Farm, the food was served on a seashell or a sheet of birchbark. We can have fun with the presentation, like their morels sitting on a bed of forest moss. I especially liked the smoked trout on a cross-cut of wood and bark from the forest.

Furniture doesn't have to match. We sat on wood stumps that came from the forest, which was perfect. Today, the interior design trend is to seat guests on dining room chairs that are mismatched to add an air of informality and fun. We could use our existing Parsons chairs and then find a couple of Eigensinnesque natural wood chairs for each end of our dining table.

Your birthday dinner could be made with a variety of sustainable and organic foods. And I could include some of the foraged herbs that we sampled at the farm. I feel like I've only barely been introduced to Eigensinn Foraging 101.

We thanked the Stadtländers for this sensational meal, but maybe the greatest thank-you would be to join them in their cause. That sounds like a win-win to me. Good environment, good eating.

The chef's peanut butter wild cherry miso cookies were astonishing. I think they'd be a big hit at your birthday dinner.

Thanks for coming with me. Don't worry—we can diet later.

XOXO

J.

EPILOGUE

Dear John,

Thank you so much for your kind thoughts—for my birthday dinner, the dining room ideas, and the book. You have really gone all out for me.

Of course, you know that we cannot incorporate all these ideas into our dining area. Our dining area is only about seventeen by twelve feet. We don't live in the White House like Jackie Kennedy!

I've always liked yellow on the walls, and your examples of brilliant yellow and gold in the dining rooms of Claude Monet, Frida Kahlo, and Downton Abbey sound wonderful. I also like the idea of an informal dining room—things like mismatched furniture, silverware, and dishware like we saw at Garth and Greg's dining room to put guests at ease. I'm looking forward to seeing what you finally decide for our dining room.

Your menu ideas for my birthday dinner sound exceptional. But as you know, I love hors d'oeuvre parties: They allow everyone to circulate and give people a chance to pick and choose what they want to eat. Maybe we can look into some of those Frank Sinatra finger foods like stuffed mushrooms, porcupine meatballs, and bacon-wrapped scallops. And those Michael Stadtländer miso peanut butter cookies would be a perfect way to say goodnight.

Oh, and I really like the idea of the beverage station—maybe near the front of the dining room. You wrote that Martha Washington and Edith Wharton greeted their guests with refreshments at the front door. I can just picture you at your own soda fountain—you might want to stand there all evening to serve our guests.

I know we're going to love our dining room and our party. And I'm dying to try out the Franny Hot Fudge Sundae that you're naming after me! Just a friendly reminder, please: lots of whipped cream on top.

XOXO

Franny

P.S. I'm glad that you're being open with people about hearing voices in houses. But as your loving wife, I am telling you, it might just be that you're the only one who hears them.

POSTSCRIPT

I DID IT.

I threw the birthday dinner for Franny with food from all the places I visited, and we shared it with our friends and family in a rejuvenated dining room. Tonight we ate, drank, and laughed, and best of all, we honored my wife with stories and toasts celebrating her past and her future.

It was especially important to Franny that she could thank everyone who helped us during her stroke and recovery. Our friends and family cooked, cleaned, and gave us medical advice and moral support through the entire ordeal. I know that everyone was thrilled that she was in good health tonight. I was too.

Franny told me she had a wonderful time, enjoying the heartfelt toasts and lively conversation in our updated dining room. It was an evening of uninhibited eating and good cheer. But right now, it's way past one in the morning and Franny has just gone upstairs to bed. I'll join her in a few minutes.

The table is still covered in dessert dishes, empty wineglasses, and rumpled napkins—the aftermath of a lovely dinner. Never mind, I can clean up in the morning. I am happy that my journey to give her a birthday dinner has come to a happy conclusion.

As a nightcap, I pour myself a a cup of warm sake to take me back to the euphoric feelings from the Nomura Samurai House experience. Each sip stirs a new memory from the evening.

Sip #1 (leaning back)

I take a big sip and take in some of the design changes I made to our dining room. Originally, I wanted to have it all—the elegance of Jacqueline Kennedy's gold chairs, the light airiness of Edith Wharton's dining room, the quiet dignity around Martin Luther King Jr.'s family table, the connection to the outdoors of Sinatra's Palm Springs house, and the subdued purity of the Nomura Samurai House in Japan.

But even though I loved all these features from my travels, I couldn't do it all. I had to edit it down. To help me make decisions, I turned to my three guidelines.

Make it a center of hospitality: To practice unconditional hospitality, we had multiple choices of dishes, with the whole meal lasting over seven hours.

I took a design cue from Greg and Garth's house: I moved our dining area to the rear of the house so that it could overlook the garden. There's something so philosophically *right* about having the dining area looking out to nature. I also wanted the dining room to be filled with bright yellow sunlight, in the spirit of Claude Monet.

But not everything went the way I envisioned it. I originally had pictured a sit-down dinner for ten guests, where I could present each course in the style of *service à la russe*. But Franny had her own ideas for her birthday.

"After all, John, it is my party," she said, with a smile.

What could I say? My Downton Abbey dreams of a multi-course meal at a long table would have to wait for another day.

And so we served the food buffet style. The message: Please help yourself. Vegans, vegetarians, gluten-free diners, and meat eaters could choose the foods that they wanted and the portion size. With people being more health-conscious and desiring more food options, I think buffet is the way of the future. We wanted the dining room to be a center of hospitality to all our guests, regardless of their food preferences.

Then, in the spirit of George and Martha Washington, whole families were invited, including children. We wanted to be inclusive. Unlike Edwardian society, we didn't think the kids would hinder the flow of conversation (in fact, they were fabulous).

Be a place to slow down: I learned at the samurai house that slowing down for dinner begins even before guests enter the house. Tonight, I hung a colorful Japanese noren curtain (my at-home traditional curtain of welcome) and a wind chime over our front door to set a welcoming atmosphere. I wanted guests approaching the house to feel good about coming to dinner.

Throughout the house I lit candles to set a festive ambience. I learned that the warm light in Edith Wharton's house and the Highclere Castle dining room enhanced a tone of relaxation and allowed a sense of escape from the commotion of everyday life. Like Garth and Greg, we played music from the sound system throughout the night.

In the vein of Martha Washington and Edith Wharton's hospitality, I greeted each guest with a drink of their choice as soon as they stepped in the front door. In addition, I set up a soda station with drinks, glasses, and ice right next to the front vestibule.

All evening, I circulated to respond to any needs of our guests.

Rejuvenate traditional ideas about the dining room: In almost all the dining rooms I visited, color and light brought the space to life, especially the bright yellow walls of Claude Monet's and Frida Kahlo's dining rooms. I also remembered the way candlelight flickered off the buffet mirror and gave a magical sparkle around Lucy Maud Montgomery's table.

But the biggest statement about light and color for me came from the gold upholstered fabric walls in the dining room at Highclere Castle. If there was anywhere that best used a strategy to reflect candlelight and the warm color off the plates, silverware, and faces of the diners, picking up the low light and making the walls shimmer, it was at Highclere Castle.

Unfortunately, the cost of wrapping our walls in gold Downton-style upholstery was out of reach for me. I didn't know what to do—and then one day, it came to me. Over the years, I had seen a stunning antique gold screen that was used as a backdrop for traditional dance performances and ceremonies at the Japanese Canadian Cultural Centre in Toronto. The cost of a gold leaf screen was astronomical, but then I had an idea.

I ordered a blank, seven-foot-high canvas screen and had it upholstered in shiny gold fabric.

Voilà! This gold screen backdrop now sits proudly in our dining room and, along with our candelabra that I spray-painted gold, it all worked to further catch the candlelight tonight.

And I'm still having fun looking for a traditional wine cooler caddy. They're not easy to find.

Sip #2 (ahhh):

Here was the menu:

Corn tortilla chips with a black bean mole dip (inspired by the Frida Kahlo birthday dining room)
Assorted sushi appetizers (Franny is, of course, a big sushi fan, and this samurai tatami room dish was devoured by vegetarians, vegans, gluten-free, and omnivore diners)
Stuffed mushrooms (the Frank Sinatra Twin Palms patio–era mushrooms had us eating mid-century modern)
Bellevue salad (inspired by the elegant Jackie Kennedy state dinner for André Malraux)
Salmon rémoulade skewers (Franny loves salmon, and this dish would have pleased George and Martha Washington)
Southern fried tofu with candied sweet potato (an example of the new vegan Southern cooking inspired by the Martin Luther King Jr. dinner)
Beef tenderloin skewers (to echo Edith Wharton's roast beef dinner; Franny likes it with creamed horseradish)
Saskatchewan mustard potato salad (a taste of the prairies from the Greg and Garth dinner)

Saskatoon berry crisp with ice cream (another prairies request from Franny, the highlight of the night)
Wild cherry miso peanut butter cookies (the must-have from Chef Stadtländer's forest dining room)

And for drinks we had a range of nonalcoholic potables (sparkling water, soft drinks, and Martha Washington lemonade) at the beverage station. But we also had some specialty alcoholic drinks, reminiscent of some of the famous dining rooms on my travels. We offered sake to accompany the sushi platter, as a memory from the samurai house tatami room; Claude Monet would have enjoyed some of the French wines on offer; there was champagne and nonalcoholic bubbly for the toast, à la Jacqueline Kennedy's White House dining room.

Sip #3 (darn, this is good):

We turned up the volume on the sound system and sang along to a booming rendition of the Mexican folk song "La Bamba" in honor of Frida Kahlo's heritage.

Baamba, Bamba! Baamba, Bamba! . . .

As we demolished our mole corn tortilla chips and drinks, we sang so loudly, I thought they'd be able to hear us in Mexico City. At first, I was concerned that things were getting a little too raucous. I thought the neighbors might call the police.

"Don't worry, John," shouted my neighbor Dave over the music. "All the neighbors are here."

Sip #4 (a gulp):

Did I ever find the perfect dining room for Franny? Well, that depends on a person's perspective.

Martin Luther King Jr.'s family dinners and dining room were perfect to set the scene for the family's open political discussions. But they would not have been the menu or space for Claude

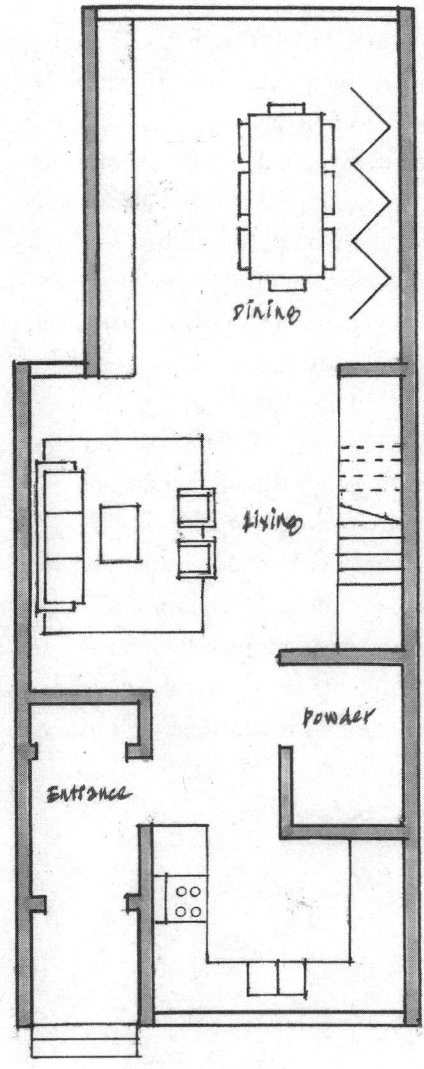

Rowe-Ota house

Monet, who adored the color yellow, or for artist Frida Kahlo, who wanted to promote Mexican nationalism.

But what I did learn along the way was that it's not about serving the perfect dish or sitting in the perfect chair or wearing the perfect clothes.

As Franny said tonight, "It's really about gathering. I loved being together with our friends, sitting around the house and enjoying each other's company."

From my perspective, the ingredients for a perfect night are hospitality, generosity, and a comfortable atmosphere. With all of these things, people open up, reveal themselves, and exchange ideas, bonds are formed, and relationships are reaffirmed.

And dinner can change history. The ritual of dining together has affected where we are today.

Tonight was a great way to celebrate Franny's recovery. We never know what the future will bring. So that's an outstanding reason to party with wonderful food and friends in a special place. All out. Like Frida Kahlo—no inhibition.

I had a great time traveling and writing this book. It has been a thrill to share the incredible tastes, aromas, and dining rooms with you. But what I enjoyed most were the people I met, cooked with, and ate with. Any differences there might have been disappeared in the joy and companionship of the dining room.

Dinner brings us together.

RECIPES

THE FOLLOWING RECIPES ARE GIVEN in formats close to their original, edited minorly for clarity. I hope you agree that the different styles and formats give a small insight into the personality of the author, the type of dining room where they served, and their historical period, in a reflection of the evolution of recipe writing and the dining experience.

Chapter 1: MORRIS-JUMEL MANSION

Cherry Pie

Makes one 10-inch double-crust pie

1 recipe Common Pie Crust (see page 315)
1 cup red currant jam
5 cups fresh sour cherries, preferably Morello, pitted, or 3 jars (1 lb., 9 oz. each) preserved Morello cherries, drained with about ¼ cup of juice reserved
About 1 cup sugar, plus more for sprinkling over crust (optional)
¼ tsp salt
4 Tbsp arrowroot
1 Tbsp butter, chilled and diced

1. Preheat the oven to 400°F.
2. On a lightly floured surface, roll the pie-crust dough into a circle about ¼-inch thick and place in a lightly greased pie pan, gently pressing it into the pan. Set aside in the refrigerator.
3. Heat the red currant jam, stirring until it begins to soften, about 2 minutes. Stir into the cherries, mixing together well. Combine the sugar and salt, and stir into the cherry and jam mixture to dissolve. Taste the mixture, and add more sugar if it seems too tart.
4. Combine the arrowroot with half of the reserved juice, and then blend in the remainder. Add to the cherries, and mix until well combined.
5. Pour the cherries into the prepared pie shell. Dot the butter over the filling. Place the top crust over the filling, folding

the bottom edges up over the top piece of dough and then pinching together to seal. If desired, sprinkle additional sugar over the top.

6. Bake for 20 minutes. Then reduce the temperature to 375°F, and bake for another 25 to 30 minutes, or until the filling is bubbly and the crust is golden brown.
7. Remove from the oven, and set on a rack to cool thoroughly before slicing. The juices will thicken as the pie cools.

(John Ota notes: Both fresh and jarred cherries work well here; if using fresh, set the pitted cherries aside for at least 2 hours so they release their juice.)

Common Pie Crust

Makes enough for one double-crust 9- or 10-inch pie

2½ cups all-purpose flour
1 tsp salt
½ cup (1 stick) unsalted butter, chilled and cut into pea-size pieces
¼ cup lard or vegetable shortening, chilled
5 to 6 Tbsp ice water

1. Sift the flour and salt together.
2. With a pastry blender or by hand, work the butter and lard into the flour until the mixture is well combined and resembles coarse breadcrumbs.
3. Blend in about 5 Tbsp of the water, mixing until the dough comes together. Add up to 1 more Tbsp of water, if needed.

4. Divide the dough in half, and shape into disks. Wrap individually in waxed paper, and refrigerate for at least 2 and up to 24 hours. Wrapped disks can be sealed in a plastic bag and frozen for later use.

Source: Nancy Carter Crump, adapted from Hannah Glasse's recipe in *Dining with the Washingtons: Historic Recipes, Entertaining, and Hospitality from Mount Vernon*, edited by Stephen A. McLeod (Mount Vernon Ladies' Association, 2011). Thanks to the Mount Vernon Ladies' Association, culinary historian Nancy Carter Crump, Mary V. Thompson, and Julie Coleman Almacy of Mount Vernon.

Chapter 2: SAMURAI HOUSE

Broiled Black Cod

Serves 4

Marinade

2 Tbsp (30 mL) shoyu (soy sauce)
1½ tsp (7.5 mL) sugar
2 Tbsp (30 mL) mirin
1½ tsp (7.5 mL) fresh shoga (ginger), grated

4 small cod fillets
Grated daikon (long white radish) for garnish (optional)

1. In a bowl, mix together the marinade ingredients until sugar dissolves. Pour the marinade over the cod fillets and refrigerate for at least 40 minutes to give time to absorb flavor.
2. Meanwhile, soak bamboo skewers for at least 30 minutes (or overnight) to avoid them burning during cooking. Thread the marinated cod on the skewers. Broil or barbecue the cod, skin side first, basting often while broiling. When the cod is just over halfway cooked, about 2–3 minutes, flip over.
3. Serve with grated daikon as garnish.

Source: John Ota, adapted from Broiled Fish recipe in *Just Add Shoyu*, Japanese Canadian Cultural Centre, Toronto.

Chapter 3: THE MOUNT

Mock Turtle Soup, of Calf's Head

Scald a well-cleansed calf's head, remove the brain, tie it up in a cloth, and broil an hour, or until the meat will easily slip from the bone; take out, save the broth; cut it in small square pieces, and throw them into cold water; when cool, put it in a stewpan, and cover with some of the broth; let it boil until quite tender, and set aside.

In another stewpan melt some butter, and in it put a quarter of a pound of lean ham, cut small, with fine herbs to taste; also parsley and one onion; add about a pint of broth; let simmer for two hours, and then dredge in a small quantity of flour; now add the remainder of the broth, and a quarter bottle of Madeira or sherry; let all stew quietly for ten minutes and rub it through a medium sieve; add the calf's head, season with a very little cayenne pepper, a little salt, the juice of one lemon, and, if desired, a quarter teaspoon of pounded mace and a dessert-spoon sugar.

Having previously prepared force meat balls (see page 319), add them to the soup, and five minutes after serve hot.

Green Turtle Soup

One turtle, two onions, a bunch of sweet herbs, juice one lemon, five quarts of water, a glass of Madeira.

After removing the entrails, cut up the coarser parts of the turtle meat and bones. Add four quarts of water, and stew four hours with the herbs, onions, pepper and salt. Stew very slowly, do not let it cease boiling during this time. At the end of four hours strain the soup, and add the finer parts of the turtle and the green fat, which has been simmered one hour in two quarts of water. Thicken with brown flour; return to the soup pot, and simmer gently for one hour longer. If there are eggs in the turtle; boil them in a separate vessel for four hours and throw into the soup before taking up. If not, put in the force meat balls (see below); then the juice of the lemon and the wine; beat up at once and pour out.

Some cooks add the finer meat before straining, boiling all together five hours; then strain, thicken and put in the green fat, cut into lumps an inch long. This makes a handsomer soup than if the meat is left in.

Green turtle can now be purchased in air-tight cans.

Force Meat Balls

Six tablespoons of turtle meat chopped very fine. Rub to paste, with the yolk of two hard-boiled eggs, a tablespoon of butter, and if convenient, a little oyster liquor.

Source: *The White House Cook Book* by Hugo Ziemann and F.L. (Fanny Lemira) Gillette (Chicago: The Werner Company, 1887).

Chapter 4: CLAUDE MONET'S GIVERNY HOME

Classic Tarte Tatin

Pâte Foncée Shell

137 g T55 flour
83 g butter
3.3 g salt
6.6 g sugar
44 g cold water
(base recipe at 110%, for one 8–9-inch Tatin)

Caramel

150 g sugar
50 g water

Apples!

4 apples
A squirt of lemon juice
Butter, for glazing
Sea salt or cassonade sugar, for sprinkling

Prepare the dough:

- Sift the flour, sugar, and salt together.
- Cut in cold butter (in small chunks) with a *coupe-pâte* (French pastry knife).
- *Sablage* (sand) the flour, sugar, salt, and butter by mixing together by hand.
- Make a well in the center of the dough and pour the salt, sugar, and cold water into the well.

- Use your fingers to swirl the salt and sugar together in the water until the salt and sugar have dissolved. Then continue to pull in the flour and butter "sand" mixture until a dough starts to form.
- Use a *coupe-pâte* to incorporate and continue to mix.
- Perform a *frassage* technique to create flaky crust: Use the heel of your hand to smear the butter into the flour (to create a gritty texture) 3 times and cut-test, in order to be sure all of the butter is well incorporated.
- By hand, form the dough into a ball, then flatten by hand into a disk 1 inch thick. (This allows the gluten to relax and the butter to firm up.)
- Wrap and chill for 30 minutes or 1 hour, overnight preferred. Tart shell dough should be worked quickly, touching as little as possible to avoid heating the butter with your hands.

Alternatively, this dough can be made in a stand mixer:

- Sift flour, sugar, and salt together directly into your mixer bowl.
- Cut cold butter directly over top with a knife, and mix on medium-low speed with a paddle attachment until you see a sandy texture.
- Stop the mixer to scrape the bottom and sides, being sure that everything is evenly mixed.
- Start the mixer again on low and slowly add the water, until a dough ball forms. Be careful not to over mix! Check with a spatula to be sure everything is mixed in.
- Remove dough, form into a ball, and then flatten by hand into a disk 1 inch thick.
- Wrap and chill. Tart shell dough should be worked quickly, touching as little as possible to avoid heating the butter with your hands.

Make the caramel:

- Heat sugar and water in a small saucepan, first on high, then, once it starts to bubble, down to medium, until it gets a medium-dark color (between 180–185°C in color.) Should be foamy and a bit smoky.
- Pour into a cake pan and tilt around so that the caramel coats the edges.
- Blast freeze or chill to cool it down quickly.

Prepare the apple slices:

- Peel, quarter, and core your apples. Leave ½ of an apple for the middle.
- Squirt some lemon juice over the apples to keep them from turning brown.
- Once the caramel is cooled and set, place the apples in your pan, fitting them in as tightly as possible, leaving a space in the center. Place the reserved apple half in this space.
- Dab the top of the apples with generous pats of butter and sprinkle with sea salt and/or cassonade sugar, to taste.
- Wrap the top in a double layer of tin foil and poke a few holes.

Bake the tart:

- Bake the tart in a 180°C oven for about 40 minutes. Rotate partway through baking to ensure even cooking.

Fonçage and démoulage (lining and demolding):

- Roll out your chilled dough disk in quarter turns. Prick with a fork, delicately flip over, and cut a circle roughly the size of your pan.
- Place the dough circle overtop of the apples in the pan.

Tuck the edges in around the apples and bake for about 25 minutes or until golden brown.

- This is the trickiest part. You want to wait until the apples and caramel have cooled enough to reset and “stick,” but not so cool that the caramel won’t release from the pan. Place your plate firmly over the pie and flip. *Et voilà!*

Source: Chef Lisa Arielle Allen, Tarts & Truffles, Paris, France.

Chapter 5: HIGHCLERE CASTLE

Mincemeat

Original recipe from *Modern Cookery for Private Families*

Ingredients: Of a fresh boiled ox-tongue, or inside of roasted sirloin, 1 lb.; stoned raisins and minced apples—each 2 lbs.; currants and fine Lisbon sugar, each 2½ lbs.; candied orange peel, lemon or citron rind, 8 to 16 oz.; boiled lemons 2 large; rinds of two others grated; salt ½ oz.; nutmegs 2 small; pounded mace, 1 large tspful, and rather more of ginger; good Sherry or Madeira ½ pint; Brandy ½ pint. The lemons will be sufficiently boiled in from one hour to one and a quarter.

To one pound of an Oxford-tongue, boiled tender and cut free from the rind, add two pounds of fine stoned raisins, two of beef kidney suet, two pounds and a half of currants well cleaned and dried. Two of good apples. Two and a half of fine Lisbon sugar, from half to a whole pound of candied peel according to taste, the grated rind of two large lemons, and two more boiled quite tender, and chopped up entirely, with the exception of the pips, two small nutmegs, half an ounce of salt, a large tsp of pounded mace, rather more of ginger in powder, half a pint of brandy, and as much good Sherry, or Madeira. Mince these ingredients separately and mix the others well before the brandy and the wine are added, press the whole into a jar or jars and keep it closely covered. It should be stored for a few days before it is used, and will remain good for many weeks. Some persons like the flavoring of cloves in addition to the other spices; others add the juice of two or three lemons, and a larger quantity of brandy. The inside of a tender and well roasted sirloin of beef will answer quite as well as the tongue.

Very Short Crust for Tarts

Original recipe from *Modern Cookery for Private Families*

Break lightly, with the least-possible handling, six ounces of butter into eight of flour. Add a dessert spoonful of pounded sugar, and two or three of water. Roll the paste, for several minutes, to blend the ingredients well, folding it together like puff-crust, and touch it as little as possible.

Ingredients: Flour 8 oz.; butter 6 oz.; pounded sugar, 1 dessertspoonful; water 1 to 2 spoonsful.

Mincemeat

Modern interpretation by Sherry Murphy

Makes enough for 20 tarts

6 oz. or ¾ cup (180 mL) roasted sirloin
4 oz. or ½ cup (125 mL) suet
½ lb. or 2 cups (500 mL) currants
2 lemons
½ lb. or 1½ cups (375 mL) Sultana raisins, minced
2 lbs. or 2 to 5 apples
1 lb. or 2 cups (500 mL) granulated white sugar
5 oz. or ⅔ cup (160 mL) mixed orange & lemon candied peel
1 Tbsp candied citron peel
1 Tbsp ginger, ground
1 tsp each of cinnamon & nutmeg, ground
1 tsp salt
4 oz. or ½ cup (125 mL) each of brandy & sherry or port

1. Rinse currants thoroughly, soak in warm water for 5 to 10 minutes, then dry on a tea towel. Add to a large bowl.

2. Boil one lemon briefly; remove seeds and chop into small pieces. Grate the rind off the other lemon and reserve it. Add to the bowl and stir.

3. Grind or finely chop meat. Add to the bowl and stir.

4. Shred suet. Add to the bowl and stir.

5. Mince the raisins. Add to the bowl and stir.

6. Peel, core, and mince the apples. Add to the bowl and stir.

7. Mince candied orange, lemon, and citron pieces. Add to the bowl and stir.

8. To the large bowl, add the sugar, ginger, cinnamon, nutmeg, salt and liquor, stirring to combine after each addition.

9. When the mixture is complete, each cook takes a turn to stir and make a New Year's wish!

Very Rich Short Crust for Tarts
Modern interpretation by Sherry Murphy
Makes enough for 20 tarts

½ lb. or 1½ cups (375 mL) all-purpose white flour
3 Tbsp (90 mL) granulated white sugar
6 oz. or ¾ cup (180 mL) butter
4 to 5 Tbsp ice water

1. Preheat oven to 350°F (180°C).

2. Combine the flour with the sugar in a bowl. Cut butter into the flour or break up pieces of butter into the flour, and with your hands rub in the butter with the flour mixture until it resembles oatmeal.

3. Immediately blend the ice water into the flour and knead briefly until you have a smooth ball of dough.

4. Chill for a few minutes, then roll out to ¼-inch thick; cut with cutter (larger size for bottom and smaller for top).

5. Line muffin tins, leaving the edges flush or a touch over the edges.

6. Fill each with mincemeat, leaving ¼-inch around the edge.

7. With fingers dipped in water, brush edges of each filled tart and place a pastry lid on each, pinching edges around the tin.

8. With a small knife, cut a slit in middle of pastry on each tart. Brush tops of tarts with beaten egg yolks to give color (optional).

9. Bake for 25 minutes or until the pastry looks golden.

Sources: *Modern Cookery for Private Families* by Eliza Acton (1845); and Sherry Murphy, Culinary Historian, Culinary Historians of Canada.

Chapter 6: LUCY MAUD MONTGOMERY

Sunshine Salad

1 Tbsp gelatin
¼ cup cold water
1 cup pineapple juice
½ cup orange juice, strained
¼ cup white vinegar
1 cup orange pieces
1½ cups cooked (canned) pineapple, cut in small cubes
1 cup raw young carrot, grated or chopped fine
Lettuce
Mayonnaise

Soften gelatin in cold water for 5 minutes. Heat the pineapple juice and add it, and stir until the gelatin is dissolved. Combine with orange juice and vinegar. Cool and set in icebox to chill. When mixture begins to set add orange, pineapple and carrot. Chill in one large mold or individuals. When firm serve on lettuce with dressing (mayonnaise).

Watermelon Rind Pickles

Rind of watermelon, cut in oblong pieces
Iced water
3 Tbsp alum
2 Tbsp ground cinnamon
2 Tbsp ground cloves
2 Tbsp ground ginger
5 lb. brown sugar
4 cups vinegar

1. Cut rind of large watermelon in oblong pieces. Set in large pot and cover with iced water. Add alum. Soak overnight. Drain. Cover with fresh water. Boil 1 hour. Drain.

2. Tie ground cinnamon, cloves, and ginger in a fine net bag. Bring brown sugar to boil with vinegar with bag in it. Add rind and cook an hour or till quite tender.

3. Set in cellar overnight. Boil 15 minutes and bottle in sterilized jars.

Source: *Aunt Maud's Recipe Book: From the Kitchen of L.M. Montgomery*, by Elaine Crawford and Kelly Crawford (Norval: Moulin Publishing, 1996). Published by Crawford's, 2809 Hwy. 7 W., Norval, Ontario, Canada. For copies contact lucymaudmontgomery.ca. Thanks to the authors for the recipes. Thanks also to Kathy Gastle and Melanie Whitfield.

Chapter 7: MARTIN LUTHER KING JR.

Fried Chicken

4 pounds of chicken (thighs, breasts)
Salt and pepper
1 cup flour
1 tsp cornstarch
1 cup panko breadcrumbs
1 Tbsp paprika
Peanut oil, to fry

1. Place chicken pieces in buttermilk and season with salt and pepper. Let stand for at least 30 minutes.

2. Set up breading station: In a dish, thoroughly mix together the flour, cornstarch, and salt and pepper with a fork. In a separate dish combine the panko breadcrumbs and paprika.

3. Dredge the wet chicken pieces in flour mixture and then pat with the breadcrumb mixture until fully coated. Fry in peanut oil until golden brown and floating. Should take 6–8 minutes depending on the size of chicken pieces. Either cut into a piece to make sure it is cooked all the way through or stick with a thermometer and make sure the internal temp is greater than 165°F. Serve hot and enjoy.

Collard Greens with Kale

½ stick of butter
½ cup olive oil
2 lbs. mushrooms sliced
3 lbs. collard green cut into ribbons, main stalks removed
2 lbs. kale cut into ribbons
1 gal vegetable or chicken stock
3 Tbsp Greens Seasoning (storebought)

In a large stock pot heat butter, olive oil, and sauté mushrooms until tender. Add collard greens and kale with the stock to the pot, and bring to a boil. Season with Greens Seasoning and simmer for 20–25 minutes, stirring often.

Candied Yams

1 stick of butter
1–2 cups dark brown sugar
1 sweet potato or yam per person thinly sliced
4 cups water
Salt and pepper to taste

In a large saucepan, melt butter and add brown sugar. Sauté sweet potatoes in butter and brown sugar. Add the water, salt, and pepper. Bring to a boil. Cook until tender and water is reduced. Serve hot.

Source: Chef Rick Westbrook, The Cooking Schools, Atlanta, Georgia, United States.

Chapter 8: FRIDA KAHLO

Nopal Cacti Salad

16 nopales paddles, remove needles, cut in strips
4 tomatoes, chopped
1 large onion chopped
3 jalapeño chiles, chopped
¼ cup cilantro
½ cup olive oil
2 Tbsp vinegar
2 Tbsp Mexican lime juice
Salt to taste
Queso fresco (cheese), crumbled

Simmer nopales in water to tender. Remove slippery coating. Cut in strips. Plate with tomatoes, onion, chiles, cilantro, oil, and vinegar in salad bowl. Garnish with crumbled queso fresco. Optional: sliced avocado, thinly sliced onion.

Black Bean Soup

Beans

1 Tbsp baking soda
1 Tbsp + 1 tsp salt
1 cup dry black beans
2 branches epazote
1 Tbsp Mexican oregano
2 cloves garlic
2 bay leaves

1. Prepare the beans: Dissolve the baking soda and 1 teaspoon of salt in 6 cups of water. Add the dry beans and let sit overnight.

2. The next day, drain the water from the beans. Add the beans, epazote, Mexican oregano, garlic, bay leaves, and 1 Tbsp of salt into a large pot with 6 cups of water and bring to a rapid boil. Boil the beans until fully cooked, about 45 minutes. Strain the beans and set aside!

Soup

2 tomatoes, roasted
½ onion, chopped
2 garlic cloves, chopped
1 tsp Mexican oregano
Salt to taste
2 chipotle chiles in adobo sauce, chopped (optional)
2 Tbsp vegetable oil
3 cups cooked black beans (see above)
6 cups water
½ pound panela cheese, crumbled
Tortillas, toasted and sliced in slivers

Puree tomatoes with onion, garlic, oregano, salt. Sauté until thickened. Puree beans with water and add to tomato mixture. Simmer 10 minutes. Serve garnished with crumbled cheese and toasted tortilla strips. Optional: sliced avocado, Mexican crema.

Source: Chef Tim Dubitsky, Mexico City.

Chapter 9: FRANK SINATRA

Bo Bo Balls

Bo Bo Balls

1 lb. lean ground pork
⅓ cup chopped green onion
¼ cup diced shrimp
¼ cup diced water chestnuts
1 clove garlic, diced
½ tsp diced ginger
1 egg, lightly beaten
¼ cup all-purpose flour

Batter

1 cup all-purpose flour
1 egg
2 tsp baking powder
1 tsp vegetable oil
½ cup whole milk

Oil for deep fat frying
Your favorite dipping sauce (such as sweet-and-sour or plum) (optional)

1. Make the filling: In a bowl, add the pork, green onion, shrimp, water chestnuts, garlic, ginger, egg, and flour and mix well.

2. Using clean hands, form the pork mixture into golf ball–sized balls and set aside.

3. Set a nonstick pan over medium-low heat, and add the meatballs, flipping every 2–3 minutes until golden brown (10–12 minutes total). Set aside.

4. Heat about 2 inches of vegetable oil in a deep pot, until the oil reaches a temperature between 350–375°F.

5. Batter and fry: Meanwhile, in a medium bowl, mix the flour, egg, baking powder, and oil and enough milk to make the batter a medium-thick consistency.

6. Coat the meatballs in batter, then using a spider or slotted spoon, gently lower them into the fryer and fry until golden, about 2–3 minutes. Set aside on a paper towel–lined plate to drain excess oil.

7. Serve with toothpicks and your favorite dipping sauce, such as sweet-and-sour or plum.

(John Ota notes: After the end of World War II, thousands of American military personnel remained stationed in the South Pacific. While there, many fell in love with the local cultures and brought an assortment of South Pacific experiences back home with them. What emerged was a vague impression of South Pacific culture. American servicemen opened up tiki bars, placed tiki torches and pink flamingos on their patios, and enjoyed bo bo balls. My mother first tasted bo bo balls at the Ports of Call Tiki Bar in Toronto and immediately replicated the recipe for our family. These would have been a perfect finger food to nosh on around Frank Sinatra's new pool patio in 1947.)

Source: Sachi Ota, inspired by the Ports of Call Tiki Bar, Toronto.

Chapter 10: JACQUELINE KENNEDY

Sea Bass Stuffed with Spinach

This dish consists of 4 components:

1. Spinach stuffing
2. Fried mushrooms
3. Baked fish
4. Sauce

1 Tbsp vegetable oil
2 Tbsp chopped shallots
1 clove garlic, minced
3 cups spinach leaves
¼ cup chopped fresh basil
¼ cup chopped parsley
French sea salt to taste
Ground black pepper to taste
1 tsp grated lemon zest
1 Tbsp butter and 1 Tbsp veg oil (to fry mushrooms)
5 cups sliced mushrooms
4 tsp chopped thyme
2 Tbsp butter (for sauce)
1 leek—white section, chopped
1 cup fish stock
1 cup white wine
2 small sea bass (1½ lb. each)
2 Tbsp butter (for dotting inside and outside of fish)
1 cup whipping cream
1 lemon, cut in quarters

1. Spinach stuffing: In a large frying pan, heat oil, shallots, and garlic. Add spinach, basil, parsley, salt, pepper, and lemon zest. Heat through until soft. Cool. Reserve.

2. Fried mushrooms: In a frying pan, heat oil and butter. Add mushrooms and thyme, and fry to golden brown. Reserve. Reheat before serving.

3. Sauce: In a saucepan, heat butter and fry leeks until soft. Add stock and wine. Bring to a boil. Reduce to ½ cup. Optional: Pass through sieve.

4. Fish: Fill fish cavities with spinach stuffing. Dot with butter inside and outside. Bake at 400°F until inside is flaky (approximately 14 to 18 minutes). Return to the sauce in the saucepan. Add cream and bring to a boil. Reduce to 1 cup. Season with salt and pepper.

5. Serve the fish with the mushrooms, lemon wedges, and sauce on the side.

(John Ota notes: I've adapted this complex recipe into something friendly for the home cook—to superb results, if I may say so. You will need 2 frying pans, a saucepan, a baking dish and a serving platter. It will put you right in the Blue Room of the White House with Mrs. Kennedy.)

Source: John Ota, adapted from Letitia Baldrige, *In the Kennedy Style*, menus and recipes by Chef René Verdon (New York: Madison Press, Doubleday, 1998).

Chapter 11: GARTH NORBRATEN AND GREG LICHTI'S HOUSE

Saskatoon Berry Crisp

4 cups Saskatoon berries
½ cup sugar
1 Tbsp flour
1 Tbsp lemon juice (optional)

Crisp Topping
1 cup flour
1½ cups rolled oats
¾ cup packed brown sugar
1 cup chilled, unsalted butter, cut into small pieces

Vanilla ice cream or whipped cream (for serving) (optional)

1. Preheat oven to 350°F. Lightly grease an 8-by-8-inch baking dish.
2. Rinse berries in a colander, drain thoroughly, and pat dry. Toss berries, sugar, flour, and lemon juice (if using) in a large bowl. Pour berry mixture into the prepared baking dish and set aside.
3. Mix the flour, rolled oats, and brown sugar in a bowl. Using an electric mixer or a whisk, gradually beat in butter pieces and blend until mixture is crumbly.
4. Top berries with crumble mixture, and bake for 30 to 35 minutes until golden.
5. Serve warm with ice cream or whipped cream.

Source: Barb and Dale Hauser.

Chapter 12: THE FOREST DINING ROOM

Peanut Butter Miso Cookies with Sour Cherries

252 g (1¾ cups plus 3 Tbsp) all-purpose flour (organic)
1 tsp baking powder
1 tsp baking soda
8 Tbsp (1 stick) unsalted butter (organic), at room temperature
199 g (1 cup) packed dark brown sugar (organic)
122 g (½ cup plus 1 Tbsp) white sugar (organic)
88 g (¼ cup plus 2 Tbsp) peanut butter (organic, smooth), at room temperature
75 g (¼ cup) white miso (organic, low sodium)
2 tsp toasted sesame oil or roasted peanut oil
1 large egg
2 tsp vanilla extract
62 g (⅓ cup) turbinado sugar
199 g (1 cup) dried sour cherries (organic)

1. In a medium bowl, whisk together the flour, baking powder, and baking soda. In a stand mixer with the paddle attachment, beat the butter, brown sugar, and white sugar on medium high until well combined, about 3 minutes. Add the peanut butter, miso, and oil, then beat, scraping the bowl once or twice, until light and fluffy, about 2 minutes. Add the egg and vanilla and beat again, then scrape the bowl.
2. With the mixer on low, gradually add the flour mixture. Mix, scraping the bowl as needed, just until the dough is evenly moistened, 1 to 2 minutes. Using a spatula, mix the dough by hand to ensure no pockets of flour remain; the dough will be very soft. Press a sheet of plastic wrap against the surface

of the dough and refrigerate for at least 2 hours or up to 24 hours.

3. When ready to bake, heat the oven to 350°F with a rack in the middle position. Line 2 baking sheets with kitchen parchment. Put the turbinado sugar in a small bowl. Divide the dough into 18 portions, about 3 tablespoons each, then roll into 1½-inch balls.
4. Push the sour cherries into the dough balls. Dip each in the turbinado sugar to coat one side; set sugared side up on the prepared baking sheets, 9 per sheet. Bake the first sheet for 10 minutes.
5. Remove the baking sheet from the oven and firmly rap it twice against the counter to deflate the cookies. Bake for another 5 to 7 minutes, until the cookies have fissured and are golden at the edges. Cool the cookies on the baking sheet on a wire rack for 10 minutes. Using a metal spatula, transfer the cookies to the cooling rack and cool completely.
6. Repeat with the second batch of cookies.

(John Ota notes: The salty-savory miso rounds out the sweetness of a conventional peanut butter cookie and heightens the nuttiness. Tapping the baking sheet deflates the half-baked cookies, which gives them a chewy-crisp texture. Turbinado sugar is a course amber sugar that gives the cookie glitter and crunch. Chef Stadtländer adapted this recipe from Milk Street *magazine's take on Falco Bakery's miso peanut butter cookie.)*

Source: Chef Michael Stadtländer.

ACKNOWLEDGMENTS

I AM LUCKY TO HAVE BEEN part of a great *Dining Room* team. If we were all gathered for a thank-you dinner at a round (of course, for maximum inclusivity) table, the circumference would be very large. There are so many people to thank for their help with this book. Unfortunately, there is not enough space here to name everyone, but I hope you know who you are and know that you also have a seat at the table.

Sitting very near me would be Robert McCullough, publisher of Appetite, Penguin Random House Canada, for his incredible support in taking a chance with this book.

Just to the left of me would be my literary agents, Kris Rothstein and Carolyn Swayze. I feel so grateful to them for their sage advice and belief in me.

Not too far away from me would be my brother and travel companion, Chris Ota.

Also nearby would be my dedicated readers Maria Coletta McLean, Eddy Yanofsky, and Valerie Hurley.

All around the table would be Lorraine Bell, Vincent Carbone, Catherine Hughes, Jun Hayashi, Anne Schuyler, Sabrina Siarri,

Lisa Arielle Allen, Melanie Whitfield, Kathy Gastle, Diane Burgoon, Samantha George, Mya Sangster, Sherry Murphy, Sylvia Lovegren, Rick Westbrook, Sonya Jones, Estefania Morlett, Tim Dubitsky, Javier Martinez, Carol Moore-Ede, Jim Keffer, Garth Norbraten, Greg Lichti, the Stadtländers (Michael, Nobuyo, and Hermann), Nancy Riley, and the Culinary Historians of Canada. These people are the fabulous chefs, historians, curators, writers, and architects who made important contributions to this book. Thanks to Ashley Shifflett McBrayne, Archival and Special Collections, McLaughlin Library, University of Guelph, for her advice concerning the journals of Lucy Maud Montgomery.

Also at the table would be my friends, neighbors, relatives, and acquaintances who encouraged me to write and shared their thoughts about and experiences with dining rooms.

But most important, to my immediate right at this table would be my wife, Frances Mary Rowe. My constant companion and best friend in life, Franny has patiently endured cancelled vacations, suffered failed recipes, and counseled me on my excruciating anxieties in the middle of the night as I lay with my eyes wide open staring at the bedroom ceiling—she does not even send me a bill in the morning. Thank you, Franny.

Also important, to the immediate left of me would be my editor, Whitney Millar. It is impossible to describe the many ways that I am thankful to Whitney for her professional manner, generosity in advice, editing skills, and willingness to help at every turn. Just knowing there was a positive, keen, and knowledgeable person within easy reach was a great comfort and inspiration to me. Thank you, Whitney.

And finally, and most sincerely, thank you to *you*, for reading this book. I am so grateful that we could spend time together in *The Dining Room*.

SOURCES AND FURTHER READING

Chapter 1: GEORGE AND MARTHA WASHINGTON'S GARDEN AND DINING ROOM AT MORRIS-JUMEL MANSION

An inspiring source of information for me in writing about the history of the dining room came from reading *The Rituals of Dinner* by Margaret Visser (Toronto: Harper Collins Publishers, 1991). Historical background on the Morris-Jumel Mansion can be found in the book *Morris-Jumel Mansion* (Images of America series) by Carol S. Ward (New York: Arcadia Publishing, 2015). Details on the history of the early North American dining room came from the excellent master's thesis "The Evolution of the Nineteenth-Century American Dining Room: From Sitting Room to Separate Room" by Leslie Susan Berman (University of Pennsylvania, 1997). Historical recipes and further information on the Washingtons came from *Dining with the Washingtons: Historic Recipes, Entertaining, and Hospitality from Mount Vernon*, edited by Stephen A. McLeod (Mount Vernon: Mount Vernon Ladies' Association, 2011). An essay that fueled my passion for cherry pie is written by Sam Worley, "Cherry Pie: A Tart Appreciation," Epicurious, July 7, 2016.

Chapter 2: NOMURA SAMURAI HOUSE

The architectural background on traditional houses in Japan was sourced in the following books: *Japanese Homes and Their Surroundings* by Edward

S. Morse (Dover Publications, 1961); *The Japanese House* by Nakagawa Takeshi (Tokyo: International House of Japan, 2005); and *Japanese Houses* by Kiyoyuki Nishihara (Tokyo: Japan Publications, 1967). A beautiful and informative book on kaiseki dining is *Kaiseki* by Kaichi Tsuji (Tokyo: Kodansha International, 1972).

Chapter 3: EDITH WHARTON'S DINING ROOM AT THE MOUNT
Edith Wharton's design philosophy at The Mount can be traced to her book *The Decoration of Houses*, a manual of interior design written by Wharton with Ogden Codman (Charles Scribner's Sons, 1897). More on Edith Wharton's life at The Mount can be found in the following: "Guesthouse of Mirth: Summer Entertaining Tips from Edith Wharton" by Kate Bolick, *Slate*, July 31, 2014, slate.com/culture/2014/07/entertaining-tips-from-edith-wharton-whose-summer-home-the-mount-was-in-lenox-massachusetts.html; "10 Decorating Lessons from Edith Wharton" by Mayra David, *Domino*, December 18, 2015, domino.com/content/decorating-lessons-from-edith-wharton; "Edith Wharton's The Mount," *Victoria* magazine, August 17, 2016, victoriamag.com/edith-whartons-mount; "I Am Going to Leave Her Here: The Rebel Yell of Edith Wharton's The Mount" by Robin Catalano, *Once More to the Shore*, December 27, 2022, oncemoretotheshore.com/i-am-going-to-leave-her-here-edith-whartons-the-mount. Further detail came from The Mount website (edithwharton.org/discover/the-main-house) and, on mock turtle soup, *The White House Cook Book* by Hugo Ziemann and F.L. (Fanny Lemira) Gillette (Chicago: The Werner Company, 1887), gutenberg.org/files/13923/13923-h/13923-h.htm#Page_27. An excellent article on the history of turtle soup is "Our Taste for Turtle Soup Nearly Wiped Out Terrapins" by Shoshi Parks, July 18, 2019 (npr.org).

Chapter 4: CLAUDE MONET'S DINING ROOM
The cooking lesson for the tarte Tatin was led by Lisa Arielle Allen, owner and operator of Tarts & Truffles Paris (tartsntruffles.com). An excellent source of information on the Impressionist artists and their approach to color is the book *Mystical Landscapes: From Vincent van Gogh to Emily Carr*, edited by Katharine Lochnan (AGO/Musée d'Orsay). Background information on

the Monet garden and house can be found in the book *Monet at Giverny* by Adrien Goetz (Giverny: Fondation Claude Monet, 2015). Two cookbooks that were used as sources of culinary information are *Monet's Table* by Claire Joyes (New York: Simon and Schuster, 1989) and *Monet's Palate Cookbook* by Aileen Bordman and Derek Fell (Layton, Utah: Gibbs Smith, 2015).

Chapter 5: HIGHCLERE CASTLE'S "DOWNTON ABBEY" DINING ROOM

The mincemeat tart cooking class was led by Mya Sangster and Sherry Murphy, members of the Culinary Historians of Canada (culinaryhistorians.ca/wordpress). Samantha George, curator at Parkwood National Historic Site in Oshawa, Ontario (parkwoodestate.com), was a most helpful consultant about Edwardian table manners. Lady Carnarvon is a prolific writer, and her publications provided historical detail from the books *Highclere Castle* by Fiona Carnarvon (Newbury: Highclere Enterprises, 2013); *Christmas at Highclere* by Lady Carnarvon (London: Preface Publishing, Penguin Random House, 2019); and *Lady Almina and the Real Downton Abbey* by The Countess of Carnarvon (New York: Broadway Paperback, 2011). The relationship and etiquette between family and staff was clearly outlined in the online articles "Downstairs in Downton Abbey: The Servants," Jane Austen's World, January 5, 2011, janeaustensworld.com/2011/01/05/downstairs-in-downton-abbey-the-servants; and "A Guide to Downton Abbey Etiquette," The British School of Excellence, thebritishschoolofexcellence.com/british-culture/a-guide-to-downton-abbey-etiquette. An excellent source for Edwardian recipes and culinary information is *The Official Downton Abbey Cookbook* by Annie Gray (San Rafael: Weldonowen, 2019).

Chapter 6: LUCY MAUD MONTGOMERY'S MANSE DINING ROOM

There are five volumes of remarkable Lucy Maud Montgomery diary entries in the series of *The Selected Journals of L.M. Montgomery* by Mary Rubio and Elizabeth Waterston (Don Mills: Oxford University Press, 1987); the volumes used for this book were Volume II: 1910–1921 and Volume III: 1921–1929. A biography that chronicles Montgomery's entire life is *Lucy Maud Montgomery: The Gift of Wings* by Mary Henley Rubio (Toronto: Anchor Canada, 2008), while the book *A Home of Her Own* by Conrad Boyce, Leaskdale, The Lucy Maud Montgomery Society of Ontario, 2016, is an excellent source for her life during the Leaskdale years. Background information on Montgomery's culinary life came from *Aunt Maud's Recipe Book: From the Kitchen of L.M. Montgomery* by Elaine Crawford and Kelly Crawford (Norval: Moulin Publishing, 1996). Montgomery's most famous novel, *Anne of Green Gables*, which has sold more than fifty million copies worldwide, was first published by L.C. Page and Co., Boston, 1908. Further detail came from "The Story of a Classic: Anne and After" by Joseph Gerard Brennan in *American Scholar* 64, no. 2 (1995), page 253, and through interviewing Melanie Whitfield, president of the Lucy Maud Montgomery Society of Ontario.

Chapter 7: DR. MARTIN LUTHER KING JR.'S CHILDHOOD DINING ROOM

The Southern food cooking class was led by Rick Westbrook at The Cooking Schools (thecookingschools.com). Sweet Auburn Bread Company's website is at sweetauburnbread.com. King's "I Have a Dream" speech can be found in its entirety at the NPR website (npr.org/2010/01/18/122701268/i-have-a-dream-speech-in-its-entirety). Reflections on King's life in his own words can be found in *The Autobiography of Martin Luther King Jr.*, edited by Clayborne Carson (New York: IPM Intellectual Properties Management Inc., in association with Grand Central Publishing, 1998). The sources of Southern food traditions can be found in *Soul Food: The Surprising Story of an American Cuisine One Plate at a Time* by Adrian Miller (Chapel Hill: The University of North Carolina Press, 2013).

Chapter 8: FRIDA KAHLO'S CASA AZUL DINING ROOM

The Mexican cooking class was led by Tim Dubitsky and Javier Martinez. A highly informative and beautiful book on the life of Kahlo is *Frida Kahlo: Her Universe* by Mara Garbuno (Mexico City: Museo Frida Kahlo—Museo Casa Azul, 2022). Recipes and a culinary history of Kahlo's life are described in *Frida's Fiestas: Recipes and Reminiscences of Life with Frida Kahlo* by Guadalupe Rivera and Marie-Pierre Colle (New York: Clarkson Potter, 1994). Information was also sourced from a three-part PBS documentary series

Becoming Frida Kahlo, which delves into her art, personal life story, and dedication to Mexican culture (pbs.org/show/becoming-frida-kahlo).

Chapter 9: FRANK SINATRA'S TWIN PALMS PATIO

The most revealing book on Sinatra was written by his daughter Nancy Sinatra, *Frank Sinatra: An American Legend* (Santa Monica: General Publishing Group, 1995). Other sources of information were the books *Sinatra Treasures* by Charles Pignone (New York: Bulfinch Press, 2004) and *The Way You Wear Your Hat* by Bill Zehme (New York: Harper Collins, 1997). For hardcore Sinatra fans, *Frank Sinatra Has a Cold* by Gay Talese (New York: Penguin Books, 1961) is a renowned literary piece for its portrayal of Sinatra, his environment, and those around him. The book *Hollywood Modern* by Alan Hess and Michael Stern (New York: Rizzoli, 2018) provides a page-turning profile of Twin Palms and other famous Palm Springs houses. The stories and eccentricities of post–World War II cuisine are delightfully presented in the book *Fashionable Food* by Sylvia Lovegren (Chicago: University of Chicago Press, 1995). This chapter also includes information from the Palm Springs Designation Statement (October 13, 2011). "Somethin' Stupid" was written by C. Carson Parks.

Chapter 10: JACQUELINE KENNEDY'S STATE DINING ROOM AT THE WHITE HOUSE

Letitia Baldrige, who was Mrs. Kennedy's social secretary from 1961 to 1963, provides candid insights into the planning and atmosphere of the Malraux Dinner in her book *In the Kennedy Style: Magical Evenings in the Kennedy White House* (New York: Madison Press, Doubleday, 1998). The definitive work and excellent journalism on the history and background of the Malraux Dinner can be found in the article "The Two First Ladies" by Margaret Leslie Davis, *Vanity Fair*, November 2008. Information on the Malraux Dinner was also sourced from the John F. Kennedy Presidential Library and Museum in Boston, Massachusetts; the exhibition *Jacqueline Kennedy Entertains: The Art of the White House Dinner* ran from April 12, 2007, until April 03, 2008, curated by Frank Rigg (https://www.jfklibrary.org/visit-museum/exhibits/past-exhibits/jacqueline-kennedy-entertains-the-art-of-the-white-house-dinner;

see video: jfklibrary.org/asset-viewer/jacqueline-kennedy-entertains). History on the construction of the White House can be found in *The White House: An Historic Guide* (Washington: The White House Historical Association, 1962). *The White House Chef Cookbook* by René Verdon (New York: Doubleday, 1967) is a rare book that provides over five hundred recipes and menus by the White House chef during the Kennedy years.

Chapter 11: THE NORBRATEN AND LICHTI DINING ROOM
A groundbreaking early book on Canadian modernism is *Canadian Architecture 1960/70* by Carol Moore-Ede (Toronto: Burns and MacEachern, 1971). Further detail on contemporary Canadian architecture can be found in the books *Canadian Modern Architecture: A Fifty Year Retrospective, from 1967 to the Present* by Elsa Lam (Princeton Architectural Press and Canadian Architect, 2019) and *Canadian Architecture: Evolving a Cultural Identity* by Leslie Jen (Victoria: Figure 1 Publishing, 2021). Garth Norbraten's thoughts on architecture can be accessed at Vincent Hui's podcast *Architectural Education: Off the Record*, June 14, 2020, creators.spotify.com/pod/profile/vincent--hui/episodes/Guest-Interview--Garth-Norbraten-efdt4j.

Chapter 12: CHEF MICHAEL STADTLÄNDER'S EIGENSINN FARM
A book that was highly inspirational to Michael Stadtländer in his path to organic farming is *The Natural Way of Farming* by Masanobu Fukoka (Tokyo: Japan Publication, 2017) that details Fukoka's philosophy and techniques of working with nature rather than against it. The Stadtländers stayed with Fukoka at his farm on the island of Shikoku in southern Japan, reading his books and working his land. Details for the chapter were sourced from a 2014 documentary titled *The Singhampton Project*, in which the Stadtländer family and a landscape architect create seven gardens on his farm where they grow, cook, and serve a seven-course tasting menu to hundreds of guests over twenty nights, showcasing their organic farming methods. More background was accessed from a 2006 film titled *The Islands Project*, where the Stadtländers and apprentices journey in a kitchen-equipped school bus to the West Coast of Canada to cook with famous chefs and serve artists, farmers, environmentalists, and loggers who are dedicated to environmentally sustainable business practices.

ABOUT THE AUTHOR

John Ota has been involved with architecture and design since 1978, with degrees from Columbia University, the University of Toronto, and the University of British Columbia. His bestselling book *The Kitchen* was a 2021 Taste Canada Awards finalist and a 2021 Paris Gourmand Cookbook finalist in the book design category. After working in architecture in Toronto, New York, and Vancouver, John now loves to travel the world visiting historic houses, cooking regional food, and meeting people of all backgrounds.